Practice*Planner*

Arthur E. Jongsma, Jr., Series Editor

Helping therapists help their clients...

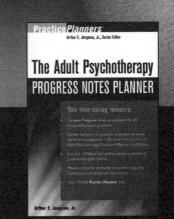

Over 250,000 Practice*Planners* sold . . .

TheraScribe®

The Treatment Planning and Clinical Record Management System for Mental Health Professionals.

TheraScribe®—the latest version of our popular treatment planning, patient record-keeping software. Facilitates intake/assessment reporting, progress monitoring, and outcomes analysis. Supports group treatment and multiprovider treatment teams. Compatible with our full array of **PracticePlanners**® libraries, including our *Treatment Planner* software versions.

- This bestselling, easy-to-use Windows®-based software allows you to generate fully customized psychotherapy treatment plans that meet the requirements of all major accrediting agencies and most third-party payers.

- In just minutes, this user-friendly program's on-screen help enables you to create customized treatment plans.

- Praised in the *National Psychologist* and *Medical Software Reviews,* this innovative software simplifies and streamlines record-keeping.

- Available for a single user, or in a network version, this comprehensive software package suits the needs of all practices—both large and small.

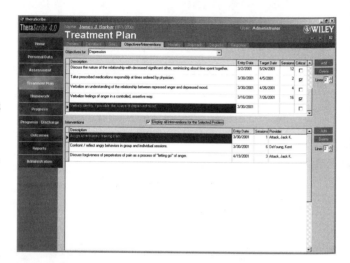

Treatment Planner Upgrade to Thera*Scribe*®

The behavioral definitions, goals, objectives, and interventions from this *Treatment Planner* can be imported into Thera*Scribe*®. For purchase and pricing information, please send in the coupon below or call 1-866-888-5158 or e-mail us at planners@wiley.com.

For more information about **TheraScribe**® or the Upgrade to this *Treatment Planner,* fill in this coupon and mail it to: R. Crucitt, John Wiley & Sons, Inc., 7222 Commerce Center Dr., Ste. 240, Colorado Springs, CO 80919 or e-mail us at planners@wiley.com.

- ❑ Please send me information on **TheraScribe**®
- ❑ Please send me information on the *Treatment Planner* Upgrade to **TheraScribe**®
  Name of *Treatment Planner* _____
- ❑ Please send me information on the network version of **TheraScribe**®

Name _____

Affiliation _____

Address _____

City/State/Zip _____

Phone _____ E-mail _____

For a free demo, visit us on the web at: therascribe.wiley.com

Practice*Planners*®

Treatment Planners cover all the necessary elements for developing formal treatment plans, including detailed problem definitions, long-term goals, short-term objectives, therapeutic interventions, and DSM-IV™ diagnoses.

❑ **The Complete Adult Psychotherapy Treatment Planner,** Third Edition
0-471-27113-6 / $49.95

❑ **The Child Psychotherapy Treatment Planner,** Third Edition
0-471-27050-4 / $49.95

❑ **The Adolescent Psychotherapy Treatment Planner,** Third Edition
0-471-27049-0 / $49.95

❑ **The Addiction Treatment Planner,** Second Edition
0-471-41814-5 / $49.95

❑ **The Couples Psychotherapy Treatment Planner**
0-471-24711-1 / $49.95

❑ **The Group Therapy Treatment Planner**
0-471-37449-0 / $49.95

❑ **The Family Therapy Treatment Planner**
0-471-34768-X / $49.95

❑ **The Older Adult Psychotherapy Treatment Planner**
0-471-29574-4 / $49.95

❑ **The Employee Assistance (EAP) Treatment Planner**
0-471-24709-X / $49.95

❑ **The Gay and Lesbian Psychotherapy Treatment Planner**
0-471-35080-X / $49.95

❑ **The Crisis Counseling and Traumatic Events Treatment Planner**
0-471-39587-0 / $49.95

❑ **The Social Work and Human Services Treatment Planner**
0-471-37741-4 / $49.95

❑ **The Continuum of Care Treatment Planner**
0-471-19568-5 / $49.95

❑ **The Behavioral Medicine Treatment Planner**
0-471-31923-6 / $49.95

❑ **The Mental Retardation and Developmental Disability Treatment Planner**
0-471-38253-1 / $49.95

❑ **The Special Education Treatment Planner**
0-471-38872-6 / $49.95

❑ **The Severe and Persistent Mental Illness Treatment Planner**
0-471-35945-9 / $49.95

❑ **The Personality Disorders Treatment Planner**
0-471-39403-3 / $49.95

❑ **The Rehabilitation Psychology Treatment Planner**
0-471-35178-4 / $49.95

❑ **The Pastoral Counseling Treatment Planner**
0-471-25416-9 / $49.95

❑ **The Juvenile Justice and Residential Care Treatment Planner**
0-471-43320-9 / $49.95

❑ **The Psychiatric Evaluation & Psychopharmacology Treatment Planner**
0-471-43322-5 / $49.95 (available 8/03)

❑ **The Probation and Parole Treatment Planner**
0-471-20244-4 / $49.95 (available 3/03)

❑ **The School Counseling and School Social Work Treatment Planner**
0-471-08496-4 / $49.95

❑ **The Sexual Abuse Victim/Offender Treatment Planner**
0-471-21979-7 / $49.95

Progress Notes Planners contain complete prewritten progress notes for each presenting problem in the companion Treatment Planners.

❑ **The Adult Psychotherapy Progress Notes Planner**
0-471-34763-9 / $49.95

❑ **The Adolescent Psychotherapy Progress Notes Planner**
0-471-38104-7 / $49.95

❑ **The Child Psychotherapy Progress Notes Planner**
0-471-38102-0 / $49.95

❑ **The Addiction Progress Notes Planner**
0-471-10330-6 / $49.95

❑ **The Severe and Persistent Mental Illness Progress Notes Planner**
0-471-21986-X / $49.95

Name_____

Affiliation_____

Address_____

City/State/Zip_____

Phone/Fax_____

E-mail_____

On the web: practiceplanners.wiley.com

To order, call 1-800-225-5945
(Please refer to promo #1-4019 when ordering.)

Or send this page with payment* to:
John Wiley & Sons, Inc., Attn: J. Knott
111 River Street, Hoboken, NJ 07030

❑ Check enclosed ❑ Visa ❑ MasterCard ❑ American Express

Card #_____

Expiration Date_____

Signature_____

*Please add your local sales tax to all orders.

Child and Adolescent Client Education Handout Planner

Practice*Planners*® Series

Treatment Planners

The Complete Adult Psychotherapy Treatment Planner, 2e
The Child Psychotherapy Treatment Planner, 2e
The Adolescent Psychotherapy Treatment Planner, 2e
The Continuum of Care Treatment Planner
The Couples Psychotherapy Treatment Planner
The Employee Assistance Treatment Planner
The Pastoral Counseling Treatment Planner
The Older Adult Psychotherapy Treatment Planner
The Behavioral Medicine Treatment Planner
The Group Therapy Treatment Planner
The Gay and Lesbian Psychotherapy Treatment Planner
The Family Therapy Treatment Planner
The Severe and Persistent Mental Illness Treatment Planner
The Mental Retardation and Developmental Disability Treatment Planner
The Social Work and Human Services Treatment Planner
The Crisis Counseling and Traumatic Events Treatment Planner
The Personality Disorders Treatment Planner
The Rehabilitation Psychology Treatment Planner
The Addiction Treatment Planner, 2e
The Special Education Treatment Planner
The Juvenile Justice and Residential Care Treatment Planner
The School Counseling and School Social Work Treatment Planner
The Sexual Abuse Victim and Sexual Offender Treatment Planner

Progress Notes Planners

The Child Psychotherapy Progress Notes Planner
The Adolescent Psychotherapy Progress Notes Planner
The Adult Psychotherapy Progress Notes Planner
The Addiction Progress Notes Planner
The Severe and Persistent Mental Illness Progress Notes Planner

Homework Planners

Brief Therapy Homework Planner
Brief Couples Therapy Homework Planner
Chemical Dependence Treatment Homework Planner
Brief Child Therapy Homework Planner
Brief Adolescent Therapy Homework Planner
Brief Employee Assistance Homework Planner
Brief Family Therapy Homework Planner
Grief Counseling Homework Planner
Group Therapy Homework Planner
Divorce Counseling Homework Planner
School Counseling and School Social Work Homework Planner
Child Therapy Activity and Homework Planner

Client Education Handout Planners

Adult Client Education Handout Planner
Child and Adolescent Client Education Handout Planner
Couples and Family Client Education Handout Planner

Documentation Sourcebooks

The Clinical Documentation Sourcebook
The Forensic Documentation Sourcebook
The Psychotherapy Documentation Primer
The Chemical Dependence Treatment Documentation Sourcebook
The Clinical Child Documentation Sourcebook
The Couple and Family Clinical Documentation Sourcebook
The Clinical Documentation Sourcebook, 2e
The Continuum of Care Clinical Documentation Sourcebook

Child and Adolescent Client Education Handout Planner

Laurie Cope Grand

WILEY

John Wiley & Sons, Inc

Library of Congress Cataloging-in-Publication Data:

0471-20233-9

Printed in the United States of America

10 9 8 7 6 5 4 3 2 1

For David Cope, Charles Cope, Mary Cope Brennan, Holly Cope Jacoby,
Heidi Cope Roy, Susan Back, and Karen Grand Ball.
You helped make me who I am and I am grateful that you are my family.

Contents

Practice*Planners*® Series Preface

The practice of psychotherapy has a dimension that did not exist 30, 20, or even 15 years ago—accountability. Treatment programs, public agencies, clinics, and even group and solo practitioners must now justify the treatment of patients to outside review entities that control the payment of fees. This development has resulted in an explosion of paperwork.

Clinicians must now document what has been done in treatment, what is planned for the future, and what the anticipated outcomes of the interventions are. The books and software in this Practice*Planners*® series are designed to help practitioners fulfill these documentation requirements efficiently and professionally.

The Practice*Planners*® series is growing rapidly. It now includes not only the new editions of the original *Complete Adult Psychotherapy Treatment Planner*, *The Child Psychotherapy Treatment Planner*, and *The Adolescent Psychotherapy Treatment Planner*, but also *Treatment Planners* targeted to specialty areas of practice, including: addictions, the continuum of care, couples therapy, employee assistance, behavioral medicine, therapy with older adults, pastoral counseling, family therapy, group therapy, neuropsychology, therapy with gays and lesbians, and more.

In addition to the ***Treatment Planners***, the series also includes Thera*Scribe*®, the best-selling treatment planning and clinical record-keeping software, as well as related books, including ***Homework Planners*** for a wide number of client populations (*Adult, Chemical Dependence, Couples, Child, Adolescent, Family, Divorce, Group*, and *Grief Therapy*), ***Client Education Handout Planners*** that provide ready-to-use handouts for client education and community service, as well as marketing purposes, and ***Documentation Sourcebooks*** containing forms and resources to aid in mental health practice management covering *Clinical, Forensic, Child, Couples* and *Family, Continuum of Care*, and *Chemical Dependence* populations. The goal of the series is to provide practitioners with the resources they need in order to provide high-quality care in the era of accountability—or, to put it simply, we seek to help you spend more time on clients, and less time on paperwork.

ARTHUR E. JONGSMA, JR.
Grand Rapids, Michigan

Acknowledgments

I am grateful for the support of Peggy Alexander and Cristina Wojdylo at John Wiley & Sons. Thanks also to Kelly Franklin, who opened the door for me.

Introduction

The *Child & Adolescent Client Education Handout Planner* is a valuable resource for therapists that will enable you to provide information to your clients in a condensed, user-friendly format. The handouts are an excellent therapeutic tool, provide a valuable community service, and are an effective marketing tool as well.

The *Child & Adolescent Client Education Handout Planner* includes a set of ready-to-use handouts on 60 different topics. 39 of the topics correspond to the problems and disorders found in *The Child Psychotherapy Treatment Planner* (2nd ed.)* and *The Adolescent Psychotherapy Treatment Planner* (2nd ed.).† In addition to these problem-focused topics, there are 21 others that address various important life skills. You can choose from these topics to provide information for your clients to read and study in between sessions. You can also refer to them during your sessions and use them as a teaching and discussion tool.

The back section of each handout includes a list of other related handouts from this book. This makes it easy for you to provide additional handouts to clients. You can tailor the choice of handouts to each client's unique issues and interests.

This book includes a CD with PDF files containing the complete text of every handout. The documents on the CD are laid out as you see them in this book. You can open and print each handout provided that you have Adobe Acrobat Reader on your computer. This is a free software download that you can obtain in a few minutes from the Adobe web site. Look for the "Get Adobe Acrobat" icon on the opening page and click it. Follow the instructions to download the software to your computer. Now you can open any document with a PDF extension.

You can print each handout right from your computer. There is a blank space on the original handout where you can place your business card before you have copies made. You can also type information regarding your practice onto the original and have your printer make copies. This personalizes your handouts.

---

*Jongsma, Arthur E. Jr., Peterson, L. Mark, and McInnis, William P. *The Child Psychotherapy Treatment Planner* (2nd ed.). New York: John Wiley and Sons, 2000.
†Jongsma, Arthur E. Jr., Peterson, L. Mark, and McInnis, William P. *The Adolescent Psychotherapy Treatment Planner* (2nd ed.). New York: John Wiley and Sons, 2000.

A simple and fast alternative is to photocopy the handouts right from the book. Make one original and place your business card on the blank space provided before you have copies made. You can also type your practice information in the blank space. Copying the handouts from the book like this will work, but the resulting handouts will be less professional looking.

HOW THESE HANDOUTS CAN BENEFIT YOU AND YOUR CLIENTS

You can use these handouts to educate your clients as part of your treatment plan. You can place them in your waiting room or give them to clients in session as a way of extending the therapy process beyond your office. You can also include them in newsletters, and distribute them as handouts when you give presentations, seminars, and workshops. Using the text of any handout as your source, you can also write your own articles, perhaps for publication in your local paper or newsletter. The information can also be tied to your web site and other marketing efforts.

WHY DISTRIBUTING HANDOUTS IS AN EFFECTIVE THERAPY MARKETING TECHNIQUE

Distributing educational handouts can be a very effective way to increase your visibility. By making your practice literature available to your community, you make yourself more accessible to potential clients and referral sources. Sending a useful, professional handout on a regular basis enables you to:

- Reach out to new potential clients and referral sources
- Stay in touch with current and past clients
- Bring back past clients
- Educate people about your area of specialization
- Provide added value to your counseling services
- Showcase your knowledge
- Highlight your skills
- Enhance your credibility
- Stimulate referrals
- Inform readers of facts they may not have known
- Keep you in front of people's minds
- Publicize your practice to the media
- Network with community businesses and organizations
- Tie in with information on your web site

WHEN AND HOW OFTEN TO SEND HANDOUTS

Sending handouts to referral sources on a regular basis should be one part of your overall marketing plan. According to one marketing expert, people begin to remember your marketing message after they have seen it 7 to 10 times. This means that you have to repeat your message and be sure that people see it in more than one place. Your educational handouts, along with your print and radio ads, flyers, postcards, brochures, newspaper coverage, and other media, can be an important part of your marketing message.

When you send educational handouts to referral sources on a regular basis, you establish recognition for your practice. Ideally, you should plan to send mailings between 4 and 12 times each year. If you can discipline yourself to produce a monthly educational handout and can afford the mailing and production costs, you will soon establish a name for yourself. Every other month or quarterly is fine, too. The important thing is to design a plan and follow it. Starting a handout program and stopping after two or three issues only makes you look unprofessional, and you will quickly be forgotten.

When you set up your plan for sending out handouts, it's best to schedule it for an entire year. Identify the topics for each mailing, choosing from those in this book or combining two or three to make a customized issue to match the needs and interests of your referral sources and clients.

Some marketing experts advise that you avoid the months when potential referral sources and clients are likely to be busy with other activities and less likely to contact you for counseling services. Depending on your target client, these months usually include August, November, and December. On the other hand, you may decide to send your handouts at regular intervals regardless of the time of year. This will steadily build your visibility and name recognition so that when people are ready to seek the services of a mental health professional, they will think of you first.

DEVELOPING YOUR MAILING LIST

You may already have a mailing list if you work for a counseling center or group practice. For those of you who are just starting to market your services or who are on your own, there are several places to begin. If you are a member of your local chamber of commerce, you can most likely purchase mailing labels for all or some of the members for a reasonable fee. Other organizations, clubs, and professional associations may offer the same service. You can also build your own list by going through your local Yellow Pages and the directories of organizations you belong to. Add the name and business address of anyone who may be a potential client or referral source. Be sure to include businesses and professionals who specialize in areas where your clients are likely to be. For example, if you specialize in working with children, the names of day care providers, nursery schools, pediatricians, and children's clothing stores should be on your list.

If at all possible, build and maintain your mailing list on your own computer. Microsoft Works, which comes loaded on many computers today and is inexpensive to purchase, has a very simple-to-use database tool that will help you to manage your mailing list. You can easily update it and print address labels each time you produce a new issue.

Another option, if you have the budget, is to contact a mailing list broker and purchase a list that is tailored to the demographics of your specific target client. This can be expensive, but it can also be especially effective.

MEASURING THE EFFECTIVENESS OF YOUR HANDOUT MAILINGS

It is difficult to precisely measure the effectiveness of a marketing effort, especially when it is for a small business or individual private practice. However, there are a few things you can do to evaluate the impact of your handout mailings.

When a new client contacts you for the first time, always ask how he or she heard about you. Keeping track of these responses and determine which of your marketing efforts are producing your clients.

You may also wish to include an offer for a free consultation or a discount on ongoing sessions. Keeping track of the responses to these offers is another way to determine how effective your campaign is.

Even if you are unable to identify any clients who came to you directly from your mailing campaign, this doesn't mean it is not a success. In the mental health business, it takes several years to build a reputation and name recognition. Your educational handout program should be just one part of a larger effort designed to let people know who you are and how you can help them.

MAKE THESE HANDOUTS YOUR OWN

You may use the content in the handouts in this book in any way you wish. It is not necessary to cite the author of this book (Laurie Cope Grand). You may use this information as if you had written it yourself. However, where the work of *another* author is cited, please be sure to give credit to that author when you use it. For example, the handout "Helping Kids Recover from Loss" cites the work of Elisabeth Kübler Ross. Please be sure to cite her and her book as noted in the sample handout. Very few handouts quote specific authors, but please be sure to give them credit when they do appear. Also, if you add any ideas from an author other than yourself, be sure to cite your sources.

The content of this book is designed for you to use as you see fit in your counseling practice. Please feel free to make it your own. If you want to, you can type, scan, or copy it into a word processing program on your computer. Then you can reword, reformat, edit, delete, or add your own opinions and examples. If you dislike or disagree with anything in any handout, please change it to suit your own preferences. If you have a professional photo of yourself, you can insert that along with your name and practice information. You can also change the handout titles to suit your own style. You will need to copy them from the PDF document and insert them in your word processing program. If you have limited computer skills, however, this is not recommended, because it may be extremely frustrating to accomplish. You may want to find someone else who can do this for you.

These source materials are intended to make it easy for you to create useful and attractive handouts without starting from zero. You may use them exactly as they are written, or you may perform major surgery on them.

HOW TO SET UP YOUR HANDOUTS FOR PRINTING

The text of all 60 handouts is included on the CD in the back of the book. As they appear in the book, the handouts are divided into two sections: problem-focused and life skills. These are the steps to follow when you are ready to prepare them for use in your practice:

1. Download Adobe Acrobat Reader from www.Adobe.com if you don't already have it on your computer. It is free and takes only a short time to download.

2. Copy all of the files onto your hard drive. Don't work from the CD. Keep it in a safe place in case you accidentally delete a file or make changes that you regret. You can always recopy it to your hard drive later.

3. Open the first file you want to print from.

4. Print the appropriate pages.

PRODUCING YOUR HANDOUTS

It can be costly to create a set of handouts if you rely on others to produce them. The more you can do yourself, the less it will cost. If you are fairly skilled at using your computer, you can produce your handouts yourself without having to pay someone else to do it.

The handouts are designed to be printed on two sides of 8½- by 11-inch paper as a trifold brochure like the one in this illustration.

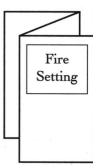

You may wish to purchase small folders for them and make stickers with your practice information for the front of each folder. Insert the handouts or brochures into the folders for an interesting, eye-catching marketing tool. For ideas on special papers and folders, visit www.PaperDirect.com.

I hope you will find this book useful and that you will enjoy providing client education and marketing your practice with these handouts. If you have any questions, feedback, or suggestions, you can send e-mail to Laurie@LaurieGrand.com. I will be happy to answer your handout questions via e-mail and would also appreciate hearing your success stories.

MATCHING THE HANDOUTS WITH TOPICS IN THE CORRESPONDING TREATMENT PLANNERS

The following table lists the recommended handouts for various client issues. Some clients may benefit from more than one handout, since many people have more than one kind of problem. The Life Skills handouts listed following these topic and handout lists may be appropriate for many other client problems.

THE COMPLETE CHILD PSYCHOTHERAPY TREATMENT PLANNER (2ND ED.)

Problem:	Handout:
Academic Underachievement	When Kids Underachieve
Adoption	Dealing with Common Adoption Issues
Anger Management	Helping Kids Manage Angry Feelings
Anxiety	Anxiety in Children
Attachment Disorder	Attachment Disorder
ADHD	Attention-Deficit-Hyperactivity Disorder (ADHD)
Autism/Pervasive Developmental Disorder	Autism
Blended Family	Managing the Stepfamily
Conduct Disorder/Delinquency	Conduct Disorder
Depression	Depression in Children and Teens
Disruptive/Attention Seeking	Attention-Seeking with Disruptive Behavior
Divorce Reaction	Helping Children in Divorcing Families
Enuresis/Encopresis	Enuresis, Encopresis (two separate handouts)
Fire Setting	Fire Setting
Gender Identity Disorder	Gender Identity Disorder
Grief/Loss Unresolved	Helping Kids Recover from Loss
Low Self-Esteem	How to Build Your Child's Self-Esteem

Medical Condition	Living with Your Child's Serious Medical Condition
Mental Retardation	Mental Retardation
Oppositional Defiant	Oppositional Defiant Disorder (ODD)
Peer/Sibling Conflict	Managing Sibling Conflict
Physical/Emotional Abuse Victim	How to Help Victims of Child Abuse
PTSD	Posttraumatic Stress Disorder (PTSD)
School Refusal	When Kids Don't Want to Go to School
Separation Anxiety	Separation Anxiety
Sexual Abuse Victim	Helping a Child Recover from Sexual Abuse
Sleep Disturbance	Sleep Disturbances
Social Phobia/Shyness	Social Anxiety Disorder (Shyness)
Specific Phobia	Phobias
Speech/Language Disorders	Childhood Speech and Language Disorders

THE COMPLETE ADOLESCENT PSYCHOTHERAPY TREATMENT PLANNER (2ND ED.)

Problem:	**Handout:**
Academic Underachievement	When Kids Underachieve
Adoption	Dealing with Common Adoption Issues
Anger Management	Helping Kids Manage Angry Feelings
Anxiety	Anxiety in Children
Attachment Disorder	Attachment Disorder
ADHD	Attention-Deficit/Hyperactivity Disorder (ADHD)
Autism/Pervasive Developmental Disorder	Autism
Blended Family	Managing the Stepfamily
Chemical Dependence	What to Do About Teen Chemical Dependence
Conduct Disorder/Delinquency	Conduct Disorder
Depression	Depression in Children and Teens
Divorce Reaction	Helping Children in Divorcing Families

LIFE SKILLS HANDOUTS

Assertiveness Skills (for Teens)

Building People Skills (for Teens)

Building Positive Teen Relationships

Dealing with Peer Pressure (for Teens)

Expressing Feelings Responsibly (for Teens)

Goal Setting (for Teens)

Helping Your Child or Teen Manage Stress

Helping Your Child Succeed in School

Helping Your Kids Manage the Relocation Blues

Helping Your Kids to Be Self-Confident

How to Cope When Parenting Seems Overwhelming

How to Help a Friend through a Crisis (for Teens)

I'm Planning to Come Out to My Family. What Should I Expect?

Life Skills (for Teens)

Listening Skills (for Teens)

Personal Negotiation Skills (for Teens)

Positive Reinforcement (for Parents)

Teaching Your Child to Respect Others

Understanding Body Language (for Teens)

What Teens Need to Know about HIV and AIDS

Workplace Skills (for Teens)

Child and Adolescent Client Education Handout Planner

Section I

Problem-Focused Handouts

Anxiety in Children

INTRODUCTION

Every human feels anxiety on occasion; it is a part of life. All of us know what it is like to feel worry, nervousness, fear, and concern. This is true for adults and children alike. Kids feel nervous on their first day at school or when they have to take a test. We all know it's normal to feel a surge of fear when we unexpectedly see a photo of a snake or look down from the top of a tall building. Most of us manage these kinds of anxious feelings fairly well and are able to carry on with our lives without much difficulty. They don't disrupt our lives.

But millions of people (an estimated 15 percent of the population) suffer from devastating and constant anxiety that severely affects their lives, sometimes forcing them to live in highly restricted ways. Many of these victims are children. They experience panic attacks, phobias, extreme shyness, obsessive thoughts, and compulsive behaviors. The feeling of anxiety is a constant and dominating force that disrupts their lives. Some become prisoners in their own homes, unable to leave to go to school or visit the mall. For these children, anxiety is much more than just an occasional wave of apprehension.

SEE THESE HANDOUTS ON RELATED TOPICS

Depression in Children and Teens

How to Build Your Child's Self-Esteem

Phobias

How to Cope When Parenting Seems Overwhelming

Separation Anxiety

Social Anxiety Disorder (Shyness)

When Kids Don't Want to Go to School

---

person has an anxiety disorder in combination with another disorder (such as ADD or depression), treatment may be more complicated and take longer.

While a treatment plan must be specifically designed for each individual, there are a number of standard approaches. Mental health professionals who specialize in treating anxiety most often use a combination of the following treatments (there is no single correct approach):

Cognitive Therapy. The patient learns how to identify and change unproductive thought patterns by observing his or her feelings and learning to separate realistic from unrealistic thoughts.

Behavior Therapy. This treatment helps the patient alter and control unwanted behavior.

Systematic Desensitization. A type of behavior therapy, this is often used to help people with phobias, OCD, and agoraphobia. The patient is exposed to anxiety-producing stimuli one small step at a time, thereby gradually increasing his or her tolerance to situations that have produced disabling anxiety.

Relaxation Training. Many children and adolescents with anxiety disorders benefit from self-hypnosis, guided visualization, and biofeedback. Relaxation training is often part of psychotherapy.

Medication. Antidepressant and antianxiety medications can help restore chemical imbalances that cause symptoms of anxiety. This is an effective treatment for many children and adolescents, especially in combination with psychotherapy.

The treatment for an anxiety disorder depends on the severity and duration of the problem. The patient's willingness to actively participate in treatment is also an important factor. When a child or adolescent with panic is motivated to try new behaviors and practice new skills and techniques, he or she can learn to change the way the brain responds to familiar thoughts and feelings that have previously caused anxiety.

WHERE CAN I GO FOR MORE INFORMATION?

Anxiety Disorders Association of America (www.adaa.org)

Anxiety Network (www.anxietynetwork.com)

Anxiety Panic Internet Resource (TAPIR) (www.algy.com)

Free self-help for people with anxiety disorders (www.Anxieties.com)

Beck, Aaron, Emery, Gary, and Greenberg, Ruth. *Anxiety Disorders and Phobias: A Cognitive Perspective.* New York: Basic Books, 1990.

Freeman, Arthur, and DeWolf, Rose. *Woulda, Coulda, Shoulda: Overcoming Regrets, Mistakes, and Missed Opportunities.* New York: Harperperennial Library, 1992.

WHAT IS ANXIETY?

An estimated 15 percent of the U.S. population suffers from devastating and constant anxiety, including panic attacks, phobias, extreme shyness, obsessive thoughts and compulsive behaviors.

An anxiety disorder affects a child's behavior, thoughts, feelings, and physical sensations. The most common anxiety disorders include the following:

Social anxiety also called social phobia. This is a fear of being around other people. Children who suffer from social anxiety always feel self-conscious around others. They always have the feeling that everyone is watching and staring at them and being critical in some way. Because the anxiety is so painful, they learn to stay away from social situations and avoid other people. Some eventually need to be alone at all times, in a room with the door closed. The feeling is pervasive and constant and even happens with people they know.

COMMON PANIC SYMPTOMS

- Racing or pounding heart
- Trembling
- Sweaty palms
- Feelings of terror
- Chest pains or heaviness in the chest
- Dizziness and lightheadedness
- Fear of dying
- Fear of going crazy
- Fear of losing control
- Feeling unable to catch one's breath
- Tingling in the hands, feet, legs, arms

Older children and adolescents who have social anxiety know that their thoughts and fears are not rational. They are aware that others are not actually judging or evaluating them at every moment. But this knowledge does not make the feelings disappear.

Panic disorder. This is a condition where a person has panic attacks without warning. According to the National Institute of Mental Health, about 5 percent of the adult American population suffers from panic attacks. Some experts say that this number is actually higher, since many people experience panic attacks but never receive treatment.

A panic attack typically lasts several minutes and is extremely upsetting and frightening. In some cases, panic attacks last longer than a few minutes or strike several times in a short time period.

A panic attack is often followed by feelings of depression and helplessness. Most people who have experienced panic say that the greatest fear is that the panic attack will happen again.

Many times, the person who has a panic attack doesn't know what caused it. It seems to have come "out of the blue." At other times, people report that they were feeling extreme stress or had encountered difficult times and weren't surprised that they had a panic attack.

Generalized anxiety disorder. Quite common, generalized anxiety disorder affects an estimated 3 to 4 percent of the population. This disorder fills a child's life with worry, anxiety, and fear. Children and adolescents who have this disorder are always thinking and dwelling on the "what ifs" of a situation. It feels like there is no way out of the vicious cycle of anxiety and worry. The person often becomes depressed about life and his or her inability to stop worrying.

Children and adolescents who have generalized anxiety usually do not avoid situations, and they don't generally have panic attacks. They can become incapacitated by an inability to shut the mind off and are overcome with feelings of worry, dread, lack of energy, and a loss of interest in life. The person usually realizes these feelings are irrational, but the feelings are also very real. The person's mood can change from hour to hour, or even day to day. Feelings of anxiety and mood swings become a pattern that severely disrupts the victim's quality of life.

Children and adults with generalized anxiety disorder often have physical symptoms including headaches, irritability, frustration, trembling, inability to concentrate, and sleep disturbances. They may also have symptoms of social phobia and panic disorder.

WHAT ARE THE OTHER TYPES OF ANXIETY DISORDERS?

Other types of anxiety disorders include:

- Phobia—fearing a specific object or situation

- Obsessive-compulsive disorder (OCD)—a system of ritualized behaviors or obsessions that are driven by anxious thoughts

- Posttraumatic stress disorder (PTSD)—severe anxiety that is triggered by memories of a past traumatic experience

- Agoraphobia—disabling fear that prevents one from leaving home or other safe places

HOW IS ANXIETY TREATED?

The treatment for an anxiety disorder depends on the severity and length of the problem. The child's willingness to actively participate in treatment is also an important factor.

Most children and adolescents who suffer from anxiety disorders begin to feel better when they receive the proper treatment. It can be difficult to identify the correct treatment, however, because each person's anxiety is caused by a unique set of factors. It can be frustrating for the patient when treatment is not immediately successful or takes longer than hoped for. Some patients feel better after a few weeks or months of treatment, while others may need a year or more. If a

Attachment Disorder

WHAT IS ATTACHMENT DISORDER?

An attachment disorder develops during the first two years of a child's life. Normally, children bond or attach with their primary caretakers and learn to trust and feel secure with them. This positive attachment experience enables a child to form other trusting relationships and is an important part of his or her ability to function productively in the world.

When the quality of care provided by the primary caretaker is extremely abusive and neglectful during the first two years of life, the child may develop attachment disorder. This is a mental condition in which the child has difficulty trusting and loving the caretaker or anyone else. Children with attachment disorder are afraid to trust and love and develop controlling behaviors that keep other people at a distance. They are unable to relate to others and develop symptoms like the following:

- Their behavior may be at either extreme of inhibited and avoidant or inappropriately friendly with strangers.

WHERE CAN I GO FOR MORE INFORMATION?

Gil, Eliana. *Outgrowing the Pain*. Rockville, MD: Laurel Press, 1983.

Jaratt, Claudia Jewett. *Helping Children Cope with Separation and Loss*. Harvard, MA: Harvard Common Press, 1982.

Turecki, Stanley. *The Difficult Child*. New York: Bantam Books, 1985.

SEE THESE HANDOUTS ON RELATED TOPICS

Helping Kids Recover from Loss
How to Build Your Child's Self-Esteem
How to Cope When Parenting Seems Overwhelming
Positive Reinforcement (for Parents)

- Starting at a young age (before age five), they do not relate appropriately to other people.
- They do not interact socially in ways that are consistent with their developmental stage.
- They may be hypervigilant and guarded.
- Their responses to others may seem ambivalent, confused and contradictory.

> Children with attachment disorder are afraid to trust and love. They develop controlling behaviors that keep other people at a distance.

The failure to develop a secure attachment to one's mother or primary caregiver is extremely damaging to a child. When a very young child is neglected, shifted from one primary caregiver to another, and never experiences comfort, stability, security, and love, he or she is at risk for developing this serious disorder. Such children lack the emotional base needed to develop into healthy, productive adults. As they grow up, they develop a wide array of problems in all areas of development: social, cognitive, physical, mental, spiritual, moral, developmental. Sadly, they are at great risk for passing along the same problems to their own children.

> Children with attachment disorder are afraid to trust and love, and develop controlling behaviors that keep other people at a distance. They are unable to relate to others.

Children who live in unstable, unloving environments as infants suffer not only emotionally, but their brain chemistry is affected as well. The extremely high levels of stress hormones in their brains can impair their physical development, affecting both brain and body. As a result of the impact on the brain, these children are more likely to have problems such as these:

- Behavior problems and conduct disorders
- Low self-esteem
- Anger, lack of impulse control, violent behavior
- Sociopathic (criminal) behavior
- Depression
- Learning disabilities
- Poor physical health
- Inability to trust; inability to form and maintain relationships

Attachment disorder may be a symptom of the dramatic increase in the number of abused and neglected children treated by the social service system in the past 20 years. If not treated, these children will perpetuate the cycle of neglect and abuse when they have their own children.

WHAT CAUSES ATTACHMENT DISORDER?

Attachment disorder is caused by abusive and neglectful parenting. The following kinds of behaviors on the part of the primary caregiver are some examples:

- Drug or alcohol use during pregnancy
- Premature birth
- Physical, emotional, or sexual abuse
- Parental neglect: ignoring the child's needs for food, love, safety, and security
- Moving frequently
- Parental mental illness
- Being separated from one's mother or primary caretaker because of death or illness
- Untreated illness

WHAT IS THE TREATMENT FOR ATTACHMENT DISORDER?

The goals of treatment are to help the child establish and maintain a positive relationship with his or her primary caretaker and to learn to relate to others in healthy and appropriate ways. The treatment may include the following components:

> The goals of treatment are to establish and maintain a positive relationship with the primary caretaker and to learn to relate to others in healthy and appropriate ways.

Individual counseling. A qualified mental health professional can work with the child to address the behavioral and emotional issues. It is important to seek the services of a professional who specializes in working with children with attachment disorders.

Family therapy. A family therapist can work with the family to strengthen the relationship of the family members.

School assessment. Since learning and social behavior are strongly affected by attachment disorder, parents should work with the school psychologist and teacher to assess the child's needs and develop a treatment plan.

Attention-Deficit/Hyperactivity Disorder (ADHD)

 **WHAT IS ADHD?**

ADHD stands for Attention-Deficit/Hyperactivity Disorder. This disorder prevents many bright students from doing well in school because it is so difficult for them to focus and pay attention. They are distracted, impulsive, and have a hard time sitting still. If their disorder has not been diagnosed, they may be seen as troublemakers and underachievers. When ADHD is properly diagnosed and treated, most of these children can learn to focus and become good students.

As many as 5 percent of school-age children have ADHD. It begins before children are seven years old and may last into adulthood. The disorder runs in families; it is estimated that up to 25 percent of ADHD childrens' parent(s) have it.

Some children are diagnosed with attention deficit disorder (ADD), which is similar but lacks the hyperactivity component.

 **WHAT ARE THE SYMPTOMS OF ADHD?**

ADHD symptoms include the following:

- Inattentive behavior
- Difficulty staying focused
- Disorganization
- Trouble concentrating on repetitive tasks

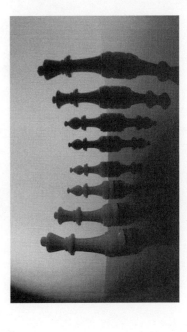

---

5. **Learn to manage impulsive behavior.**
   - Have coaching conversations with yourself.
   - Change the subject. Think about something else.
   - Change the situation. Leave the room and do something else.
   - Distract yourself with background noise like television or radio.

6. **Learn to manage strong feelings.**
   - Have supportive coaching conversations with yourself.
   - Express your feelings to a supportive person.
   - Get some exercise.
   - Change the situation. Leave the room and do something else.

7. **Learn to manage disappointment.**
   - Change the situation. Leave the room and do something else. You can revisit the problem later.
   - Have supportive coaching conversations with yourself.
   - Express your feelings to a supportive person.
   - Arrange for someone else to handle the problem.

8. **Learn to keep your work life interesting with action and variety.**
   - Have many projects going and work on them each day.
   - Interact with lots of different people.
   - Look for work that provides a sense of accomplishment.
   - Choose a work situation where you feel appreciated.
   - Look for ways to express your creativity.
   - Be in control of yourself and your time.
   - Choose work where you can exert yourself.
   - Look for a situation where there is some structure.
   - Work in a structure of deadlines and quotas.

WHERE CAN I GO FOR MORE INFORMATION?

Children and Adults with Attention-Deficit/Hyperactivity Disorder (chadd.org)

The National Attention Deficit Disorder Association (add.org)

Hartmann, T. *Attention Deficit Disorder: A Different Perception.* Grass Valley, CA: Underwood, 1997.

Hallowell, E., and Ratey, J. *Answers to Distraction.* New York: Bantam Books, 1996.

Hallowell, E., and Ratey, J. *Driven To Distraction.* New York: Pantheon Books, 1994.

Kelly, K., and Ramundo, P. *You Mean I'm Not Lazy, Stupid, or Crazy?* Cincinnati, OH: Scribner, 1995.

SEE THESE HANDOUTS ON RELATED TOPICS

Attention-Seeking with Disruptive Behavior

Helping Your Child Succeed in School

How to Build Your Child's Self-Esteem

How to Cope When Parenting Seems Overwhelming

Positive Reinforcement (for Parents)

When Kids Underachieve

- Procrastinating
- Impulsive behavior
- Fidgeting; difficulty sitting still
- Experiencing strong emotions
- Emotional outbursts
- Difficulty concentrating while driving

WHAT IS THE MEDICAL TREATMENT FOR ADHD?

Many people with ADHD find that their symptoms decrease or are eliminated when they take appropriate medication. The following types of medication are typically used for children:

> These medications enable the ADHD patient to stay focused on tasks, minimizing distraction and impulsive behavior.

- **Stimulants.** This type of medication includes Ritalin, Adderall, Cylert, Dexedrine, and Desoxyn. These medications cause increased levels of dopamine and norepinephrine in the brain, and are generally effective in calming the restless patient. They enable the ADHD patient to stay focused on tasks, minimizing distraction and impulsive behavior. Many patients respond dramatically to stimulants in the beginning, but the effect of the medicine sometimes lessens over time, requiring an adjustment of the dose. Two disadvantages of stimulants are that most of them must be taken more than once a day to be effective, and the patient must obtain a prescription for refills in person, making them less convenient.

- **Antidepressants.** These medications are helpful for some patients with ADHD, but they are used less commonly than stimulants. Antidepressants are more convenient for the patient than stimulants because the doctor can call in the prescription and authorize refills by telephone. They are also mostly taken just once daily. On the negative side, some antidepressants take a few weeks to become effective.

WHAT IS THE NONMEDICAL TREATMENT?

Counseling and Coaching

Working with a licensed counselor or therapist can be very helpful for a child or adolescent with ADHD. It is important to find a therapist who understands ADD and has experience in successfully helping other ADHD clients.

> An effective counseling method for children and adolescents with ADHD is a problem-solving or coaching type of approach.

An effective counseling method for children and adolescents with ADHD is a problem-solving or coaching type of approach. The therapist can coach the client to solve problems by improving organizational skills and focusing on life areas where ADHD issues often arise. The most common areas to focus on appear in the following list (skills that will help a child or adolescent with ADHD are listed within each area; some of the skills are more applicable to the needs of older children and adolescents):

1. **Learn skills for building and maintaining relationships.**
   - Make eye contact when you speak to another person.
   - Ask questions to demonstrate that you are listening.
   - Nod and smile to show that you are interested.
   - Share and explore your feelings with others.
   - Learn conflict management skills.
   - When you are upset, take a time-out. Take a deep breath and leave the situation for a moment if you need to.

2. **Learn to manage monotonous tasks.**
   - Set deadlines and monitor your progress regularly.
   - Assign the tasks to someone else.
   - Break the task into smaller subtasks.
   - Find a partner to work with.
   - Create some variety by doing more than one task at a time.

KEY SKILL AREAS

- Learn skills for building and maintaining relationships.
- Learn to manage monotonous tasks.
- Learn to manage information.
- Learn organizational skills.
- Learn to manage impulsive behavior.
- Learn to manage strong feelings.
- Learn to manage disappointment.
- Learn to keep your work life interesting with action and variety.

3. **Learn to manage information.**
   - Have a notebook for each key life area and write everything down.
   - Observe another person performing a task you want to learn.
   - Remember that you can learn in ways other than by reading written directions.
   - Ask questions until you understand.
   - Connect new information to something you already know.
   - Find a quiet place where you can study and stay focused.
   - Break the information into manageable chunks.

4. **Learn organizational skills.**
   - Write notes to yourself. Keep lists, a calendar, a daily planner, and so forth.
   - Structure each day by setting goals and having a to-do list.
   - Set priorities. Know which items you want to accomplish first and which are less important.
   - Focus on one thing at a time.
   - Delegate tasks to others.
   - Have deadlines for things and check them off as you finish them.

Attention-Seeking with Disruptive Behavior

WHAT IS ATTENTION-SEEKING WITH DISRUPTIVE BEHAVIOR?

There are times when every child wants attention and does something to get it. Often it is something positive, such as doing well at school or doing something nice for someone else. Some children, however, don't seem to know how to get attention in positive ways. They seem to resort to negative behavior, such as talking out of turn in class, making jokes, refusing to sit still, arguing, disagreeing, or causing conflict. Children who engage in such behaviors much of the time need special attention and interventions to help them return to positive, appropriate behavior. Without such intervention, these children may alienate their friends and require strong discipline from their parents and teachers. This results in damage to their self-esteem and begins an unfortunate cycle of events, putting the child on the wrong track in life.

WHERE CAN I GO FOR MORE INFORMATION?

Dreikurs, Rudolf, and Soltz, Vicki. *Children: The Challenge.* New York: Plume, 1991.

Dreikurs, Rudolf, Cassel, Pearl, and Kehoe, David. *Discipline without Tears.* New York: Plume, 1992.

SEE THESE HANDOUTS ON RELATED TOPICS

Anxiety in Children

Helping Kids Manage Angry Feelings

Helping Kids Recover from Loss

Helping Your Child Succeed in School

How to Build Your Child's Self-Esteem

How to Cope When Parenting Seems Overwhelming

Positive Reinforcement (for Parents)

Teaching Your Child to Respect Others

When Kids Underachieve

TIPS FOR MANAGING DISRUPTIVE BEHAVIOR

The following ideas may help you manage your child's disruptive behavior:

1. Figure out what need your child is trying to meet by behaving inappropriately.

2. If you can, ignore the disruptive behavior.

3. Tell the child that you will spend time with him or her later.

4. When the child behaves in a positive way, reinforce that behavior with attention and praise. Look for the good moments and praise them.

5. State clearly what behavior you expect from your child.

6. When the child misbehaves, state specifically what you don't like and then describe what you want to see instead. Keep it short and specific.

7. Give the child a few options. Let him or her choose from among them and accept the consequences of each.

8. When things don't go well, wait until you've both cooled down before discussing what happened.

Child psychologist Rudolph Dreikurs suggests that in addition to these ideas, adults manage misbehavior by trying the following:

1. Teach the child acceptable ways of getting attention.

2. Increase the chances that the new behavior will be used, by prompting the child to use it.

3. Schedule one-on-one time with the child. Develop a plan that will enable the child to earn even more individual time.

4. If the child needs help with schoolwork, arrange for someone to help him or her.

5. If the child tries to get your attention inappropriately, remind him or her what to do instead.

WHAT CAUSES ATTENTION-SEEKING WITH DISRUPTIVE BEHAVIOR?

Children's behavior problems may be caused by a variety of factors, including obvious ones like stress, abuse, conflict at home, ineffective parenting, and inherited personality factors. Some kids misbehave because they are not properly disciplined at home and have not been subject to limits. When they reach the classroom, they must learn how to behave appropriately. For other kids, the source of their attention-seeking behavior may be difficult to identify. It could be any combination of the following:

- Some children with behavior problems have been parented well. In some cases, children have a difficult time with the structure of the classroom environment. They have learned to behave appropriately at home and in small groups, but they fall apart when they are one of 25 or 30 children.

- Some children respond differently with different teachers. Some teachers give kids more leeway than do others. When a child moves from the classroom of one teacher to that of another, the new rules may be quite different and the child will respond in a disruptive way.

- Some children arrive at school without having learned to consider the needs of others. They are focused on their own needs and draw attention to themselves. These kids need to learn the skills of cooperation and sharing the spotlight.

- In some cases, the disruptive child is expressing his or her desire for contact with others, however inappropriately. These children generally need to learn more appropriate ways of meeting their needs for contact.

- The child may not be challenged enough or may not have the maturity or social skills to deal with the situation properly.

- The child may have problems focusing in class because of a learning disability or some other problem.

DREIKURS: FOUR GOALS OF MISBEHAVIOR

Children who behave badly don't usually have a serious personality disorder or bad parents. In most cases, kids behave badly because they misunderstand the situation they are in and choose the wrong behavior to meet their needs. Child psychiatrist Rudolf Dreikurs has said that all behavior has a goal. He has further stated that there are only four possible goals of misbehavior: (1) attention, (2) power, (3) revenge, and (4) inadequacy.

According to Dreikurs, an adult can identify the child's goal by paying attention to how you are feeling as a result of the child's misbehavior. He says that:

If you are feeling **upset** or angry, the child's goal is probably to get you to pay more **attention** to him or her. If you are feeling **helpless**, the child's goal is probably to get more **power** or control.

If you are feeling **hurt**, the child's goal is probably to get **payback** for something.

If you are feeling **immobilized**, the child's goal is probably to demonstrate that he or she is **incapable**.

Dreikurs suggests that the adult speak directly about the child's mistaken goal. For example, "It seems like you might be wanting to hurt me by what you just said. Is that possible?"

For more information, see Dreikurs' classic book, *Children: The Challenge*.

It is important to identify the causes of the disruptive behavior and choose the most appropriate course for solving it. This may be as simple as meeting with the child's teacher and discussing his or her views of the situation. In more serious or complicated cases, the services of the school psychologist or another mental health professional may be required. By attending to the behavior early on and by putting together a supportive treatment plan, the child's problems can be resolved quickly, with minimal damage to his or her school experience.

WHAT CAN I DO ABOUT ATTENTION-SEEKING WITH DISRUPTIVE BEHAVIOR?

There are many things a parent and teacher can do to help a child who is behaving in an inappropriate, attention-seeking way at school. Depending on the situation, any of the following ideas may help resolve the situation:

1. Talk to your child and try to understand the reasons for the disruptive behavior. Ask him or her to tell you about it. Ask the child's teacher if you may observe a few hours of class time to learn what is going on.

2. Schedule a meeting with the child's teacher and ask for his or her point of view about the problem. Depending on the situation, it may be a good idea to include the child in all or part of the meeting.

3. Regardless of what anyone tells you, it is important to trust your instincts about what is going on.

4. Be your child's advocate. Learn as much as you can about the issues your child is facing and search for the right answers for his or her unique situation. Be persistent and don't give up.

5. Blaming yourself or others will not help you solve the problem.

6. Making excuses for your child will not help you solve the problem. Every child has a unique set of challenges and you must help your child learn to deal with his or hers.

7. Don't give up until you get to the bottom of the problem. Be willing to try things. If you don't like the answers you get from one source, look for another.

> Some children don't seem to know how to get attention in positive ways. They need special attention and interventions to help them return to positive, appropriate behavior.

Autism

WHAT IS AUTISM?

Autism is a developmental disorder that affects the brain's functioning. The symptoms can range across a spectrum from mild to severe. People with autism have a hard time communicating with others both verbally and nonverbally. They also find it difficult to relate to others and may become aggressive or even hurt themselves. They sometimes respond in odd ways to other people and may make repeated body movements such as rocking themselves or flapping their hands. They are often highly sensitive to smell, touch, sound, sight, and taste. They tend to be quite rigid and resist any change in their routines.

It is estimated that autism occurs in as many as 1 in 500 people, generally appearing before a child is three years old. It occurs in about four times as many boys as girls, across all social and ethnic groups.

WHAT ARE THE SYMPTOMS OF AUTISM?

The symptoms of autism vary widely from one child to the next. Unlike most other disorders, there is no typical or standard group of symptoms; each person develops a unique combination

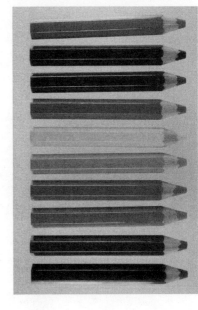

---

mathematics. Some savants, for example, can perform complex mathematical operations in their heads in a short amount of time or memorize complex lists of information.

she may eventually be able to live a productive life. However, most people with autism have impaired communication ability and difficulty interacting with others throughout their lives.

The treatment for a child with autism should be highly structured and should include training on how to function safely and independently in the world. Since every person with autism has unique needs, the treatment program should be designed specifically to meet the individual's needs. Some of the components of the program may include the following:

- Speech and language therapy
- Occupational therapy
- Physical therapy
- Vision therapy to normalize vision
- Sensory integration therapy to treat sensory impairments
- Medication (Ritalin is most often prescribed)
- Special diets and vitamins (Vitamin B6 and magnesium are often recommended)
- Music therapy and auditory integration training
- Behavior modification
- Communication skills training
- Social skills training
- Family education and therapy

With proper treatment, most children with autism can live at home. Other options are group homes and residential facilities designed for people with autism.

WHERE CAN I GO FOR MORE INFORMATION?

Autism Society of America (www.autism-society.org)

Attwood, Tony, and Wing, Lorna. *Asperger's Syndrome: A Guide for Parents and Professionals*. London, England: Jessica Kingsley Publishers, 1997.

Wing, Lorna, Klin, Ami, and Volkmar, Fred. *The Autistic Spectrum: A Parents' Guide to Understanding and Helping Your Child*. Berkeley, CA: Ulysses Press, 2001.

SEE THESE HANDOUTS ON RELATED TOPICS

How to Cope When Parenting Seems Overwhelming

Living with Your Child's Serious Medical Condition

Positive Reinforcement (for Parents)

of symptoms and each of these may be mild, moderate, or severe. The symptoms may also vary from day to day because of anxiety, fatigue, or other factors. Because autistic children find it hard to make sense of the world around them, they may become anxious, confused, and depressed as a result of the great effort that ordinary living requires. They may also be unaware that others do not respond to the world in the same way that they do.

> More than 500,000 people have autism or another pervasive developmental disorder.

The main groups of symptoms include the following:

PERVASIVE DEVELOPMENTAL DISORDERS

Autism is the most common of the pervasive developmental disorders. Others in this group of disorders include the following:

Asperger's Disorder involves having a difficult time relating to others and having limited interests and activities.

Rett's Disorder occurs mostly in females. These children develop normally and then regress to an earlier stage of development. They lose the use of their hands and develop repetitive hand movements before age four.

Childhood Disintegrative Disorder, in which a child develops normally for the first two years and then regresses to an earlier stage of development.

- **Communication is impaired.** The child may not be develop the ability to speak and understand language or may develop slowly. He or she may use words in an odd way and seem to be talking *at* others without reacting to their responses. May use gestures to communicate. The autistic child has a short attention span, and he or she may use gestures to communicate.

- **Interacting with others is affected.** The child may prefer to be alone and may not form friendships with others. Many of these children do not respond to normal social cues like smiling or making eye contact. Instead of looking at others directly, some autistic children use their peripheral vision to see those around them.

- **Aggressive or unusual behavior interferes with interacting with others.** Some autistic children are extremely passive; others are aggressive and volatile. The autistic child may throw a tantrum with no provocation, resist changes in routine, and seem to lack common sense.

- **Play skills are lacking.** The child does not engage in normal playing with other children or alone. He or she does not imitate the behavior of others or engage in pretending.

- **All five senses may be highly sensitive to stimuli.** Some autistic people find it painful to be near or touched by other people and may withdraw from them. Others seem to have under-developed senses. This sensory impairment may make it difficult for them to process information properly, and they also may have a hard time tolerating normal sensory stimulation (e.g., sound, touch, light).

Even though these symptoms are distressing and challenging, many people with autism develop the ability to compensate for their difficulties and learn to live independently.

The symptoms usually begin to appear when a child is between 18 months and three years old.

AUTISM AND SAVANT SKILLS

It is estimated that about 10 percent of people with autism also have savant skills. This means that they have extraordinary abilities or talents in areas such as music, art, or

Sometimes the child shows signs of autism from the time of birth by doing things like avoiding physical contact by arching his or her back away from the caregiver or going limp when being picked up.

As signs of autism begin to appear, the child may begin to develop more slowly than other children of the same age and show deficits in the ability to communicate, interact with others, and learn. The child may also begin to show some autistic behaviors, such as rocking, head banging, and/or avoiding eye contact.

WHAT CAUSES AUTISM?

While there does not seem to be a single cause of autism or other pervasive developmental disorders, it is believed that the source may be a biological or neurological difference in the brain of an autistic person. It is also thought that the disorder has a genetic basis. Other factors that may contribute to the development of the disorder include viruses, vaccinations, toxins, pollution, food allergies, and immune system disorders.

When diagnosing autism, there is no medical test to confirm that a child has the disorder. Since it is so complex and variable, it is important to consult a group of specialists who are experts in autism.

WHAT IS THE TREATMENT FOR AUTISM?

It is important to seek treatment as early as possible in the child's life. The correct diagnosis and treatment can result in a very positive outlook. The child's symptoms may be lessened and he or

Childhood Speech and Language Disorders

WHAT ARE CHILDHOOD SPEECH AND LANGUAGE DISORDERS?

Communication (speech and language) disorders affect about 10 percent of the U.S. population. This group of disorders encompasses a wide range of problems, including difficulty with producing sounds, making sounds incorrectly, substituting sounds, being unable to understand others, and stuttering.

When a child has a speech disorder, others find it difficult to understand him

The fact that the child is unable to send and/or receive communication properly means that he or she may be prevented from relating to others and learning.

Children who may have communication disorders should be evaluated by a pediatrician and then referred to a speech and language pathologist. These professionals are trained to work with the child and act as a resource for the family and the child's teacher. Depending on the results of the evaluation, treatment by a speech and language pathologist or other professional may be recommended.

WHERE CAN I GO FOR MORE INFORMATION?

American Speech-Language-Hearing Association (www.ASHA.org)

Learning Disabilities Association of America (www.LDAnatl.org)

Apel, Kenn, and Masterson, Julie. *Beyond Baby Talk.* New York: Prima Publishing, 2001.

Martin, Katherine. *Does My Child Have a Speech Problem?* Chicago: Chicago Review Press, 1997.

Sowell, Thomas. *Late-Talking Children.* New York: Basic Books, 1998.

When a child has a speech disorder, others find it difficult to understand him or her. A child with a language disorder has problems understanding words or using them properly.

or her. A child with a language disorder has problems understanding words or using them properly.

These children may use words incorrectly or may have improper grammar. They seem to have a smaller vocabulary and may have a difficult time following instructions. Many patients have a combination of these problems. Communication skills include *receptive skills* (what a child understands) and *expressive skills* (how well a child speaks and uses language). Children with delayed communication skills lag noticeably behind the development of children the same age. They become quite frustrated because they are unable to understand others and be understood.

Communication skills include receptive skills (what a child understands) and expressive skills (how well a child speaks and uses language).

WHAT CAUSES SPEECH AND LANGUAGE DISORDERS?

There are many kinds of speech and language disorders and just as many possible causes. The cause could be any of the items on the following list:

- Autism
- Birth defects
- Brain injury before, during, or after birth
- Brain injury caused by an accident
- Cerebral palsy
- Chronic ear infections during childhood
- Cleft lip
- Cleft palate
- Drug abuse
- Hearing loss
- Mental retardation
- Neurological disorders
- Physical abnormality
- Premature birth resulting in delayed development
- Sensory processing disorder
- Stroke

Some children experience a delay in speech and language development for no obvious reason, and the cause is never determined.

THE IMPORTANCE OF EARLY ASSESSMENT AND INTERVENTION

Children who have any of the risk factors just listed should be evaluated early in life by a speech and language pathologist for communication disorders. The evaluation may include observation, testing, and interviews with family and teachers. Several professionals may participate in the evaluation process.

HOW ARE SPEECH AND LANGUAGE DISORDERS TREATED?

It is very important to respond quickly when a child shows symptoms of a speech or language disorder. The fact that the child is unable to send and/or receive communication properly means that he or she may be prevented from relating to others and learning. Children learn communication skills best before they turn five, so it is crucial that any problems preventing them from acquiring those skills be addressed immediately.

Children, Teens, and Suicide

HOW COMMON IS SUICIDE?

It is reported that suicide, the act of deliberately ending one's own life, is a cause of death for about 30,000 people (including 5,000 between the ages of 15 to 24 years old) each year in the United States. Since many suicides are not reported as such, the actual number is most likely much higher. Suicide often goes unreported because of its stigma or because family members find it too painful to confront the truth.

---

cide. Hopelessness may be part of clinical depression, or it may be the result of an illness or other dire circumstance. When a person feels hopeless, he or she feels trapped, and suicide may seem like the only way out.

Anger. After a long, unhappy relationship and years of building anger, some people see suicide as a dramatic way to send a message of retribution.

A sudden loss. The shock and grief of an enormous loss—of a person or a job— may precipitate suicide in some people.

A scandal or extreme embarrassment. Mortifying events lead some people to feel so trapped in their situation that they can think of no other way out.

WHAT IS THE TREATMENT FOR SUICIDAL TENDENCIES?

The treatment of a suicidal person varies, depending on how severe the condition is and what the underlying cause is. Treatment can range from immediate hospitalization to weekly psychotherapy with a licensed mental health professional. It may also include antidepressant medication or treatment for drug or alcohol addiction.

WHAT SHOULD I DO IF SOMEONE IS SUICIDAL?

Always take statements about death and suicide seriously. If you suspect that your child or teen is thinking about suicide, don't be afraid to ask direct questions such as, "Do you ever think about hurting yourself?" "Have you ever thought about taking your own life?" "Tell me about what you have thought of doing," and so forth. Listen to the child's answers and respond without judgment.

Take immediate action by having the child or adolescent evaluated by a qualified mental health professional. Depending on the urgency of the situation, call your doctor, hospital, mental health center, suicide hotline, or police emergency number (911).

WHERE CAN I GO TO LEARN MORE?

Eric Marcus. *Why Suicide? Answers to 200 of the Most Frequently Asked Questions About Suicide, Attempted Suicide, and Assisted Suicide.* San Francisco: Harper San Francisco, 1996.

SEE THESE HANDOUTS ON RELATED TOPICS

Anxiety in Children

Depression in Children and Teens

Helping Kids Manage Angry Feelings

Helping Kids Recover from Loss

How to Build Your Child's Self-Esteem

How to Help a Friend through a Crisis (for Teens)

The rate of suicide in the United States is about 12 per 100,000 people, making it the ninth-leading-cause of death in the country during the years from 1993 to 1995. According to the American Association of Suicidology (which studies suicide and its prevention), there are between 8 and 20 attempts at suicide for each death from suicide. This means that there are anywhere from 240,000 to 600,000 suicide attempts each year in the United States. This rate jumps to 200 attempts for every completed suicide when young people (ages 15 to 24) are involved. In fact, it is the third-leading-cause of death for the 15 to 24 year-old age bracket. Here are some other facts about suicide:

- Very few young children commit suicide, but it is much more common among adolescents.
- Adolescent boys are at greater risk than adolescent girls.
- More suicides happen in the spring than at other times of the year.
- The most lethal days of the week for suicide are Monday and Friday.
- Suicide is an equal-opportunity killer, and is chosen by people from every group imaginable.
- Sixty percent of people who commit suicide do so with guns.

✳ **WHY DO PEOPLE ATTEMPT SUICIDE?**

There are many reasons why people kill themselves, and we often never know why some people choose this route. The fact that teens are vulnerable to suicide may be because they are especially vulnerable to feelings of confusion, self-doubt, fear, and other stresses. When some teens experience these emotions and stresses, they may view suicide as a logical solution.

WHAT ARE THE WARNING SIGNS OF SUICIDE?

One expert says that 8 out of 10 people who kill themselves have given clear warnings that they were considering suicide. While these warning signs can be evident for almost anyone at some point in their life, it is important to be aware of them and take them seriously when you see them.

- Making a threat of suicide. "I wish I were dead," "I'm going to end it."
- Expressing hopelessness.
- Expressing helplessness.
- Expressing worthlessness.
- Having previous suicide attempts.
- Seeming depressed, moody, or angry.
- Having trouble at school or at work.
- Abusing alcohol or drugs.
- Taking risks.
- Withdrawing from other people.
- Behaving differently or oddly.
- Difficulty sleeping.
- Loss of appetite.
- Giving away prized possessions.
- Suddenly seeming happy after exhibiting several of the behaviors listed above.

Various factors seem to play a role in many suicides, but none of them guarantees that a person will end his or her life. Often it is a combination of factors that seem to interact with a person's circumstances, and the factors are unique for each person. Some of these factors include:

Clinical depression. This type of depression is much more than just a simple case of the blues; it is severe and debilitating. It may surprise you to know that people who suffer from depression are at the greatest risk for suicide after they have begun treatment and are beginning to feel better. The reason for this is that when a person is severely depressed, he or she may simply lack the energy to carry out a suicide. But when such people begin to recover and feel better, their energy begins to return and they may carry the act out then.

Alcoholism and drug abuse. These substances are associated with a higher suicide rate because they impair judgment. Over half of all adolescent suicides and suicide attempts are associated with alcohol. When a person is under the influence of alcohol, he or she has fewer inhibitions and may also think and act in ways that would never happen when he or she is sober. Alcoholism and drug abuse also create additional stresses in the lives of users and may result in depression and a tendency toward desperate behavior.

Mental illness. People who have certain mental disorders such as schizophrenia have a higher risk of suicide.

Physical illness. The despair accompanying terminal illness or the illnesses common as people age are often factors that contribute to people taking their own lives.

Feeling hopeless. This condition is very common among people who commit sui-

> Suicide is the third-leading-cause of death for the 15 to 24 year-old age bracket.

Conduct Disorder

WHAT IS CONDUCT DISORDER?

Half of all crimes are committed by a small number of people—about 5 percent of all adults and adolescents. The criminal behavior of this group of individuals is so disruptive and harmful that it is considered a mental disorder. When children and adolescents engage in extremely antisocial behavior, it is called a *conduct disorder*. In adulthood, a pattern of such behavior is called *antisocial personality disorder*.

CHILDREN WITH CONDUCT DISORDER ARE MORE LIKELY TO HAVE:

- Parents with antisocial personality disorder
- Young mothers
- Mothers who smoked while they were pregnant
- A lack of parental supervision
- Physical and sexual abuse

---

extremely important to seek help for any child who engages in these behaviors.

WHAT IS THE TREATMENT FOR CONDUCT DISORDER?

It is difficult to treat children and adolescents with conduct disorder. It may be difficult to obtain the trust and cooperation of the child and his or her parents. Treatment usually lasts a long time and includes a combination of the following:

1. Behavior modification therapy to help the child learn new ways of handling life situations in an acceptable way

2. Anger management training

3. Special education services if the child has learning disabilities

4. Medication, if the child has attention deficits and depression

WHERE CAN I GO FOR MORE INFORMATION?

Katherine, Anne. *Boundaries: Where You End and I Begin.* New York: Simon and Schuster, 1991.

Rosellini, Gayle, Worden, Mark, and Rosell, Garth. *Of Course You're Angry: A Guide to Dealing With the Emotions of Substance Abuse.* San Francisco: Harper Hazelden, 1986.

Williams, Redford, and Williams, Virginia. *Anger Kills: Seventeen Strategies for Controlling the Hostility That Can Harm Your Health.* New York: Time Books, 1993.

SEE THESE HANDOUTS ON RELATED TOPICS

Anxiety in Children

Depression in Children and Teens

Helping Kids Manage Angry Feelings

Helping Kids Recover from Loss

Helping Your Child Succeed in School

How to Build Your Child's Self-Esteem

How to Cope When Parenting Seems Overwhelming

Positive Reinforcement (for Parents)

Teaching Your Child to Respect Others

- Low socioeconomic status
- Less verbal ability

Children and adolescents who have a conduct disorder show a lack of regard for the rights of others. Without help, they will further develop a pattern of antisocial behavior, and as adults, they will be self-seeking and selfish. Such behavior is viewed as unacceptable in our society.

More boys than girls engage in antisocial behavior. In children between the ages of 9 and 17, about 6 percent of boys and 3 percent of girls are conduct disordered.

WHAT IS CONDUCT DISORDER?

Conduct disorder results in a significant impairment of functioning. It involves a **pattern** of behavior that includes several of the following:

- Breaking the rules
- Lying
- Getting into physical fights
- Physically harming another person with a weapon
- Threatening or intimidating people
- Being physically cruel to people or animals
- Forcing sexual activity on another person
- Deliberately destroying property
- Deliberately setting fires
- Stealing things from people, such as in robbery or mugging
- Stealing things when others are not present, such as in shoplifting or forgery
- Breaking into a car, house, or building
- Lying to get things from others
- Staying out at night without parental permission
- Running away from parents' or guardians' home and staying away overnight
- Frequently skipping school

WHAT CAUSES CONDUCT DISORDER?

Children who develop conduct disorder often grow up in families with the following characteristics:

Family beginnings. Antisocial behavior starts in the family. It is generally passed from one generation to the next. This is because people who engage in antisocial behavior patterns are generally inadequate parents who treat their children in harmful ways. They lack the ability to properly supervise and discipline their children. Their parenting is inconsistent and unpredictable. They tend to be extremely lenient at some times and extremely strict at others.

Parenting problems. Men who are antisocial almost never parent their own children and rarely stay in contact with them. Antisocial mothers and fathers often inflict harsh physical punishment with their children, and it may even be considered child abuse. Antisocial parents are also more likely to inflict sexual abuse on their children. As a result of such hurtful and dangerous parenting, it is no surprise that the children in these families develop conduct disorder in a much higher proportion than do kids in normal families.

An early start. Conduct disorder usually starts in childhood or adolescence. The earlier such behavior begins, the more likely it will continue into adulthood. It often begins with crimes against property and becomes more aggressive, involving crimes against people, violence toward animals, and other hurtful acts. When a person first engages in antisocial behavior at puberty or after, the crimes tend to be less aggressive and it is less likely that the behavior will continue into adulthood. Being diagnosed with childhood conduct disorder is the strongest predictor that a person will develop antisocial personality disorder in adulthood. Unfortunately, a high percentage of such children have unsuccessful work and social lives as adults. People diagnosed with adolescent-onset conduct disorders tend to engage in less aggressive behavior and have a more positive outlook for success as an adult.

COSTS AND RISKS

Kids who have conduct disorder have a greater chance of:

- More illness during their lifetimes
- More injuries and accidents
- Dying young

But not always. Engaging in antisocial behavior as a child or adolescent does *not* guarantee that these negative behavior patterns will continue as an adult. Some children and adolescents will overcome their problems and develop into productive adults. The most dangerous signs of future problems in children and teens are setting fires and harming animals. It is

Dealing with Common Adoption Issues

 ## WHAT ARE COMMON ISSUES RELATING TO ADOPTION?

Adopted children and adolescents and their families may struggle with any of the following issues:

- Feeling like one does not fit into one's adoptive family, in a way that is more extreme than the normal adolescent feeling of not belonging
- Rejecting the values and lifestyle of one's adoptive family beyond what is normal for one's age group and developmental stage
- Engaging in limit-testing behavior that is beyond normal behavior for one's age group and developmental stage
- Falling far short of one's ability level at school
- Not reaching normal developmental milestones

Some of these are simply normal behaviors for children and adolescents. However, if they are extreme, going beyond the normal adolescent experience, the child or adolescent needs some help resolving them. These issues are more likely to cause problems for

---

SEE THESE HANDOUTS ON RELATED TOPICS

Anxiety in Children

Attachment Disorder

Depression in Children and Teens

Helping Kids Manage Angry Feelings

Helping Kids Recover from Loss

How to Build Your Child's Self-Esteem

---

2. Let the subject of adoption come up naturally. Don't force it on your child. But be ready to discuss it openly when the child is ready and receptive.

3. Don't provide more information than the child is ready for at the time. Go slowly and see what your child wants to know.

4. Your child may seem disinterested in discussing adoption because he or she is hurt and doesn't want to show it.

5. Some children avoid talking about adoption because they sense that their parents are not comfortable with the topic. It is essential that adoptive parents resolve their own feelings about infertility and adoption with a mental health professional who understands these special issues.

6. Parents may be uncomfortable discussing adoption not because of unresolved issues, but because they fear saying it wrong or hurting the child. Just be yourself and make it clear that you support your child. It is critical to convey that you accept your child's feelings about the adoption and allow him or her to express them.

7. Adoption is an experience that originates in loss for everyone involved. Dealing with loss is difficult for everyone, and you must expect that there will be feelings of sadness and hurt. It is unrealistic to expect that your child will always feel happy about being adopted.

 ## WHERE CAN I GO FOR MORE INFORMATION?

Adopting.org (www.adopting.org).

Raising Adopted Children (www.raisingadoptedchildren.com).

Brodzinsky, David, Schechter, Marshall, and Henig, Robin Marantz. *Being Adopted: The Lifelong Search for Self.* New York: Doubleday, 1992.

Lifton, Betty Jean. *Lost and Found: The Adoption Experience.* New York: Harper and Row, 1979.

Melina, Lois Ruskai. *Making Sense of Adoption.* New York: Harper and Row, 1989.

Melina, Lois Ruskai. *Raising Adopted Children,* (rev. ed.). New York: HarperCollins, 1998.

Melina, Lois Ruskai, and Roszia, Sharon Kaplan. *The Open Adoption Experience: A Complete Guide for Adoptive and Birth Families—From Making the Decision Through the Child's Growing Years.* New York: Harper-Collins, 1993.

Silber, Kathleen, and Dorner, Patricia Martinez. *Children of Open Adoption.* San Antonio, TX: Corona Publishing, 1990.

Silber, Kathleen, and Speedlin, Phyllis. *Dear Birthmother (Thank You For Our Baby).* San Antonio, TX: Corona Publishing, 1982.

the adoptee and his or her family if the subject of adoption has not previously been openly discussed between them or if the parents have not resolved their feelings about adoption.

EVERY ADOPTEE FACES LIFE ADJUSTMENTS

Every adopted person has to accomplish certain tasks throughout the life span. According to authors Brodzinsky, Schechter, and Henig in *Being Adopted: The Lifelong Search for Self* (see book list), these tasks include adjusting to the following:

- Moving to a new home when one is adopted
- Forming secure attachments
- Learning about one's adoption and realizing the implications
- Realizing that one looks different from one's adoptive family
- Dealing with the stigma of being adopted
- Responding to other children's reactions to one's being adopted
- Coping with the losses of adoption
- Exploring the meaning of being adopted
- Including the fact of adoption in one's identity
- Thinking about searching for or getting to know one's birth family
- Learning about one's genetic history
- Thinking about having one's own family

These are just a few of the issues that adoptive parents can help their adopted children face and deal with. It is essential that parents be aware of these issues and be prepared to help their children deal with them as they arise during childhood, adolescence, and young adulthood.

HOW CAN PARENTS HELP THEIR ADOPTED KIDS DEAL WITH THESE ISSUES?

While every adopted child carries an extra set of issues to deal with throughout life, there are certain

---

Things to Do during Adoptee's Childhood

1. Talk about your child's adoption right from the beginning. Even though children do not understand the idea of reproduction until age six or later, it is important for them to begin hearing about their adoption from the beginning and not in the form of a taunt from a neighbor child or cousin.

2. When you begin telling your child stories, tell him or her the story of when he or she was adopted.

3. As your child gets older, continue to tell the story and add details.

4. When the child asks questions, answer them.

5. Don't make the adoption story sound too different from what children normally experience. Always include that the child was born the same way all children are born: that he or she grew inside a woman's body and was born in the same way as others are.

Things to Do during Adoptee's Middle Childhood

1. Expect your child to ask more questions about the adoption between the ages of 7 and 11.

2. Be prepared to share the details of your child's birth family, including who they are and any details you know about them.

3. Expect your child to feel sad or upset about the fact that he or she was placed for adoption by his or her birth parents. Your child may feel like he or she was rejected and may wonder how secure the adoptive home is, too. This is hard for many children to understand and it may take time for your child to process it.

4. If it makes sense to bring up the subject of adoption, do so. It is important for your child to know that you are not afraid to talk about it

---

things the adoptive parents can do as the child grows up to minimize the chances that the issues will become problems. Author and adoptive parent Lois Ruskai Melina suggests many of these in her books, which are listed at the end of this handout.

5. If you don't know the answer to some of your child's questions, say so. There are some facts you may not know and some questions you won't know how to answer.

> *Don't make the adoption story sound too different from what children normally experience. Always include that the child was born the same way all children are born: that he or she grew inside a woman's body and was born in the same way as others are.*

Things to Do during Adoptee's Adolescence:

1. Expect your teen to be thinking about you and your other children, if you have them (adopted or birth). Your teen may want to know about you and may be thinking about how you are similar and different.

2. As your teen becomes more interested in sex, he or she may be reminded of the fact of his or her adoption. Stay alert to signs that he or she is open to talking about it.

3. When you see an opening to bring it up, do so.

4. Always demonstrate that you are available to listen and answer questions. If your teen feels safe talking to you about adoption issues, he or she is much more likely to do so openly and not feel the need to go underground with it.

General Guidelines:

1. While many adopted children show interest and curiosity about their birth families and adoption stories, others seem to lack interest. This should not be a cause for concern, as long as the adoptive parents have been open about the facts and periodically make it clear that they are willing to discuss the subject when the child is ready.

Depression in Children and Teens

WHAT IS DEPRESSION?

Depression is a serious illness, not a harmless part of life. It is a complex disorder with a variety of causes. It is never caused by just one thing. It may be the result of a mix of factors, including genetic, chemical, physical, and sociological causes. It is also influenced by behavior patterns learned in the family and by cognitive distortions.

Depression is not just an adult disorder; it affects as many as 5 percent of children in this country. It is always troubling, and for some children it can be disabling. Depression is more than just sadness or "the blues." It can have an impact on nearly every aspect of a child's or adolescent's life. Children who suffer from depression may experience feelings of despair and worthlessness, and these can have an enormous impact on the child's relationships. Several factors may cause depression in children and adolescents, and there are many different strategies for preventing it.

Depression can have an impact on nearly every aspect of a child's or adolescent's life.

When a child or adolescent suffers from depression, it can affect every part of his or her life, including the

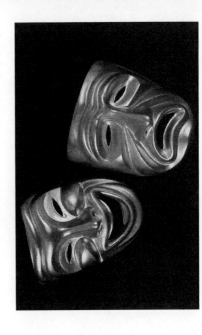

3. **The child's ability to function is impaired by depression.** Seek help before the patient's life situation deteriorates to a serious level.

4. **The child or adolescent has become severely isolated.** An isolated child has no one with whom to reality test. Advise that the patient seek someone out to share thoughts and feelings with. This could be a mental health professional, clergy member, teacher, or friend.

5. **Depressive symptoms have become severe.**

HOW CAN DEPRESSION BE PREVENTED?

Depression can often be prevented. It is especially important to take or more of the following preventive actions if a child or adolescent has predisposing factors such as those identified earlier in this handout:

SIGNS THAT PROFESSIONAL HELP IS NEEDED

Thoughts about death or suicide

Symptoms last a long time

Impaired ability to function

Becoming isolated

Symptoms become severe

1. **Help your child learn to manage stress.** Kids can learn proven techniques for calming and relaxing themselves. They can learn these techniques by working with a therapist, taking a stress management class, or listening to relaxation tapes.

2. **Help your child learn problem-solving skills.** Many kids and adolescents who develop depression need to learn better problem-solving skills. They need to develop the ability to view problems from many viewpoints and look for a variety of solutions.

3. **Help your child focus on the future.** Depressed people tend to be focused on the past. People who set goals and focus on the future tend to be more positive about life.

4. **Show your teen how to strengthen emotional boundaries and set limits.** Boundaries define a person's role in a social situation. They determine how one will and will not behave in given circumstances. Having clear, strong boundaries is empowering, while boundary violations make people feel victimized and helpless. Setting limits means having and enforcing rules for what behavior one expects in a relationship.

5. **Help your child build positive and healthy relationships.** Encourage your child to think about what you need from others in relationships. Teach

---

him or her to learn to read people and trust his or her instincts about whether or not they are positive influences.

6. **Help your child avoid isolation.** Encourage your child to talk to you and others about what's going on inside. If a person keeps his or her thoughts private, he or she may be unaware that they are distorted. Sharing thoughts with another person helps your teen become more objective.

WHERE CAN I GO FOR MORE INFORMATION?

American Academy of Child and Adolescent Psychiatry (www.aacap.org)

Burns, David D. *Feeling Good: The New Mood Therapy.* New York: Avon Books, 1980.

Solomon, Andrew. *The Noonday Demon: An Atlas of Depression.* New York: Scribner, 2001.

Yapko, Michael. *Breaking the Patterns of Depression.* New York: Doubleday, 1997.

SEE THESE HANDOUTS ON RELATED TOPICS

Anxiety in Children

Children, Teens, and Suicide

Helping Your Child or Teen Manage Stress

How to Build Your Child's Self-Esteem

How to Cope When Parenting Seems Overwhelming

How to Help a Friend through a Crisis (for Teens)

physical body and behavior, thought processes, and mood. It also affects the child's ability to relate to others.

WHAT ARE THE SYMPTOMS OF DEPRESSION IN CHILDREN AND ADOLESCENTS?

Depression in children and adolescents appears somewhat different from how it looks in adults. Children who are diagnosed with clinical depression have a combination of symptoms from the following list:

- Feeling sad, crying
- Isolating oneself from others
- Feeling hopeless, like a failure
- Anger, irritability, hostility
- Having a hard time getting along with others
- Fatigue, low energy
- Restlessness, boredom
- Greatly reduced interest or pleasure in most regular activities
- Low self-esteem, feeling worthless
- Excessive or inappropriate guilt
- Indecisiveness
- Thinking distorted thoughts
- Feeling sick much of the time; headaches and stomachaches
- Change in appetite
- Change in sleeping patterns
- Excessive school absences
- Reduced ability to think or concentrate
- Doing poorly in school
- Running away from home
- Recurrent thoughts of death
- Suicidal thoughts
- A specific plan for committing suicide
- A suicide attempt

When a child or adolescent is suffering from depression, these symptoms cause significant distress or impairment in every important area of functioning. This means that the patient's family and social relationships and work life are impaired. A child who once enjoyed playing with friends and participating in activities may become isolated and disinterested in almost everything. Adolescents are generally more verbal and may talk about death and suicide, while a younger child does not. Adolescents may also self-medicate by abusing alcohol and drugs.

The symptoms may be more hostile than sad. If a child begins having problems getting along with others and gets into trouble frequently, it may be a sign of depression.

When a child or adolescent is suffering from depression, symptoms such as these are *not* the result of a chronic psychotic disorder, substance abuse, a general medical condition, or bereavement.

Depression may include feelings of sadness, but it is not the same as sadness. Depression lasts much longer than sadness. While depression involves a loss of self-esteem, grief, disappointment, and sadness do not. Children or adolescents who are depressed function less productively. Kids who are sad or disappointed continue to function.

WHO BECOMES DEPRESSED?

Depression strikes people in families of all ethnic groups, educational levels, and income. Some researchers believe that depression strikes more often in females who have a history of emotional and sexual abuse, economic deprivation, or are dependent on others. It also affects children who are experiencing stress and those with other emotional and learning disorders.

Depression tends to run in families, so it is more common among the parents, children, and siblings of people who are diagnosed with depression. The average age at the onset of a depressive episode is the mid-twenties. However, children and adolescents are being diagnosed at a younger age.

WHAT ARE THE PHYSICAL CAUSES OF DEPRESSION?

Many physicians believe that depression results from a chemical imbalance in the brain. They often prescribe antidepressant medication, and many patients find relief as a result. However, there is no reliable test to identify such a chemical imbalance. It is unknown whether life experiences cause mood changes, which create changes in brain chemistry; or whether the process works in reverse. Depression may be associated with physical events such as other diseases, physical trauma, and hormonal changes. A child or adolescent who is depressed should always have a physical examination as part of the assessment process to determine the role of physical causes.

WHAT IS THE TREATMENT FOR DEPRESSION?

It is important to get help as early as possible for a child or adolescent who shows signs of depression. Depression can be very serious and dangerous, and professional help is often needed.

There are three basic ways to treat depression in children: individual psychotherapy, family therapy, and medication. Many children and adolescents respond best with a combination of two or more methods:

1. **Individual psychotherapy.** A competent therapist can help the child recover from depression. With children, this may be done with the use of games and art therapy. It is important to consult a mental health professional who specializes in working with children or adolescents.

Treatment for depression may include a combination of:
- Individual psychotherapy
- Family therapy
- Medication

2. **Family therapy.** Since the entire family is affected when a child or adolescent is depressed, everyone will benefit from treatment. An experienced therapist who specializes in working with families can help the family get through the crisis.

3. **Medication.** One's brain chemistry can be altered by taking antidepressant medication. A physician may recommend medication when the child's depression is severe, if the child has been depressed before, and if there is a family history of depression. Four types of antidepressant medication are available today:

- Tricyclic antidepressants (TCAs)
- Monoamine oxidase inhibitors (MAOIs)
- Selective serotonin reuptake inhibitors (SSRIs)
- Structurally unrelated compounds

The TCAs and MAOIs have been used for decades. The SSRIs (such as Prozac) and structurally unrelated compounds are newer and are being prescribed more and more frequently today. They have fewer and less pronounced side effects than the TCAs and MAOIs.

WHEN IS PROFESSIONAL TREATMENT NEEDED?

If a child or adolescent is depressed and exhibits any of the following signs, it is extremely important to seek the assistance of a medical or mental health professional:

1. **Thoughts about death or suicide.** This is always dangerous. The patient should see a professional therapist immediately.

2. **Symptoms of depression continue for a long time.** When this occurs, the patient may need professional help. Acute responses to events are normal, but they should not last beyond a reasonable time.

Eating Disorders

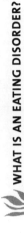

Siegel, Michelle, Brisman, Judith, and Weinshel, Margot. *Surviving an Eating Disorder: Strategies for Family and Friends.* New York: HarperCollins, 1997.

SEE THESE HANDOUTS ON RELATED TOPICS

Helping Your Child or Teen Manage Stress

How to Build Your Child's Self-Esteem

How to Cope When Parenting Seems Overwhelming

How to Help a Friend through a Crisis (for Teens)

Positive Reinforcement (for Parents)

WHAT IS AN EATING DISORDER?

Eating disorders are a group of serious and complicated illnesses that affect a small percentage of people, mostly adolescent and young adult women. These disorders present a severe threat to a person's health and can result in dangerous physical problems and even death. The three main types of eating disorders are anorexia nervosa, bulimia nervosa, and binge eating disorder:

It is difficult to escape our society's message that one's value is based on the size and beauty of one's body.

Anorexia nervosa. People who develop anorexia nervosa have an intense fear of gaining weight and dread being fat. They have a distorted view of their actual body weight, which is 85 percent or less of the normal weight for their age and height. They base their self-esteem on their evaluation of their weight. They deny the reality of their physical condition and its physical effects, which includes at least three missed menstrual cycles. There are two subcategories of anorexia nervosa: (1) the restricting type and (2) the binge eating/purging type. The person with the *restricting type* controls her weight

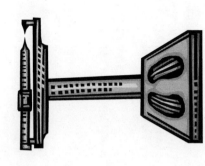

The best treatment for an eating disorder is a combination of elements tailored specifically for the individual patient. The course of treatment depends on the client's situation and needs, and on the severity of the illness. The following treatment methods are the most effective:

Medical treatment for physical symptoms. Patients who have medical complications caused by extreme weight loss or who are suffering from the effects of bingeing and purging must seek the help of a qualified physician. Many patients need treatment at a hospital or treatment center that specializes in treating people with eating disorders.

Cognitive behavioral therapy. Patients learn techniques to change their behavior and also learn to change their responses to stressful situations.

Relationship counseling. The patient learns ways to relate to others in a healthier and more productive way.

Self-help groups. Groups like Overeaters Anonymous provide support for people with eating disorders.

Medication. Many people with eating disorders also suffer from depression, anxiety disorders, and other psychiatric problems. These must be treated in conjunction with the eating disorder. Medication for these disorders can be very effective.

Education. It is critical for patients to learn the facts about eating disorders, proper nutrition, and skills for managing triggers.

WHERE CAN I GO FOR MORE INFORMATION?

Eating Disorders Association (www.UQ.ENET.AU/EDA/documents/start.html)

Eating Disorders Awareness and Prevention (www.EDAP.org)

National Association for Anorexia Nervosa and Associated Disorders (ANAD) (www.ANAD.org)

National Eating Disorders Screening Program (www.NMISP.org/eat.htm)

Costin, Carolyn. *The Eating Disorder Sourcebook: A Comprehensive Guide to the Causes, Treatments, and Prevention of Eating Disorders.* New York: McGraw Hill, 1999.

Natenshon, Abigail. *When Your Child Has an Eating Disorder: A Step-By-Step Workbook for Parents and Other Caregivers.* New York: Jossey-Bass, 1999.

by limiting the amount of food she eats and by increasing her activity. This usually means that she exercises excessively and compulsively. The person with the *binge eating/purging type* of anorexia also controls her weight by limiting the amount of food she eats, but also binges on occasion. Rather than exercising, she purges by making herself vomit or by using diuretics, laxatives, or enemas. About a third of anorexics eventually develop bulimia nervosa.

Bulimia nervosa. Most people who develop bulimia nervosa are adolescent girls or young women. Bulimics are overly concerned about their body shape and weight, basing their self-image on how they look. Unlike anorexics, bulimics may be of normal or above-average body weight. They are obsessed with food, engaging in episodes of overeating or bingeing, during which they feel out of control. After the binge, they attempt to compensate for this behavior to avoid gaining weight. They make themselves vomit, consume laxatives or diuretics, or give themselves enemas; these bulimics are considered the *purging type*. The *nonpurging types* compensate for their binge behavior by fasting or with excessive exercise. Unlike people with anorexia, most bulimics are aware that their behavior is not normal or healthy, and they often feel depressed, ashamed, and isolated. They develop a complicated way of life to accommodate the bingeing and purging cycle.

Binge eating disorder. Binge eating disorder, also known as *compulsive overeating*, is thought to be the most common type of eating disorder. It is similar to bulimia nervosa in that one eats large amounts of food in a short period of time. Unlike those with bulimia nervosa, however, people with binge eating disorder usually do not engage in purging behavior. As a result, people with binge eating disorder usually experience rapid weight gain, weight fluctuations, and obesity. They often become secretive with food, hoarding it and eating alone. They generally feel ashamed of their eating behavior and may avoid social situations that are likely to involve eating. They may also develop depression and anxiety. Unlike the other types of eating disorders, binge eating disorder affects both teens and adults.

WHO IS AT RISK FOR DEVELOPING AN EATING DISORDER?

We live in a culture that emphasizes thinness and physical beauty rather than valuing one's inner qualities. It is difficult to escape our society's message that one's value is based on the size and attractive-

ness of one's body. Young girls are most susceptible to these messages, which are even more powerful when there is a lack of emotional support from one's family and friends. People who develop eating disorders tend to have the following characteristics:

- Low self-esteem
- Need for others' approval
- High need to be in control of their environment and their feelings
- Perfectionism
- Feel undeserving of pleasure and happiness
- Feeling like a failure; disappointed in oneself
- Difficulty controlling impulses
- Depression, anxiety, loneliness
- Not expressing one's feelings
- Obsessed with thinness; extreme fear of gaining weight or being fat
- Disturbed body image
- Past experiences of being shamed for being over-weight
- Family members are or were obsessed with food and weight
- Parents had unrealistic expectations
- Transfers emotional problems to obsession with food and weight
- Past experiences of sexual or physical abuse

Most people who develop anorexia nervosa and bulimia nervosa are adolescent girls or young adult women.

WHAT IS THE TREATMENT FOR EATING DISORDERS?

Eating disorders are extremely serious and dangerous and require treatment by a qualified licensed professional. It is important to obtain treatment as early as possible to maximize chances of a complete recovery. People who allow an eating disorder to progress beyond the early stages may become seriously ill and may even die.

THE PHYSICAL EFFECTS OF EATING DISORDERS

Acid reflux disorder
Anemia
Blood sugar changes (high or low)
Blurred vision
Brittle nails
Calluses on fingers
Death
Dehydration
Depression
Diabetes
Digestive problems (cramps, bloating, constipation, diarrhea)
Dizziness
Dry skin and hair
Electrolyte imbalances
Esophagus deterioration
Extreme fatigue
Fainting
Gum disease
Hair loss
Headaches
High blood pressure
Hyperactivity
Incontinence
Insomnia
Kidney infection and failure
Lanugo (developing hair on face, back, and arms)
Liver failure
Low blood pressure
Lowered body temperature
Malnutrition
Menstrual problems, pregnancy complications, and infertility
Muscle atrophy
Osteoporosis and osteopenia
Pancreatitis
Peptic ulcers
Seizures
Stomach erosion, perforation or rupture
Swelling of the face and cheeks
Swelling of the legs and feet
TMJ Syndrome
Tooth enamel erosion

Encopresis

WHAT IS ENCOPRESIS?

Encopresis is a condition where a child over the age of four is unable to control his or her bowel movements. It is also called *soiling*. It is a difficult condition because it is embarrassing and frustrating for both the child and those who care for him or her. The condition can also cause additional physical problems such as irritation, bleeding, and enlargement of the colon, as well as wetting accidents.

SEE THESE HANDOUTS ON RELATED TOPICS

How to Build Your Child's Self-Esteem

Positive Reinforcement (for Parents)

---

5. The child should follow a regular schedule for going to the bathroom. The child should sit on the toilet and try to have a bowel movement.

6. Keep a record of bowel movements and laxatives taken.

7. Teach the child to do the Valsalva maneuver. This involves holding one's breath, contracting the abdominal muscles, and bearing down.

8. If the child does not have a bowel movement during a given day, give the child a suppository or enema.

9. If several days go by with no bowel movement, give the child a larger amount of laxative.

The information in this handout is for educational purposes only. It is important to obtain the advice and supervision of a qualified licensed health care provider.

WHERE CAN I GO FOR MORE INFORMATION?

Spock, Benjamin, and Parker, Stephen. *Dr. Spock's Baby and Child Care.* New York: Pocket Books, 1998.

WHAT CAUSES ENCOPRESIS?

Encopresis happens when feces accumulate in the large intestine (colon) over a period of time. The feces may become hard and painful. When more feces are formed they may leak out around the accumulated matter. The muscles of the rectum and colon become stretched and do not send the proper signals to the child's brain that a bowel movement is needed. As a result, the child has accidents and pain when he or she goes to the bathroom.

The problem is considered encopresis only if it is *not* caused by an illness or disability. Many children who have encopresis also have other emotional problems such as hyperactivity and attention deficits. These problems may develop in response to stresses in the home such as moving to a new location, the birth of a sibling, or other challenging situations. The condition occurs in boys more often than in girls.

> Many children who have encopresis also have other emotional problems such as hyperactivity and attention deficits.

> This problem can be caused by a number of things, including toilet training problems, physical disabilities and conditions, and emotional problems.

WHAT ARE THE SIGNS OF ENCOPRESIS?

When a child has encopresis, some of the following signs may be present:

- Having soiling accidents when not ill
- Clothing feels tight around the waist
- Feeling a hard mass around the abdomen
- Feeling pain when defecating
- Having the symptoms of constipation (a stomachache or cramps)

> It is important that the family be supportive and patient and not cause the child additional shame.

is found, you may want to consult a mental health professional who specializes in working with children and adolescents. This will help you determine if the condition is caused by emotional problems.

It may take some time to treat the problem. It is important that the family be supportive and patient and not cause the child additional shame. It is also important to praise the child when he or she is successful. Treatment may include some or all of the following steps:

1. Include plenty of fiber and fluids in the child's diet.
2. Make sure the child gets plenty of exercise each day.
3. Clean the rectum and colon with an enema.
4. Administer laxatives to clear out the feces in the bowel. This will also help the colon begin to function properly once again.

WHAT IS THE TREATMENT FOR ENCOPRESIS?

Children who soil should first be seen by a medical doctor to rule out a physical cause. If no physical cause

Enuresis (Bed Wetting)

✳ WHAT IS ENURESIS?

Enuresis or bed wetting is an upsetting experience for everyone in the family. It is very common, affecting as many as 15 percent of all kids over the age of six in the United States. It is common for children

---

SEE THESE HANDOUTS ON RELATED TOPICS

How to Build Your Child's Self-Esteem

Positive Reinforcement (for Parents)

- Wake the child during the night and take him or her to the bathroom.

- Some people have had success using a special pad with a buzzer that wakes the child when he or she begins to wet the bed. See your doctor for information about this gadget.

- Your family doctor may be able to prescribe medication to help solve the problem. In some cases, the doctor may prescribe an antidiuretic or antidepressant medication.

- If the problem is caused by family stress, seek the services of a licensed family therapist who is skilled at working with children.

The information in this handout is for educational purposes only. It is important to obtain the advice and supervision of a qualified licensed health care provider.

✳ WHERE CAN I GO FOR MORE INFORMATION?

Spock, Benjamin, and Parker, Stephen. *Dr. Spock's Baby and Child Care.* New York: Pocket Books, 1998.

under age six to wet the bed, but most learn to stay dry at night by the time they are six. Beyond the age of six, of those who continue to wet the bed, about 15 percent learn to stay dry without any treatment. For some children, however, the problem continues into puberty. It is a problem not only because it results in a lot of tiresome laundry chores, but more important, because it causes many kids to feel embarrassed and ashamed. They may be teased by other children and may not be able to participate in fun activities like sleepovers and sleep-away camp. However, it is important to know that most people with enuresis eventually stay dry at night; some just take longer than others.

> It is important to know that most people with enuresis eventually stay dry at night; some just take longer than others.

✳ WHAT CAUSES ENURESIS?

Children do not wet the bed on purpose. They usually feel embarrassed about it, and it is important that they

not be teased or punished. The cause could be any of the following:

- Bed wetting runs in families, and affects more boys than girls. In some cases, it is caused by the lack of a hormone that keeps the bladder from overfilling. Since there isn't enough of this hormone, the bladder fills up and the child wets the bed.

- Another cause of wetting the bed is that the child drinks too much liquid late in the day. If the child doesn't wake up when he or she has to urinate during the night, he or she wets the bed.

- In rare cases, the child may have a bladder or kidney problem or a sleep disorder.

- Some children wet the bed because they are dealing with emotional stresses, such as moving to a new location, a divorce or death in the family,

> Children do not wet the bed on purpose. They usually feel embarrassed about it, and it is important that they not be teased or punished.

> Bed wetting runs in families, and affects more boys than girls.

- or the birth of a new sister or brother.

- Some children begin to wet the bed after they have been toilet trained and learned to stay dry at night. Perhaps their experience of toilet training was stressful and they simply need to be trained again with patience, encouragement, and understanding.

✳ WHAT IS THE TREATMENT FOR ENURESIS?

Since wetting the bed is never anyone's fault, it is important that the child not be punished or teased when it happens. Treatment may include any of the following:

- Show your child patience and understanding.

- Praise the child for taking steps to solve the problem.

- The child should avoid drinking liquids late in the day or during the night.

- The child should go to the bathroom before going to sleep.

Fire Setting

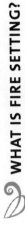

WHAT IS FIRE SETTING?

Many young children are interested in fire. Most learn to appreciate it when they see the candles lighted on their birthday cakes or when their parents light a warm, beautiful fire in the fireplace on a winter evening. Sometimes, they are attracted to and want to experiment with matches, candles, and lighters. It is important for adults to model safe fire behavior and teach their children behavior that will help everyone in the family stay safe.

WHAT IS PYROMANIA?

Fire setting is not the same as pyromania. People with pyromania experience tension before the act and relief afterward. People with this rare disorder do not set fires to benefit from insurance money or out of revenge. They are usually fascinated by fire.

SEE THESE HANDOUTS ON RELATED TOPICS

Attention-Seeking with Disruptive Behavior

Conduct Disorder

Helping Kids Manage Angry Feelings

How to Build Your Child's Self-Esteem

How to Cope When Parenting Seems Overwhelming

Oppositional Defiant Disorder (ODD)

Positive Reinforcement (for Parents)

You may be able to find help for your child by consulting your local fire department, burn center, or mental health professional.

HOW CAN FIRE SETTING BEHAVIOR BE PREVENTED?

- Be a good example for your child by demonstrating safe fire behavior.

- Teach kids that lighters and matches are not toys.

- Keep lighters and matches hidden away in a high cabinet.

- Instruct your kids to notify an adult if they find lighters or matches.

- Teach older kids to handle lighters and matches safely. Show them how to strike matches and light candles safely.

WHERE CAN I GO FOR MORE INFORMATION?

Sakheim, George, and Osborn, Elizabeth. *Firesetting Children: Risk Assessment and Treatment.* Washington, DC: Child Welfare League of America, 1994.

Fire setting is not the same as pyromania. People with pyromania experience tension before the act and relief afterward.

WHAT CAUSES KIDS TO SET FIRES?

There are several kinds of situations where children set fires. The most common include the following:

Curiosity. Sometimes curious children play with fire when they don't understand the consequences of their actions. This typically happens with boys under age seven who get themselves into trouble while playing alone. They may be experimenting with a lighter or matches in a closet or under a bed. These children do not understand what they are doing or how to react when the fire starts. They also have a false sense of security and think that nothing will happen or they won't get hurt. When a fire starts, they become frightened and try to hide. As a result, there is an even greater chance of injury and destruction.

Trauma. Another dangerous situation is when a child between 5 and 10, usually a boy, sets fire to clothing or things that belong to someone in the house. He is alone in the house and has probably recently experienced stress. His fire setting is not the result of curiosity, but due to some kind of crisis in his life. He may be setting fire to clothing or objects belonging to a person associated with the crisis, such as the perpetrator of child abuse.

Aggression. Boys between 7 and 12 years old set fires randomly for no obvious reason.

Vandalism. Older children (between the ages of 10 and 14); often acting in groups, set fires out of boredom or to impress others. These acts of delinquency are often committed by groups of both boys and girls. The fire is often set outside, to grass or a trash can.

> Sometimes curious children play with fire when they don't understand the consequences of their actions.

addressed immediately. Fires can kill people and destroy property, so any behavior that goes beyond mild curiosity must be stopped. Setting fires deliberately is arson, and more than half of all arson arrests are juveniles.

WHAT IS THE TREATMENT FOR FIRE SETTING BEHAVIOR?

When your child has set a fire, your course of action will depend on the answers to several questions:

- Did the child set the fire out of curiosity or was it deliberate?
- Was the child seeking to destroy property or injure someone?
- Why did the child set the fire? Was it an attempt to punish someone who has abused the child, a response to sibling jealousy, or a way to create some excitement?
- What did the child do after he set the fire—seek help, escape, or watch and enjoy?
- How many times has the child set fires in the past?
- What other negative behavior has the child shown recently?

> Setting fires deliberately is arson, and more than half of all arson arrests are juveniles.

It is normal for children to be curious about fire, but setting fires deliberately is a serious problem that must be

> It is normal for children to be curious about fire, but setting fires deliberately is a serious problem that must be addressed immediately.

Gender Identity Disorder

WHAT IS GENDER IDENTITY DISORDER?

Children with gender identity disorder express an intense desire to be the opposite gender. In some cases, these children actually claim that they *are* the opposite gender. They may prefer to wear clothing of the opposite gender and take on the role of that gender when playing with other children. They may gravitate toward children who are the opposite gender, participating their activities

In assessing whether a child has gender identity disorder, one must be careful to ascertain whether the child's behavior is something other than normal gender role experimentation.

the beginning of this handout, treatment should be sought.

It is important to seek early treatment for gender-disordered children. If the disorder is not properly treated, more serious problems such as transvestitism and transsexualism may develop. Treatment generally includes several types of interventions, including individual counseling, family therapy, meeting with the school psychologist, behavior modeling to teach appropriate gender role behaviors, sex education, and the use of male role models. The right therapy can help the child resolve this disorder and avoid even more serious problems later in his or her life.

WHERE CAN I GO FOR MORE INFORMATION?

Di Ceglie, Domenico, Freeman, David, and Money, John. *A Stranger*

in My Own Body: Atypical Gender Identity Development and Mental Health. London, England: Karnac Books, 1998.

Zucker, Kenneth, and Bradley, Susan. *Gender Identity Disorder and Psychosexual Problems in Children and Adolescents.* New York: Guilford Press, 1995.

SEE THESE HANDOUTS ON RELATED TOPICS

How to Build Your Child's Self-Esteem

Positive Reinforcement (for Parents)

and daydreaming about being that gender themselves. These behaviors are more extreme, persistent, and long lasting than the normal behaviors children engage in as they explore opposite gender roles during childhood play.

Gender Identity Disorder creates a high level of discomfort and stress for the child or adolescent who suffers from it. Adolescents express their feelings as being trapped in the body of the wrong gender.

Adolescents with gender identity disorder express their wish to be the other gender and are often mistaken for that gender. They further identify with the other gender and believe that they respond to life situations as if they were that gender. They are increasingly uncomfortable with their own gender and their role as a member of that gender. They are also disgusted by their genitals and wish they could be altered to resemble the genitals of the opposite gender. In

adolescence, they may begin to ask about the possibility of having their sex organs altered by surgery or with hormones.

Gender identity disorder creates a high level of discomfort and stress for the child or adolescent who suffers from it. Adolescents express their feelings as being trapped in the body of the wrong gender. This experience severely limits their ability to function normally in most areas of their lives (socially, academically, and for adolescents, in work situations). The disorder may first appear in early childhood and affects more males than females. If it continues for more than six months, or if it continues from childhood into adolescence, treatment should be considered.

WHAT CAUSES GENDER IDENTITY DISORDER?

There has been little research on gender identity disorder, and all of

the studies that have been completed have focused on boys. The research that has been done points out that boys learn about their roles as males from their fathers, and when there is no father present, or if the father is emotionally distant, some boys develop gender identity disorder. A high percentage of both mothers and fathers of boys with the disorder also have psychiatric problems, which makes it difficult for any child to develop normally.

Gender identity disorder creates a high level of discomfort and stress for the child or adolescent who suffers from it.

It is important to seek early treatment for gender-disordered children. If the disorder is not properly treated, more serious problems may develop.

WHAT IS THE TREATMENT FOR GENDER IDENTITY DISORDER?

In assessing whether a child has gender identity disorder, one must be careful to ascertain whether the child's behavior is something other than normal gender role experimentation or in the case of a girl, a tomboy phase. If the behavior has persisted for more than six months and fits the description at

Helping a Child Recover from Sexual Abuse

WHAT IS CHILD SEXUAL ABUSE?

Child sexual abuse (CSA) occurs when one person forces any unwanted sexual contact onto a child. It can involve a stranger, friend, partner, or acquaintance. It can involve any type of unwanted sexual behavior. Although as many as 80,000 cases of CSA are reported each year, the actual number of incidents is much greater. This is because many children are afraid to tell an adult about the abuse and because even when they do tell, it is difficult for adults to confirm what happened and to respond properly.

Being sexually abused involves both physical and psychological assault. CSA victims experience a range of emotions that includes fear, shame, anger, and depression. Such experiences

WHAT SHOULD I DO AFTER A CHILD TELLS ME ABOUT ABUSE?

- Report any suspicion of abuse to the police or your local child protective services.
- Provide support in the agency's evaluation of the situation.
- Take your child to the pediatrician for evaluation. The doctor can provide treatment and reassure the child that he or she will recover.
- Take the child to a licensed mental health professional who has special training and experience in working with child sexual abuse victims. Participate in designing a treatment plan that involves the entire family, if appropriate.
- If the child is asked to testify against the abuser, provide emotional support to prevent the testimony from being a second abusive experience.

While it is impossible for parents to protect their children from every kind of harm, there are some things you can do to help keep your children safe from sexual predators. One is to teach your child how to say no. Use books, educational videos, and dolls to show your child how to say no if an adult behaves inappropriately.

WHERE CAN I GO FOR MORE INFORMATION?

American Academy of Child and Adolescent Psychiatry. *Facts for Families* (www.AACAP.org).

Bass, E., and Davis, L. *The Courage to Heal: A Guide for Women Survivors of Child Sexual Abuse.* San Francisco: HarperCollins, 1988.

Bradshaw, John. *Healing the Shame That Binds*

You. Deerfield Beach, FL: Health Communications, Inc., 1988.

Kleven, Sandy. *The Right Touch: A Read-Aloud Story to Help Prevent Child Sexual Abuse.* Bellevue, WA: Illumination Arts, 1998.

SEE THESE HANDOUTS ON RELATED TOPICS

Anxiety in Children

How to Build Your Child's Self-Esteem

How to Cope When Parenting Seems Overwhelming

How to Help a Friend through a Crisis (for Teens)

are so devastating to children that proper and immediate treatment must be provided.

> The perpetrator can be a member of the child's immediate family or a teacher, priest, minister, or stranger.

WHAT ARE THE COMMON RESPONSES TO SEXUAL ABUSE?

Most CSA victims report some of the following symptoms (these responses are always devastating, even when the victim is a young child who seems not to understand what has happened):

- Experiencing sleep disturbances
- Having frightening dreams
- Withdrawing from friends and family
- Being secretive
- Feeling depressed and sad
- Experiencing low self-esteem and/or feelings of worthlessness
- Talking about death or suicide
- Avoiding or skipping school
- Acting up at school
- Being unusually aggressive
- Showing increased interest in anything sexual
- Avoiding any discussion of anything sexual
- Incorporating sexual references in games and drawings
- Behaving in a seductive manner
- Saying that one's body is bad or dirty
- Saying that something is wrong in one's genital area

Some physical symptoms of sexual abuse can only be detected by a medical professional during a physical examination.

When sexual abuse continues for a long time, the effects become even more severe. The child is likely to become even more withdrawn, depressed, and distrustful of adults. Self-hatred and suicidal behavior become more likely. The child begins to relate to others more exclusively on a sexual basis and is much more likely to also become a sexual abuser in adulthood.

> With the proper treatment and family support, most victims can recover their self-esteem and heal from the effects of the trauma.

The actual assault is often compounded when the abuser is someone the child knows and loves. The child cares about the person but probably senses that the sexual part of the relationship is wrong. The child may try to stop the sexual activity, but the abuser may threaten or coerce the child into keeping the secret and continuing the behavior. This can lead to a devastating web of emotions for the child and those who love him or her.

WHAT IS THE TREATMENT FOR CHILD SEXUAL ABUSE?

Children who are sexually abused need professional treatment as soon as the abuse is discovered. It is important that all members of the victim's family be included in the treatment plan. Without treatment, child victims are very likely to develop severe emotional problems that can last a lifetime. With the proper treatment and family support, most victims can recover their self-esteem and heal from the effects of the trauma.

> While it is impossible for parents to protect their children from every kind of harm, there are some things you can do to keep your children safe from sexual predators.

HOW SHOULD I RESPOND TO A CHILD'S REPORT OF ABUSE?

If you suspect that your child may have been abused sexually, it is important to follow these guidelines carefully. The adult's responses to the information about the abuse are critical to the child's ability to recover.

- Encourage the child to talk about what happened.
- Avoid any response that may convey disapproval.
- Show that you take the child's statements seriously.
- State that the abuse is not his or her fault.
- Tell the child that he or she is right to tell you about the abuse.
- Keep in mind that the child may have been threatened by the abuser and may be afraid of the consequences of telling.
- Take steps to protect the child from further harm, either retaliation for telling or further abuse.
- Promise the child that you will take action to stop the abuse right now.

Helping Children in Divorcing Families

WHAT ARE TYPICAL PROBLEMS OF CHILDREN IN DIVORCING FAMILIES?

The decision to divorce causes major changes in the lives of every member of the family. Some upheaval is inevitable, but devastation is not.

Divorce profoundly affects children. In *Surviving the Breakup*, authors Judith Wallerstein and Kelly Joan Berlin describe the experience of 60 divorcing families. Based on their research, they outline the following key issues for children of divorcing families:

Fear. Divorce is frightening to children, and they often respond with feelings of anxiety. Children feel more vulnerable after a divorce, because their world has become less reliable.

Wallerstein, Judith, and Kelly, Joan Berlin. *Surviving the Breakup: How Children and Parents Cope with Divorce.* New York: Basic Books, 1996.

SEE THESE HANDOUTS ON RELATED TOPICS

Anxiety in Children

Depression in Children and Teens

Helping Kids Manage Angry Feelings

Helping Kids Recover from Loss

Helping Your Child or Teen Manage Stress

How to Build Your Child's Self-Esteem

How to Cope When Parenting Seems Overwhelming

How to Help a Friend through a Crisis (for Teens)

Managing Sibling Conflict

Managing the Stepfamily

Positive Reinforcement (for Parents)

Separation Anxiety

---

who has experience and training for working with the special needs of children and adolescents.

WHAT IS THE TREATMENT?

Children of divorcing families need plenty of support and understanding. It is important that they have many opportunities to express their feelings and concerns. If professional treatment is needed, these are the most effective options:

Individual psychotherapy. A competent therapist can help the child deal with feelings about the divorce. With younger children, this may be done with the use of games and art therapy. It is important to consult a mental health professional who specializes in working with children or adolescents.

Family therapy. Since the entire family is affected by the divorce, it is important to help the entire group heal so they can recover and go on to a productive life. An experienced therapist who specializes in working with families can help the family get through the crisis.

Individual and family therapy can help the family members deal with their feelings of grief, hurt, and anger; obtain emotional support; resolve conflicts; and learn problem-solving skills.

WHERE CAN I GO FOR MORE INFORMATION?

American Academy of Child and Adolescent Psychiatry (www.aacap.org)

Wallerstein, Judith, and Blakeslee, *Second Chances: Men, Women, and Children a Decade After Divorce.* Boston: Mariner Books, 1996.

Fear of abandonment. One third of the children in Wallerstein's study feared that their mother would abandon them.

Confusion. The children in divorcing families become confused about their relationships with their parents. They see their parents' relationship fall apart and sometimes conclude that their own relationship with one or both parents could dissolve, as well.

Sadness and yearning. More than half of the children in the Wallerstein study were openly tearful and sad in response to the losses they experienced. Two-thirds expressed yearning, for example: "We need a daddy. We don't have a daddy."

Worry. In Wallerstein's study, many children expressed concern about one or both of their parents' ability to cope with their lives. They wondered if their parents were emotionally stable and able to make it on their own. Over half of the children expressed deep worries about their mothers. They witnessed their mothers' mood swings and emotional reactions to the events in the family. Some children worried about suicide and accidents.

> The children in divorcing families become confused about their relationships with their parents. They see their parents' relationship fall apart and sometimes conclude that their own relationship with one or both parents could dissolve too.

Feeling rejected. Many children who experience a parent moving out of the home feel rejected by the parent. The parent is usually preoccupied with problems and pays less attention to the child than in the past. Many children take this personally and feel rejected and unlovable.

Loneliness. Since both parents are preoccupied with their problems during the divorce process, they are less able to fulfill their parenting roles with their children. The children may feel like their parents are slipping away from them. If the father has moved away and mother has gone off to work, the children often feel profound loneliness.

Divided loyalties. The children may (accurately) perceive that the parents are in a battle with each other. The children feel pulled in both directions and may resolve the dilemma by siding with one parent against another.

Anger. Children in divorcing families experience more aggression and anger. It is often directed toward the parents, expressed in tantrums, irritability, resentment, and verbal attacks. Many children see the divorce as a selfish act and feel very resentful about the resulting destruction of their lives.

More than one third of the children in Wallerstein's study showed acute depressive symptoms such as sleeplessness, restlessness, difficulty in concentrating, deep sighing, feelings of emptiness, compulsive overeating, and various somatic complaints.

WHAT ARE TYPICAL LONG-TERM SYMPTOMS?

The symptoms that many children may have during the divorce process either moderate or

disappear within 18 months after the breakup. Of the symptoms that remain, these were the most common:

Manipulative behavior was reported by about 20 percent of the teachers of the children in Wallerstein's study.

Intense anger at one or both parents was reported by 25 percent of the children and adolescents one year after the divorce.

Depression was diagnosed in 25 percent of the children and adolescents. The symptoms of depression in children include:

- Low self-esteem
- Inability to concentrate
- Sadness
- Mood swings
- Irritability
- Secretiveness
- Isolation
- Eating disorders
- Behaving too perfectly
- Being accident-prone
- Stealing
- Skipping school
- Underachieving at school
- Sexual acting out
- Self-blame

WHEN IS PROFESSIONAL HELP NEEDED?

You should consider finding a licensed mental health professional to work your child or adolescent if he or she is experiencing the following feelings most of the time:

Loneliness	Overwhelmed by feelings
Depression	Sleeping too much or too little
Numbness	Worry
Exhaustion	Anxiousness
Hopelessness	Fear

When seeking the services of a mental health professional, it is important to find a therapist

Helping Kids Manage Angry Feelings

All children find it difficult at times to express and manage angry feelings. Let's take a look at what causes children to become angry and how you can help them respond to stressful situations more constructively.

WHAT CAUSES ANGRY FEELINGS?

Kids feel angry in response to either external or internal events. For example, your daughter may feel anger in response to the behavior of a specific person, like her brother or the child next door. Your son may feel anger in response to something that happens—not being able to watch her favorite television show or being told "no." Children may also feel angry as a result of their own thoughts and feelings—things like worry, fear, hurt, or remembering upsetting events. Any of these things can set off angry feelings.

Some experts say that anger is a secondary emotion that is triggered by another emotion such as hurt, fear, or frustration. To resolve the feelings of anger, you can help your child identify and express the primary emotions that lie beneath the anger.

Feelings of anger are neither good nor bad. The important thing is to help your children realize that they have the ability to choose their responses to their feelings

Once a child begins to feel angry, there are several things you can teach him or her to do to stop the process and keep things from spiraling out of control. Here are a few ideas:

1. **Call a time-out.** This is a very effective technique for breaking the sequence of behavior that leads to a blowup. It works best if it is discussed ahead of time and both people agree to use it. Either person in an interaction can initiate time-out. One person makes the time-out gesture like a referee in a football game. The other person is obligated to return the gesture and stop talking.

2. **Check it out.** When a friend is angry, it is okay to ask, "What's bothering you?"

3. **Make positive statements.** Teach your children to memorize a few positive statements to say to themselves when they feel their anger being triggered. These statements can remind them that they can **choose** their behavior instead of reacting in a knee-jerk manner. For example:

   - "I can take care of my own needs."
   - "His needs are just as important as mine."
   - "I am able to make good choices."

4. **Be prepared with a memorized response.** Here are a few statements and questions that will help your children deescalate anger:

   - "What's bothering me is . . ."
   - "If this continues like this, I'll have to do X to take care of myself."
   - "What do you need now?"
   - "So what you want is . . ."

 WHERE CAN I GO FOR MORE INFORMATION?

McKay, Matthew, Rogers, Peter, and McKay, Judith. *When Anger Hurts: Quieting the Storm Within.* Oakland, CA: New Harbinger Publications, 1989.

Rosellini, Gayle, and Worden, Mark. *Of Course You're Angry* (2nd ed.). Center City, MN: Hazelden Foundation, 1997.

Tavris, Carol. *Anger: The Misunderstood Emotion.* New York: Touchstone, 1989.

in any situation. Their way of dealing with angry feelings can be either positive or negative, leading to either a destructive or constructive outcome for themselves and those around them.

HOW IS ANGER HARMFUL?

Psychologists have long disagreed about the value of venting feelings. Recent research shows that expressing anger often results in more irritation and tension rather than feeling more calm. Giving vent to anger can produce the following harmful effects:

- Blood pressure rises.
- The original problem is worse rather than better.
- The person venting anger seems negative and intimidating.
- Being around an angry person drives others away.

> Psychologists have long disagreed about the value of venting feelings. Recent research shows that expressing anger often results in more irritation and tension rather than feeling more calm.

WHAT ARE THE PHYSICAL EFFECTS OF ANGER?

Children who are frequently angry tend to develop more physical problems as they become adults. For example:

Heart. Researchers at Stanford University have found that of all the personality traits found in Type A patients, the potential for hostility is the key predictor for coronary disease. The combination of anger and hostility is the most deadly.

Stomach and intestines. Anger has a very negative effect on the stomach and has even been associated with the development of ulcerative colitis.

Nervous system. Anger is bad for people (both children and adults) because it exaggerates the

associated hormonal changes. Chronic suppressed anger is damaging because it activates the sympathetic nervous system responses without providing any release of the tension. It is a bit like stepping down on a car's accelerator while slamming on the brakes.

WHY DO KIDS GET ANGRY?

Anger is our response to stress. Many times we feel anger to avoid feeling some other emotion, such as anxiety or hurt. Or we may feel angry when we are frustrated because we want something and can't have it. Sometimes, feeling angry is a way of mobilizing ourselves in the face of a threat.

Anger may be useful because it stops (blocks) stress. Here are two examples:

- Your son is up at bat at his baseball game. From the stands, you yell out his name and cheer him on. He looks up at you at glares. After the game, he snaps, "Why do you have to embarrass me when I'm trying to bat?"

- Your daughter has just finished taking an important exam. She has studied for weeks and the result is very important to her GPA. She fantasizes all the way home from school about relaxing in front of the television with her favorite show. When she gets home, her brother and his friends are using the television to play video games. She yells, "Why don't you ask me before you start hogging the TV with your stupid games?"

This explains why people often respond with anger when they experience stressful situations like being in a hurry, feeling overworked, feeling attacked, feeling forced to do something they don't want to do, feeling out of control, and so forth.

> Sometimes, feeling angry is a way of mobilizing ourselves in the face of a threat.

WHAT ARE SOME ALTERNATIVES TO BECOMING ANGRY?

There are lots of constructive things you can teach your children to do to deal with stress instead of becoming angry. Here are a few examples:

- Get some physical exercise.
- Play a game.
- Walk away.
- Listen to favorite music.
- Make a joke of the situation.
- Take a nap.
- Do something relaxing.
- Tell someone about the situation.
- Write about it.

HOW CAN I HELP KIDS DEAL WITH STRESS TO PREVENT ANGER?

An angry response often results when children are unhappy with someone else's behavior. Here are some other responses kids can choose instead of flying off the handle:

- **Teach them to set limits.** Let's say your daughter's friend hasn't returned a game she lent her. Now the friend wants to borrow another one. Your daughter could say, "I'm not going to be able to lend you this game until you return the first one."

- **Teach them to speak up.** When your child realizes that he or she is starting to feel annoyed by a situation, encourage him or her to speak up. It's better not to wait until annoyance escalates into anger.

- **Teach them to be assertive.** Show your children to say what they want to get from others—in a positive way. For example, suggest that they say things like, "Please call me when you get home" rather than "Would you mind giving me a call when you get there?"

HOW CAN CHILDREN STOP THE ANGER SPIRAL ONCE IT STARTS?

WAYS TO STOP ANGER IN ITS TRACKS

Call a time-out.
Check it out.
Make positive statements.
Be prepared with a memorized response.

Helping Kids Recover from Loss

The process of recovering from loss is always difficult. The grief process applies to all kinds of losses—loss of loved ones through death and divorce, losing a job, moving to a new place, losing a friend. These experiences are difficult for everyone, children included.

WHAT ARE THE STAGES OF RECOVERY FROM LOSS?

There are some predictable stages that most people—adults, adolescents, and kids—pass through after losing something or someone important. In her work on death and dying, Elisabeth Kübler-Ross outlined five stages of grieving.

1. **Shock and Denial.** The first reaction to loss is often the inability to feel anything. This may include feeling numb, weak, overwhelmed, anxious, not yourself, or withdrawn.

SEE THESE HANDOUTS ON RELATED TOPICS

Anxiety in Children

Depression in Children and Teens

Helping Kids Manage Angry Feelings

Helping Your Child or Teen Manage Stress

How to Cope When Parenting Seems Over-whelming

How to Help a Friend through a Crisis (for Teens)

---

10. **Avoid making extreme life changes.** Don't make any important decisions involving your child until life feels more balanced. It can be tempting to make some important changes right after a major loss in an effort to feel more in control. If you can, put off such changes and decisions until later. If you have a teen, advise him or her to do the same.

11. **Remind your child that grief will not harm him or her.** Although grief is painful, your child will survive and even grow from the experience.

12. **Expect your child to regress.** Reversal in the recovery process will occur from time to time. This is normal. It may happen unexpectedly, but it probably won't last long.

13. **Acknowledge the anniversary of the loss.** Do something special. Be available to provide support. If the loss was a significant one and your older child or adolescent is likely to be aware of it, the anniversary could be a difficult day.

WHERE CAN I GO FOR MORE INFORMATION?

Deits, Bob. *Life After Loss.* Tucson, AZ: Fisher Books, 1992.

Kubler-Ross, Elisabeth. *On Death and Dying.* New York: MacMillan, 1969.

2. **Anger.** Blaming others for the loss. Kids may be angry, irritable, and difficult to get along with.

3. **Bargaining.** "If you'll just let my mommy live, I'll promise to do my homework every day."

4. **Depression.** Feeling deep sadness, disturbed sleep and eating patterns, thoughts of suicide, excessive crying.

5. **Acceptance.** Beginning to look for the lessons of the experience.

Kübler-Ross said that the grieving process involves experiencing all five stages, although not always in this order. She also said that people often cycle back and forth through a number of the stages before coming to the stage of acceptance.

WHAT ARE SOME EXAMPLES OF LOSSES?

> Your child's responses to loss will probably be different from those of another child. You can help your child express his or her grief, but you can't tell him or her how to grieve.

These are some examples of significant losses that children and adolescents may experience:

- Loss of a person through death
- Loss of the family structure through divorce
- Loss of a friend when he or she moves away
- Loss of everything familiar when you move away

- Loss of a pet
- Loss of a body part through an accident or surgery
- Loss of a physical ability, such as when blindness strikes

Each kind of loss affects each person in a different way, but the recovery process usually follows Kübler-Ross' five stages.

HOW DO KIDS RECOVER FROM LOSS?

> Show your child how to express feelings by writing or drawing. This helps him or her express them, rather than keeping them inside.

If your child or adolescent is experiencing the grief process, the following points may help:

1. **Everyone grieves differently.** Your child's responses to loss will probably be different from those of another child. You can help your child express his or her grief, but you can't tell him or her how to grieve.

2. **Grief needs to be expressed.** Avoid sending the message that the grieving should end. The purpose of the grief process is to help one learn to accept the reality of the loss and to learn from the experience. Cutting it short prevents the process from being completed.

3. **Remind your child that the sadness will end.** Your child will not feel bad forever. He or she will heal.

4. **Help your child get plenty of rest.** Grief is extremely stressful, and it requires energy to manage the stress.

5. **Encourage your child to talk about the loss.** People sometimes avoid talking about the loss as a denial mechanism. However, this prolongs denial and the grieving process.

> It can be tempting to make some important changes right after a major loss as an effort to feel more in control. If you can, put off such changes and decisions until later.

6. **Provide opportunities for downtime.** In the days and weeks following the loss of a loved one, there is often a flurry of activity and many visitors and phone calls. Added to the stress of the loss, this can be completely exhausting for children and adults alike. Make sure your child has opportunities to go to his or her room and close the door for a while.

7. **Maintain a normal routine if you can.** There are enough changes in your child's life right now. Help your child get up in the morning, go to bed at night, and eat meals at the same times as always.

8. **Give your child extra help.** The greater the loss, the more it will be needed. If your child doesn't want to be alone, or if he or she wants to be a little less independent, make it okay for now.

9. **Show your child how to keep a journal during the grief process.** Writing about one's feelings helps to express them, rather than keeping them inside. And recording one's experiences gives your child something to remember and review in the future.

How to Build Your Child's Self-Esteem

WHAT IS SELF-ESTEEM AND WHERE DOES IT COME FROM?

Self-esteem literally means to esteem or respect yourself. Having high self-esteem means that you have a positive image of yourself. People are not born with these beliefs. They are learned during childhood and adolescence. These beliefs are based on:

- What others said about you
- What others told you
- What others did to you

A person's self-image is the result of all of the messages he or she heard about himself or herself as a child. These messages added up to a set of beliefs about who he or she is. It may have nothing to do with who the person *really* is. For example, you may believe that:

- You're not very smart.
- You're naturally passive.
- Girls aren't any good at math.

---

people (adults, children, and adolescents) feel better by identifying how faulty ways of thinking make them feel bad. Cognitive therapists believe that faulty thoughts cause us to feel bad, which in turn makes us feel bad about ourselves.

> *Review child development literature regularly to stay updated on what is normal at each age and stage.*

WHERE CAN I GO TO LEARN MORE?

Branden, Nathaniel. *The Six Pillars of Self-Esteem.* New York: Bantam, 1994.

Briggs, Dorothy Corkville. *Celebrate Your Self: Making Life Work For You.* Garden City, NY: Doubleday, 1977.

David D. Burns, *Ten Days to Self-Esteem.* New York: William Morrow, 1993.

Sher, Barbara, with Gottlieb, Annie. *Wishcraft.* New York: Ballantine Books, 1979.

SEE THESE HANDOUTS ON RELATED TOPICS

Building Positive Teen Relationships

Helping Kids Manage Angry Feelings

Positive Reinforcement (for Parents)

---

problems on this assignment" is more constructive than "You never finish anything."

- Ask your son what he thinks.
- Let your daughter be the one to choose the restaurant or movie or activity some of the time.
- Ask your son to go along with you on routine errands just because you want to spend some time with him.
- Touch your daughter when you talk to her.
- Give your son a hug at least every few days.
- Go in and say goodnight before your daughter goes to sleep. (This is easy to forget once she becomes a teenager.)
- Look up and smile when your son walks into the room.
- Introduce yourself when your daughter is with a new friend.
- Ask your daughter to tell you about the book she is reading or the movie she just saw.
- It is important to recheck your standards and expectations from time to time to be sure they are realistic for your children's ages and individual abilities.
- Look for ways to maintain your own self-esteem. If you are unhappy, discontented, or disappointed in how your life is turning out, it will be difficult for you to build the self-esteem of your children.
- Every child needs to be the object of a parent's undivided attention on a regular basis.
- Make certain that your body language matches your words. If they are out of synch, your children will be aware of it.
- Be yourself. Tell the truth.
- Be appropriate. You don't have to say everything that is on your mind or tell your children things they aren't ready to know.
- If you show that you accept yourself and your actions, you give permission to your children to do the same.

HOW DO MENTAL HEALTH PROFESSIONALS TREAT LOW SELF ESTEEM?

Every kind of psychotherapy is designed to improve the self-esteem of the client. Therapists who specialize in working with children and adolescents have a variety of methods that focus on the special needs of younger people. The experience of being listened to, empathized with, and taken seriously is an important component of every type of therapy and is a key ingredient in building the self-esteem of the client.

One of the most successful methods for helping people feel better about themselves is the process of **cognitive therapy.** Cognitive therapy helps depressed and anxious

There are hundreds of ways to convey the message "You are worthwhile" to your children.

- You're too old to start over.
- All Hamilton women are doctors.
- You're painfully shy.
- The Van Dykes never lie.

In addition to learning to believe certain things during our early years, there are certain situations that make most people feel inferior or lacking in self-esteem. Some examples are:

- Being criticized
- Not being loved
- Being rejected
- Experiencing failure

WHAT DOES LOW SELF-ESTEEM FEEL LIKE?

In situations like those just cited, it is common to feel emotions such as:

- Sadness
- Inferiority
- Anger
- Jealousy
- Rejection

HOW CAN I BUILD MY CHILDREN'S SELF ESTEEM?

There are hundreds of ways to convey the message "You are worthwhile" to your children. This list could fill a hundred books, since the ways to raise responsible, happy children are limited only by our imagination. Here are some places to begin.

- Tell your daughter on a regular basis that you love her. Actually say the words. If you think, "I don't have to tell her. She knows," you are wrong. It doesn't count if you think it but don't say it out loud.
- Tell your son that you are glad he is your child. Say the words and mean them. If you don't feel it, there is

---

Tell your child that you are glad he or she is your child. Say the words and mean them.

something wrong and you should find out what's going on. We all have moments when we have a hard time getting in touch with our positive feelings for our children. I'm not talking about those times, if you're not feeling good about being your child's parent, something is wrong. He will never feel good about himself if he senses that you are not connected to him.

- Give your daughter an example to follow. Take the time to teach her the steps. Kids need models. It's unfair to expect that she will know what to do in her daily life if you haven't shown her how to do it.
- Spend time with your son. If you are absent most of the time, he notices, and he probably thinks it's because he isn't important enough.
- Look at your daughter when you speak to her. This conveys, "This is important and you are important."
- Look at your son when he speaks to you. This conveys, "What you are saying is important. You are important."
- Explain why. It takes more time, but it conveys to your daughter that she is important enough to you for you to spend the time helping her understand. When you explain why, you are also saying, "I understand that you need to know why. I am going to help you get your needs met."
- When your son tells you about something that happened, ask him how he feels about it. Take the time to listen to his answer.
- When you ask your daughter a question, encourage her to elaborate. Say, "Tell me more about that" or ask, "What was that like?"
- When you ask your daughter a question, don't interrupt when she is answering.
- When you ask your son a question, watch your responses. Don't disagree with or criticize his answer. Doing so teaches him that it isn't safe to be candid and will make him edit what he tells you.
- Participate in the driving. The kids whose parents never help with the driving feel bad about themselves.
- Take your child seriously.

When you ask a question, watch your responses. Don't disagree or criticize his answer. Doing so teaches him that it isn't safe to be candid and will make him edit what he tells you.

- Say no when you need to say no. Kids need to know there are limits and that some things are outside of those limits.
- When you say no to your child, explain why.
- When you say yes to your child, explain why.
- Set a positive example with your own behavior. You can only expect your children to behave with dignity and self-respect if they see you doing it.
- When you lose your temper or make a mistake, apologize. Say that you are sorry; be specific about what you are sorry for; and give your child a chance to respond.
- When you know that you have disappointed your son, acknowledge it. Ask him how he feels about it.
- Spend time alone with your child. Arrange activities for just the two of you.
- Ask your son what he would like to do.
- Give your daughter a private space where she can express herself.
- Respect your child's privacy.
- If your child did a good job on something, say so.
- If your daughter didn't do such a good job on something, point out what she did well.
- After a disappointment or failure, ask your child, "What did you learn from the experience?"

When there is a problem, focus on the issue, not the child.

- When you are giving your child feedback, describe specific behavior. For example, "I like how you asked the question so politely" or "You still need to pick up the towels off the floor."
- When there is a problem, focus on the issue, not the child. For example, "You didn't do the last 10

How to Help Victims of Child Abuse

WHAT IS CHILD ABUSE?

It is an unfortunate fact that child abuse is widespread throughout the world today. In the United States, thousands of children die each year as a result of being physically abused, and hundreds of thousands more are injured either physically or emotionally. It is difficult to know exactly how many children are victims; many cases are never reported because the victims are afraid to tell. Because the problem is so extensive and the emotional damage so long-lasting, it is essential that it be recognized and treated as early as possible.

There are several kinds of child abuse and neglect, including physical, emotional, and sexual. Any act that harms the physical or emotional well-being of any child is abuse. Any child who is being so harmed should be evaluated and treated immediately.

Physical abuse is any injury to a child that is not an accident. This can include any of the following:

- Striking, hitting, or slapping
- Pushing, shoving, or throwing

Monahon, Cynthia. *Children and Trauma: A Parent's Guide to Helping Children Heal.* New York: Lexington Press, 1983.

SEE THESE HANDOUTS ON RELATED TOPICS

Anxiety in Children

Depression in Children and Teens

Helping a Child Recover from Sexual Abuse

Helping Kids Manage Angry Feelings

Helping Kids Recover from Loss

Helping Your Kids to Be Self-Confident

How to Build Your Child's Self-Esteem

How to Cope When Parenting Seems Overwhelming

How to Help a Friend through a Crisis (for Teens)

Positive Reinforcement (for Parents)

If you have harmed your own child, it is important that you talk to an adult about it and get help right away. You should ask for a referral to a qualified mental health professional who can help you and the child.

If a child tells you that he or she has been abused, follow these steps:

1. Stay calm.

2. Tell the child that you believe him or her.

3. Listen and pay close attention.

4. Tell the child that you are glad he or she told you about the abuse.

5. Tell the child that the experience is not his or her fault.

6. Reassure the child that you want to make sure it will never happen again.

7. Show the child that you are listening. Ask him or her to tell you the entire story.

8. Avoid saying negative things about the person who committed the abuse. The child may care about this person and may want to protect him or her, despite the abuse.

9. If the child needs to be seen by a doctor, make the necessary arrangements.

10. Children who have been abused need to see a licensed mental health professional. This is essential in order for the child to heal and to prevent the pattern of abuse from being repeated in the next generation.

WHERE CAN I GO FOR MORE INFORMATION?

Child Help USA (www.childhelpusa.org)

Jantz, Gregory. *Healing the Scars of Emotional Abuse.* Grand Rapids, MI: Fleming H. Revell Co., 1995.

Miller, Alice. *The Drama of the Gifted Child.* New York: Basic Books, 1996.

WHO COMMITS CHILD ABUSE?

Adults from all parts of society commit child abuse. The only common denominator among perpetrators is that they live stressful lives and are unable to respond appropriately to their stress. Most abusers are known to the child victims and they are often a parent or relative.

WHAT ARE THE SIGNS OF CHILD ABUSE?

Children who have been harmed by deliberate abuse may show any of the following signs:

Emotional Signs

- Anxiety, fear
- Depression, sadness
- Anger, aggressiveness, hostility
- Low self-esteem
- Self-destructive behavior
- Withdrawing from others
- Passivity
- Inability to connect with others
- Distrustfulness
- Sleep disturbances and nightmares
- Flashbacks
- Suicidal thoughts

Physical Signs

- Injuries (bruises, cuts, black eyes, broken bones)
- Not wanting to be touched
- Not wanting to go home after school
- Not doing schoolwork
- Not eating
- Being fearful of or avoiding certain grownups
- Being sexually promiscuous
- Self-mutilation
- Drug and alcohol abuse
- Suicide attempts

IS IT ABUSE OR STRESS?

Children who witness abuse but don't experience it themselves also may show some of these symptoms. Children who are experiencing stress at home or at school may demonstrate some of the same symptoms as children who are being abused. Examples of stressors include divorce, custody problems, moving to a new location, a death in the family, and fighting or violence in the home.

WHAT IS THE TREATMENT FOR CHILD ABUSE?

Children who are physically or emotionally abused suffer extreme emotional damage. The harm that results may not be evident until later in the child's life, during adolescence or even adulthood. Even if the effects are not visible, they are present, often leading to an inability to establish trusting relationships with others. Because of their difficulty in relating to others in a positive way, victims have a much higher chance of becoming abusive parents themselves. They also have a much greater chance of developing any of the following kinds of problems in adolescence and adulthood:

- Mood disorders (anxiety, depression)
- Alcohol abuse
- Drug abuse
- Behavioral disorders
- Academic problems
- Difficulties at work
- Physical illnesses

People who are abused as children need to receive treatment in order to heal and live productive lives. Professional treatment—the sooner the better—can help the child and his or her family recover the ability to trust others.

If you think that a child is being abused, report it to your local police or child welfare agency. You don't have to be certain that abuse is taking place, and you can report anonymously. Don't hesitate. You could be saving a child's life.

- Paddling or whipping
- Kicking
- Shaking
- Choking
- Tying up or locking inside a small space
- Burning with a match or cigarette
- Pinching
- Beating with any object
- Pulling hair
- Biting
- Starving

Emotional abuse is extremely negative behavior that harms the child's mental health. This can include:

- Screaming, yelling, shouting
- Calling a child negative, offensive names
- Telling a child that he or she is a bad, stupid, or worthless person
- Shaming, embarrassing, or belittling

Emotional abuse can harm a child as seriously as physical abuse, because it destroys the victim's self-esteem and his or her ability to trust other people. As a result, many abuse victims struggle with relationship problems throughout their adult lives.

Sexual abuse is any sexual activity between a child and an adult. See the Child Abuse handout for a complete discussion.

Neglect is not taking care of a child's physical or emotional needs. Neglect can include any of the following:

- Not supervising a child
- Abandoning a child
- Not helping a child stay clean and healthy
- Not providing shelter
- Exposing a child to danger
- Not providing appropriate clothing
- Not providing proper food
- Not providing for the child's emotional needs for love, affection, and safety

Kids Who Sexually Abuse Other Kids

SEE THESE HANDOUTS ON RELATED TOPICS

Helping a Child Recover from Sexual Abuse

How to Cope When Parenting Seems Overwhelming

Teaching Your Child to Respect Others

What Teens Need to Know about HIV and AIDS

WHAT IS SEXUAL ABUSE?

Sexual abuse or assault occurs when one person forces any unwanted sexual contact onto another person. It can involve a stranger, friend, partner, or acquaintance. It can involve any type of unwanted sexual behavior.

Most perpetrators of sexual abuse on children are male. One-third are adolescents. Of all adult child sexual abuse (CSA) perpetrators, one-half began abusing people sexually when they were adolescents. If an adolescent sexual abuse perpetrator can be identified and treated while still an adolescent, there is a much greater chance that future abuse can be prevented.

- **Cognitive behavioral counseling.** This is the most commonly used approach for CSA perpetrators.

- **Group counseling.** This may include group discussions, role playing, communication skills, and developing empathy.

- **Life skills training.** This may include self-control skills, dealing with anger, assertiveness skills, and relaxation skills.

- **Family therapy.** This may involve separate sessions for the parents and siblings. In some families, where the mothers do not believe that the child incest victim is telling the truth, treatment success is unlikely.

WHERE CAN I GO FOR MORE INFORMATION?

Morrison, Tony, Erooga, Marcus, and Beckett, Richard. *Sexual Offending Against Children: Assessment and Treatment of Male Abusers.* New York: Routledge, 1994.

WHAT CAUSES A CHILD TO SEXUALLY ABUSE ANOTHER?

It is difficult to learn exactly how and why a CSA perpetrator carries out his crimes because there is so much secrecy and shame surrounding the behavior. Victims are often coerced into silence. Since many CSA incidents are never reported, little is known about how and why the abuse takes place. In addition, not all inappropriate sexual behavior is the same. Some of this behavior takes place because children are not properly supervised and because they have never been educated about proper sexual behavior. Innocent but inappropriate behavior is quite different from sexual abuse committed by an adolescent who inflicts violence on other children and understands that he is committing a crime.

Research on CSA perpetrators concludes that these individuals have some or all of the following personality flaws:

- low self-esteem
- feeling unworthy
- helplessness
- defenselessness
- depression
- uncertainty about one's masculinity (in males)
- inability to relate well with others
- inability to contain hostile feelings

Many CSA perpetrators were themselves sexually abused as children; many are incest victims. Many grew up in families where the parents were unstable, emotionally distant, strict, and rigid. There may have been an improper lack of boundaries between parents

and children, and the customary taboo on incest may have broken down.

Depending on the facts of each individual case, CSA may be considered incest, sexual abuse, and/or pedophilia. A **pedophile** is a person over age 16 who carries on inappropriate sexual activity with a child or adolescent. The pedophile's behavior is a response to powerful sexual urges and fantasies. It is unknown what causes a person to become a pedophile, but it is possible that some pedophiles have abnormal brain structures or hormonal activity. Some believe that this behavior is a pathological way of dealing with conflict and anxiety.

WHAT ARE THE SIGNS THAT AN ADOLESCENT MAY BE A CSA PERPETRATOR?

Any combination of the following behaviors may indicate that an adolescent is a perpetrator of child sexual abuse:

> Many perpetrators were themselves sexually abused as children; many are incest victims. There may have been an improper lack of boundaries between parents and children, and the customary taboo on incest may have broken down.

- Knows more about sex than others in his age group
- Has sexual relationships with family members
- Has sex frequently
- Masturbates frequently
- Has a sexually transmitted disease
- Engages in ritualistic or degrading sexual behavior
- Pushes himself on others sexually
- Has underdeveloped social skills
- Spends time with people who are significantly older or younger
- Gives alcohol or drugs to children
- Is under stress in other areas of his life
- Has friends who are children who show signs of child sexual abuse

WHAT IS THE TREATMENT FOR CHILD SEXUAL ABUSE?

The choice of treatment and punishment depends, of course, on the severity of the abuser's behavior. If the abuser believes that his behavior was not unacceptable, any treatment will be ineffective.

The treatment of a CSA offender should be based on an assessment of the act(s) of abuse, the abuser's family history, and an exploration of his motivation for the behavior. As mentioned at the beginning of this handout, early treatment is imperative to prevent the behavior from being repeated.

All treatment must be administered in a way that guarantees the safety of the victim. Treatment may be inpatient or outpatient, depending on the situation, and it may include any of the following components, depending on the diagnosis and the circumstances:

- Has a hostile attitude
- Behaves aggressively or violently
- Has committed several minor offenses or crimes
- Behaves in a sexual way not appropriate for his age

Living with Your Child's Serious Medical Condition

WHAT ARE THE CHALLENGES OF LIVING WITH A SERIOUS MEDICAL CONDITION?

If you have recently discovered that your child or teen has a serious medical condition, both

support for people with your child's condition and also for the parents who care for them. These groups, which may meet in person or via chat groups on the Internet, offer emotional support and practical advice from people who are facing the same issues you are. They are also a place for you to candidly express your feelings and fears to people who understand what you are going through.

Depending on your situation, your child's condition may have a serious impact on the lives of those outside your immediate family. They may need information and support as much as you do. It is important to ask not only for their help and understanding, but to seek support and information for them. This will help them help you as you face the issues surrounding your child's medical condition.

WHERE CAN I GO FOR MORE INFORMATION?

Capossela, Cappy, and Warnock, Sheila. *Share the Care: How to Organize a Group to Care for Someone Who Is Seriously Ill.* New York: Fireside Books, 1995.

Kübler-Ross, Elisabeth. *On Death and Dying.* New York: MacMillan, 1969.

Register, Cheri. *The Chronic Illness Experience.* Minneapolis, MN: Hazelden Information and Educational Services, 1999.

Well, Susan Milstrey, *A Delicate Balance: Living Successfully with Chronic Illness.* New York: Perseus Books, 1998.

SEE THESE HANDOUTS ON RELATED TOPICS

Depression in Children and Teens

Helping Kids Manage Angry Feelings

Helping Kids Recover from Loss

How to Build Your Child's Self-Esteem

How to Cope When Parenting Seems Overwhelming

you and your child have undoubtedly been affected both emotionally and physically. There are some predictable stages that most people pass through after they discover that they have a serious illness or medical condition such as cancer, AIDS, MS, or diabetes. The discoveries of others who have experienced such shocking news may help you and your child cope with the news.

> Your child's condition may have a serious impact on the lives of those outside your immediate family. It is important to ask not only for their help and understanding, but to seek support and information for them.

In her well-known work on the stages of grieving, Elisabeth Kübler-Ross outlined five stages that most people go through as they react to losing something important. These stages apply to almost any kind of loss, including the loss of one's healthy lifestyle. Upon being told that your child faces serious medical issues and the loss of your good health, even temporarily, you can both expect to experience the following emotional stages:

Shock and Denial. The first reaction to bad medical news is often the inability to feel anything. This may include feeling numb, weak, overwhelmed, anxious, not yourself, or withdrawn. You may also not believe the news or feel certain that it will turn out to be incorrect.

Anger. Blaming others for the development of the problem; being furious with yourself for waiting too long to take the child to a doctor; blaming the doctor for not acting quickly enough.

Bargaining. It is not uncommon to think something like this: "If you'll just let my child live, I'll promise to go to church every Sunday for the rest of my life" or "I'll never yell at her again if the illness will just go away."

Depression. It is normal to feel deep sadness. You and your child may also have disturbed sleep and eating patterns, entertain thoughts of suicide, and cry excessively.

Acceptance. At some point you will begin to look for the lessons of the experience. If your child is older, he or she may do the same.

Kübler-Ross said that the grieving process involves experiencing all five stages, although they don't always occur in this order. She also said that people often cycle back and forth through a number of the stages before coming to the stage of acceptance.

 WHAT SKILLS WILL HELP ME COPE?

After the shock of your diagnosis has worn off, you will begin to look for ways to control the situation. There are many things you can do to cope:

COPING SKILLS

- Educate yourself and your child.
- Get the best doctor.
- Make a list of questions to ask your doctor.
- Take care of your child's emotional health.
- Join a support group.
- Ask your family and friends for support.

Educate yourself and your child. You will be better able to make plans for your future if you know as much as possible about your child's medical condition. You will also eliminate many fears that are based on inaccurate information. Ask your doctor for books and web sites that will help you learn about the condition and how to cope with it.

Get the best doctor. You are going to need to feel comfortable asking questions and getting answers. Look for a doctor who is board-certified to treat your child's specific condition and who is able to work well with someone your child's age. Make sure you are seeing a doctor who has the interpersonal skills to be able to talk to you and your child like a human being, not a disease.

Make a list of questions to ask your doctor. It is important that you ask everything that is on your mind. Keep an ongoing list as your child's situation develops. Ask your child to add questions to the list, too.

Take care of your child's emotional health. A serious illness or medical condition takes a toll on anyone's psyche. It is important that you locate a licensed mental health professional who can help you, your child, and your family deal with the emotional aspects of your situation. Some mental health professionals specialize in working with children who have specific physical disorders. If you need a referral, ask your doctor.

Join a support group. There are support groups today for just about every situation and condition. Ask your doctor, hospital, or mental health counselor for a referral. You can also look on the Internet for groups that provide information and

Managing Family Conflict

INTRODUCTION

Every family and relationship has conflicts. In some families, differences and conflicts are a serious problem. In others, differences seem to be resolved fairly easily, without resulting in battles or serious arguments. Kids learn to deal with conflict in the family and use the same behaviors in their relationships with their peers. Since the family is the primary place where these skills are learned (for better or worse), it is important to model and teach them at home throughout your children's childhood and adolescence.

> Since the family is the primary place where these skills are learned, it is important to model and teach them at home throughout your children's childhood and adolescence.

SEE THESE HANDOUTS ON RELATED TOPICS

Attention-Seeking with Disruptive Behavior

Dealing with Common Adoption Issues

Helping Kids Manage Angry Feelings

How to Build Your Child's Self-Esteem

How to Cope When Parenting Seems Overwhelming

Positive Reinforcement (for Parents)

Teaching Your Child to Respect Others

---

foot. Do your best to convey openness with your body.

7. **Watch your language.** Use specific words and facts. Stay away from generalities. For example, "You were an hour late," instead of "You're always late" or "I can never count on you."

HOW CAN YOU PREVENT FAMILY CONFLICTS?

Think of situations in your life where there don't seem to be many conflicts. What might be happening there? Chances are, you are practicing one of the following conflict-prevention skills:

1. **Address issues before they become problems.** For example, if you know that you need to attend a business dinner next Tuesday evening, talk to your spouse about it now and ask him or her to be home early to feed the kids. Don't wait until the last minute.

2. **Be aware of triggers.** For example, your teen's lack of eye contact makes you upset. During a calm moment, talk to him or her about it. Explain that it triggers your anger and ask him or her to try to look at you when you are having serious discussions. When he or she does, praise the improvement.

3. **Have a process for resolving conflicts.** During a calm moment, discuss the process with your family and get agreement on what members should do when there are differing viewpoints.

WHERE CAN I GO FOR MORE INFORMATION?

Gordon, Thomas. *Parent Effectiveness Training: The Proven Program for Raising Responsible Children.* New York: Three Rivers Press, 2000.

Ury, William. *Getting Past No: Negotiating Your Way from Confrontation to Cooperation.* New York: Bantam Doubleday Dell, 1993.

Think about the kinds of conflicts that happen in your family on a typical day. These are some common ones:

- **Disagreeing over who should do what.** For example, who should do the dishes? Who should be allowed to take the car on Friday night? Who should stay home when the kids are sick?

- **Conflicts about how things should be done.** For example, should homework be done right after school or can the kids wait until after dinner?

- **Conflicts of personality and style.** Mom thinks teenage son Tom is too bossy with his younger brother. Dad thinks Mom should be more assertive with the car repair guy, but Mom prefers the soft approach.

WHAT ARE SOME TYPICAL MISTAKES WHEN DEALING WITH CONFLICT?

Most often, conflict becomes a problem when family members respond in ineffective ways. Here are some examples of nonproductive responses to conflict:

1. **Avoid the conflict.** "If I don't talk about how much the repair cost, maybe he'll forget about it."

2. **Change the subject.** "Yes, I got the car fixed. What a relief! Oh, yes—let me show you Lisa's grades!"

3. **React emotionally**—become aggressive, abusive, hysterical, or frightening. "Stop criticizing me! I'm sick of you picking on me! Leave me alone!"

4. **Find someone to blame.** "Well, if you wouldn't have waited so long to get it fixed, it wouldn't have cost so much."

5. **Make excuses.** "Lisa's grades are bad because of that horrible teacher. It isn't her fault. The teacher has her completely intimidated."

6. **Let someone else deal with it.** "Carmen, will you ask Amanda to turn the stereo down?"

All of these responses to conflict have two things in common: All of them are nonproductive, and all are destructive, some physically. This is why learning to manage conflict is so important.

HOW DO WE LEARN TO MANAGE CONFLICT?

> *The skills involved in managing conflict are learned behaviors. None of us is born knowing how to deal with differences of opinion or arguments or turf wars.*

The skills involved in managing conflict are learned behaviors. None of us is born knowing how to deal with differences of opinion or arguments or turf wars. Some of the factors that affect how we behave in the face of conflict are:

1. **Behavior learned in families.** In some families, conflict and confrontation are a communication style. In others, conflict always remains hidden. Whether it is out in the open or concealed, the way of dealing with conflict is usually passed on from one generation to the next, for better or worse.

2. **Behavior learned from role models.** New ways of managing conflict can be learned at any time in life. People who have had a teacher or boss who modeled effective conflict resolution skills are more likely to develop these skills themselves.

3. **Status.** People in higher-status positions usually feel freer to engage in conflict and are less likely to avoid confrontation.

4. **Unwritten rules.** Some groups (including families) encourage conflict, while others have unwritten rules that it is to be contained or avoided.

5. **Gender differences.** In general, males are encouraged to be more confrontational than females.

WHAT ARE THE KEY SKILLS FOR MANAGING CONFLICT?

The following communication skills will help you deal with conflict in your family:

1. **Use "I" statements instead of "you" statements.** They sound less accusing and place the responsibility for the statement on you. For example:

> *You escalate hostile feelings when you roll your eyes, cross your arms in front of your body, or tap your foot. Instead, do your best to convey openness with your body.*

- "I would like you to empty the dishwasher before you leave," instead of "You need to empty the dishwasher before you leave."
- "I get upset when you come home an hour later than you said you would," instead of "You are late again."

2. **Avoid name-calling and put-downs.** They are inflammatory and only make the other person defensive and angry. This escalates the conflict.

3. **Soften your tone.** Listen to how you sound. A softer, friendlier tone of voice helps lessen the hostility of your message.

4. **Take a time-out.** Some families have an agreement to make the time-out sign (make a "T" with your hands) when a discussion escalates into an argument. Say, "Let's take a break and cool down." Agree on how long the time-out should be, and come back when time is up.

5. **Acknowledge the other person's point of view.** For example, "I hear what you are saying," or "I accept that you think you did the right thing." It is not necessary to agree.

6. **Watch your body language.** You escalate hostile feelings when you roll your eyes, cross your arms in front of your body, or tap your

Managing the Stepfamily

If you are a member of a stepfamily, you know how difficult it can be to integrate all of the new members and adjust to the new boundaries and rules. The following ideas may help you make a successful transition during this challenging process.

 WHAT ARE THE MOST IMPORTANT ASPECTS OF MANAGING A STEPFAMILY?

Have patience. Establishing new families takes time. Just because you love your new partner, it is unrealistic to think that you will automatically love his or her children. It is equally unrealistic to expect that your new partner's children will instantly love you. It can be difficult to accept that even though you wish to have a relationship with your stepchildren, they may not be ready for a relationship with you.

Expect to adjust. With proper help and guidance, children can recover from family disruption. All children experience a difficult adjustment period following a divorce or remarriage. It takes time, patience, and perhaps some professional assistance, but most children are able to regain their emotional

Give the kids their own space. Make physical space available for the children who don't live with you. Children need a sense of belonging. Creating a room or section of a room for visiting children will help them feel like part of your family.

Expect them to think it's temporary. Accept the fact that your children may expect you and their other birth parent to reconcile. They may fantasize that your relationship with your partner is only temporary. This is especially true in the beginning. Find a time to sit down with the children and explain that when two people are unable to live together anymore, it doesn't mean they love their children any less. This is especially important for the parent who has moved away, since the children will inevitably feel a sense of rejection.

Expect resentment. No matter how good a parent you are, you will never be the biological parent of your stepchildren. It is natural for a stepchild to feel some resentment toward you, especially when you are setting limits on his or her behavior.

Show the children love. Sometimes children need love the most at a time when it is the most difficult to give it to them. While bad behavior should never be rewarded, always praise children when they are behaving well.

 WHERE CAN I GO FOR MORE INFORMATION?

Kalter, Neil. *Growing Up with Divorce.* New York: Fawcett Books, 1991.

Norwood, Perdita Kirkness, and Wingender, Teri. *The Enlightened Stepmother: Revolutionizing the Role.* New York: Avon Books, 1999.

Visher, Emily, and Visher, John. *Stepfamilies: Myths and Realities.* Secaucus, NJ: Citadel Press, 1993.

SEE THESE HANDOUTS ON RELATED TOPICS

Helping Children in Divorcing Families

Helping Kids Manage Angry Feelings

Helping Kids Recover from Loss

How to Build Your Child's Self-Esteem

How to Cope When Parenting Seems Overwhelming

Managing Family Conflict

Positive Reinforcement (for Parents)

Separation Anxiety

bearings. It is critical that the adults manage their own emotional recovery in order to help the children adjust without trauma.

> All of the family members must learn to understand the new structure and learn to navigate the boundaries.

If you are part of a part-time stepfamily, you may need a longer adjustment period. All relationships take time to grow and develop. When stepchildren see you less often, you have less time to get to know each other. This is why it may take a part-time stepfamily longer to move through the adjustment process.

Don't expect your new family to be like your first family. If you expect that your stepfamily will be just like the family of your first marriage, you are setting yourself up for frustration. Your new family will have its own unique identity and will evolve in its own special way.

Expect confusion. Forming a stepfamily is a confusing time for everyone. Think about how confusing it is for a child to become part of two new families. All of the family members—parents and children—must learn to understand the new structure and learn to navigate the boundaries.

Allow time for grieving. Stepfamilies begin with an experience of loss, and everyone needs to grieve. The adults' losses are not the same as those of the children, and both must be respected. Adults grieve the following losses:

- The loss of a partner.
- The loss of a marriage relationship.
- Lost dreams about the way they thought it would be.
- They must adjust to changes that result from the divorce or death (e.g., moving to a new house, starting a new job, adjusting to changes in lifestyle).

Children grieve too. Their losses are usually different from those of their parents:

- They may now be living with one parent instead of two.
- They may have less time with one or both parents during times of dating and remarriage.
- There may be less stability in their homes.
- They must adjust to changes that result from the divorce or death (they may have a new place to live and go to a new school, and they may have lost friends in this process).
- They have lost the fantasy of how they wanted their family to be.

> The children who have access to both of their parents are those who adjust the best to divorce. They should be allowed to regularly speak with, visit, and write to their noncustodial parent.

Children have an especially difficult time resolving their grief when their parents are hostile to one another, when one or both of their parents remarry, and when they have trouble accepting their new stepparents.

Acknowledge the absent parent. When one of the original parents is absent, the children need a special kind of understanding. An absent parent (who has died or who lives elsewhere and doesn't visit) is part of a child's past. The child must be allowed to have memories of this parent. The children who have access to both of their parents are those who adjust the best to divorce. They should be allowed to regularly speak with, visit, and write to their noncustodial parent.

Help the kids fit in. Children of stepfamilies belong to two households. It is understandable that they will have questions about where they fit in. They are usually able to adjust to having two sets of rules as long as they are not asked to choose which one is better.

Be clear about the rules. Ideally, both sets of parents should discuss the family rules and what will happen if rules are broken. When the adults agree on the rules, they should explain them to the children. Most successful stepfamilies have learned that the rules should be decided together in the beginning, and that the biological parent should do the explaining and disciplining. The stepparent may have more involvement after the relationships with the stepchildren have been established. All of this works best when the parents can agree to be flexible and cooperative with one another. This may be difficult immediately following a divorce or remarriage, but it is important to work toward this objective.

Educate yourselves and seek emotional support. Read books about managing stepfamilies, attend classes, and participate in stepfamily support groups. Seek the counsel of an experienced mental health professional to help you through the rough spots. Marriage and family therapists have specific skills and training for working with families and stepfamilies.

> No matter how good a parent you are, you will never be the biological parent of your stepchildren. It is natural for a stepchild to feel some resentment for you.

Mania and Hypomania

WHAT ARE MANIA AND HYPOMANIA?

Mania is the "high" behavior that is part of bipolar disorder (BPD). A person with BPD alternates between extremes of mania (highs) and depression (lows). While it is unusual for a child or adolescent to develop this disorder, it does happen, especially if one or both parents have it. It is also more likely to occur when there is drug or alcohol abuse in the family. Hypomania is a BPD condition similar to mania, but with episodes that are shorter and less severe.

Characteristic BPD behavior. When a person is manic, he or she is likely to exhibit the following kinds of behavior:

- High levels of physical and mental energy (more than other children or adolescents of the same age group)
- A very positive mood (talkativeness and sociability)
- Overoptimism
- Extreme self-confidence

difficult to convince some patients to stay on their medication and continue their psychological treatment. The most effective treatment for BPD includes both medication and psychotherapy:

Medication. Lithium, the standard medication for BPD, is effective in up to 80 percent of manic and hypomanic episodes. It requires careful monitoring. It may take weeks to become effective, so immediate relief may require other types of treatment. Drugs used to treat epilepsy, such as Depakote and Tegretol, are used for some patients who cannot take lithium.

Electroconvulsive therapy (ECT). Also called *shock treatment*, ECT can be an effective treatment for patients who cannot take lithium. Following the administration of a muscle relaxant and anesthetic, ECT involves sending a small amount of current to the brain. The patient has a short seizure and may experience confusion, headache, nausea, memory lapse, and other symptoms. However, most people respond to ECT very quickly, making it an effective treatment for patients who need to be stabilized immediately or who cannot take medications.

Psychotherapy. This is another important component of the treatment for BPD. Because guilt, remorse, and depression often follow a manic phase, it is very important that patients establish and maintain a relationship with a licensed mental health professional who specializes in working with children or adolescents who have mood disorders. The therapist can encourage the patient to stay on his or her medication and help him or her build self-esteem and develop a support system. If the patient is an adolescent, the therapist may also refer him or her to a support group for teens or young adults with BPD. Such a group can be an excellent source of assistance.

Family support. The patient's friends and family members can provide some of the most important support of all. They can help by understanding that BPD is an illness, not a character defect. It is important that they learn as much as they can about BPD, listen empathetically, behave in a supportive manner, and plan ahead for the times when the patient experiences

mania or depression. They should listen for remarks about suicide and take them seriously.

WHERE CAN I GO FOR MORE INFORMATION?

National Depressive and Manic-Depressive Association (www.ndmda.org).

Fawcett, Jan, Golden, Bernard, Rosenfeld, Nancy, and Goodwin, Frederick. *New Hope for People with Bipolar Disorder.* Rocklin, CA: Prima Publishing, 2000.

Mondimore, Francis. *Bipolar Disorder: A Guide for Patients and Families.* Baltimore: Johns Hopkins University Press, 1999.

SEE THESE HANDOUTS ON RELATED TOPICS

Depression in Children and Teens

How to Cope When Parenting Seems Overwhelming

Positive Reinforcement (for Parents)

- Extreme aggressiveness
- Agitation and irritability
- Bragging and boasting; exaggerated self-importance
- Distorted thinking, with delusions
- Racing thoughts and speech
- Little need for sleep; staying awake for long periods without tiring
- Marked distractibility; difficult to follow; going off on tangents
- Impulsive or reckless behavior; showing bad judgment
- Strange or bizarre dress
- Hallucinations

The behavior of a person in the manic phase of BPD can place him or her in extreme danger. Some adolescents become paranoid or violent during manic episodes; others may be openly promiscuous.

An illness, not a character flaw. BPD is an illness caused by a chemical imbalance in the brain. It affects as many as two million Americans, mostly adults. While people who have BPD can be difficult to live with, their illness is not a character defect or sign of weakness. The disorder can be controlled with the proper treatment and maintenance.

Cycling. People with Bipolar disorder alternate (cycle) between the *poles* of mania and depression. Each mood swing can last for a few hours or a few months. The disorder can first appear when a person is a child, an adolescent, or an adult. It affects

Hypomania. Because hypomania episodes are not so extreme as manic attacks, BPD patients who have hypomania usually do not need to be hospitalized and their lives are less severely impacted by the disorder. Although they tend to be easily distracted and may not function well in the world, their disorder is less noticeable than for BPD sufferers whose moods swing from the highest high to the deepest despair. These swings are different from the normal mood changes that we all experience in that they can cause severe disruptions in one's normal life activities. For some BPD patients, hypomania is a sign that a manic phase is about to begin.

The depression component. People who suffer from BPD experience the highs of mania and the lows of depression. During periods of depression, the patient may feel extremely sad, anxious, pessimistic, worthless, hopeless, and apathetic. He or she may have suicidal thoughts. (See the Depression handout in this series for a complete description.)

Levels of severity. A person diagnosed with BPD may have any of three levels of the disorder: Bipolar I disorder (the most severe form, involving extreme manic episodes); Bipolar II disorder (less severe); or Cyclothymic disorder (still less severe mood swings of shorter duration).

How it begins. When a person has an episode of manic behavior, it usually begins suddenly, often following one or more periods of severe depression. When this happens for the first time, the person's friends and family members may be thankful to see that his or her depression has

people of both genders, of all socioeconomic groups, and of all races. It often runs in families and is thought to have a genetic link.

lifted and it looks as if life is returning to normal. However, as the manic phase continues, those around the patient begin to realize that something is not right. The person's upbeat mood is too extreme and the behavior may be odd or bizarre.

Similar symptoms. BPD is difficult to diagnose because many of its symptoms are similar to those of other disorders, including schizophrenia, ADHD, adrenal disorders, epilepsy, brain tumors, multiple sclerosis, thyroid disorders, and vitamin B12 deficiency. Manic symptoms may also be caused by certain medications.

Range of severity. BPD ranges from mild to severe, and it can be infrequent (10 or fewer manic episodes during one's lifetime) or rapid-cycling (several manic-depressive cycles in a day) and long-term. Because BPD can have such a serious impact on a person and those around him or her, and since it can result in suicide, it is critical that patients obtain proper ongoing treatment.

AN IMPORTANT NOTE

If you or someone you know has thoughts of death or suicide, take it seriously. **Immediately** contact any of the following and ask for help:

- Police (911)
- Suicide hotline
- Medical professional
- Mental health professional
- Friend or loved one
- Hospital emergency room

WHAT IS THE TREATMENT FOR MANIA OR HYPOMANIA?

The main goals of treatment for BPD are to reduce its damaging effects and to help the patient live a normal life between episodes. Unfortunately, some people *enjoy* the effects of mania and avoid treatment because they don't want to lose the creativity and exhilaration they feel during this part of the cycle. As a result, it is

Mental Retardation

WHAT IS MENTAL RETARDATION?

There are three criteria for mental retardation:

1. An IQ below 70
2. The condition begins before age 18
3. The person has very limited skills in at least two areas of daily living [the ability to communicate, take care of oneself,

Treatment may include behavioral therapy, medication for psychiatric disorders, and special education. Family therapy and support may also be recommended.

WHERE CAN I GO FOR MORE INFORMATION?

The Arc of the United States (www.thearc.org).

Burack, Jacob, Hodapp, Robert, and Zigler, Edward (editors). *Handbook of Mental Retardation and Development.* New York: Cambridge University Press, 1998.

Drew, Clifford, and Hardman, Michael. *Mental Retardation: A Life Cycle Approach.* Upper Saddle River, NJ: Prentice Hall, 1999.

Smith, Romayne, and Shriver, Eunice Kennedy. *Children with Mental Retardation: A Parents' Guide (The Special Needs Collection).* Bethesda, MD: Woodbine House, 1993.

SEE THESE HANDOUTS ON RELATED TOPICS

How to Build Your Child's Self-Esteem

How to Cope When Parenting Seems Overwhelming

Positive Reinforcement (for Parents)

---

live at home, relate socially, work, manage one's free time, take care of one's health and safety, direct one's activities, do basic school work (reading, writing and math), and use community resources].

Up to 3 percent of the population has mental retardation. The condition affects people from every racial and socioeconomic background. Over 85 percent of those diagnosed with the condition are only slightly affected and are able to live on their own as adults.

> Over 85 percent of those diagnosed with the condition are only slightly affected and are able to live on their own as adults.

The rest of the retarded population have IQs of 50 or less and require support and assistance to live independently.

WHAT CAUSES MENTAL RETARDATION?

> The most common causes of mental retardation are Down syndrome, fetal alcohol syndrome, and Fragile X. There are hundreds of other causes besides these.

Mental retardation occurs when the brain does not develop properly. This damage can occur before, during, or after birth. The most common causes of mental retardation are Down syndrome, fetal alcohol syndrome, and Fragile X (a disorder that occurs on the X chromosome). There are hundreds of causes in addition to these, including genetic conditions, problems that occur during pregnancy (alcohol abuse, malnutrition, toxins, diseases), problems that occur at birth, and childhood diseases or accidents that cause damage to the brain. Impoverished children with no access to medical care may be exposed to conditions that result in brain damage. In about 33 percent of people who have mental retardation, the cause of the condition is unknown.

> In about 33 percent of people who have mental retardation, the cause of the condition is unknown.

WHAT IS THE TREATMENT FOR MENTAL RETARDATION?

Children who may have mental retardation should be carefully evaluated by a team of specialists. The team may include a pediatrician, neurologist, child psychologist or psychiatrist, special education teacher, eye doctor, physical therapist, and speech and language specialist. The child should be given a series of tests, and a treatment plan will be developed based on the results.

Oppositional Defiant Disorder (ODD)

WHAT IS OPPOSITIONAL DEFIANT DISORDER?

Children who have oppositional defiant disorder (ODD) are more than just argumentative from time to time. All children have days when they don't obey their parents and/or teachers, perhaps refusing to cooperate or behaving in an especially hostile way. But when a child regularly engages in a pattern of defiance and hostility, and that behavior begins to affect the child's social relationships and family life, oppositional defiant disorder may be diagnosed.

psychiatric disorders as adults, such as antisocial personality disorder.

Treatment for ODD may include several different components, including the following:

- Individual counseling
- Family therapy
- Behavioral training in anger management, communication skills, and social skills
- Parenting skills training to develop skills of behavior modeling, positive reinforcement, conflict management, setting limits and consequences, and stress management.

WHERE CAN I GO FOR MORE INFORMATION?

Barkley, Russell. *Defiant Children* (2nd ed.). New York: Guilford Press, 1997.

Greene, Ross. *The Explosive Child*. New York: HarperCollins, 1998.

Koplewicz, Harold. *It's Nobody's Fault: New Hope and Help for Difficult Children and Their Parents*. New York: Random House, 1997.

SEE THESE HANDOUTS ON RELATED TOPICS

Anxiety in Children

Attention-Seeking with Disruptive Behavior

Depression in Children And Teens

Helping Kids Manage Angry Feelings

Helping Your Child or Teen Manage Stress

Helping Your Child Succeed in School

How to Build Your Child's Self-Esteem

How to Cope When Parenting Seems Overwhelming

Positive Reinforcement (for Parents)

Teaching Your Child to Respect Others

The symptoms of oppositional defiant disorder may include the following:

- Frequently losing one's temper
- Frequently arguing with parents, teachers, and authority figures
- Refusing to follow the rules
- Offending people on purpose
- Making mistakes and blaming others
- Acting up and blaming others
- Irritability
- Saying hurtful things when angry
- Looking for ways to get revenge against others

> ODD is a pattern of behavior that interferes with the child's normal functioning. It affects as many as 15 percent of school-age children.

ODD SELF-HELP STEPS

Kids with oppositional defiant disorder can help themselves by doing the following:

- Participating in counseling
- Developing a support system—people who understand and can help
- Managing their behavior with time-outs
- Learning the causes of anxiety
- Expressing feelings by talking rather than acting
- Learning ways to relax and calm down
- Setting and reviewing goals
- Expending energy through physical activity
- Learning communication and social skills
- Following a schedule
- Learning new ways to have fun
- Learning to recognize when they've made a mistake
- Identifying signs of relapse and forming a plan for responding to it

ODD is a pattern of behavior that interferes with the child's normal functioning. It affects as many as 15 percent of school-age children.

In very young children, it affects more boys than girls, but as children grow older, both genders are equally affected.

ODD seems similar to attention-deficit/hyperactivity disorder (ADHD) and conduct disorder (CD) but it is different in certain important ways. Children with ADHD are impulsive, while those with ODD are mainly aggressive. Children with CD are unsafe when not supervised, whereas kids with ODD do not have safety issues.

WHAT CAUSES OPPOSITIONAL DEFIANT DISORDER?

It is not known what causes ODD. Possible causes include a chemical imbalance in the brain and the way the family responds to the child's behavior. If the parents and other

> ODD usually begins before age three and seems to run in families.

family members have an especially difficult time managing the child and helping him or her behave properly, the condition may be aggravated.

> ODD usually begins before age three and seems to run in families.

ODD usually begins before age three and seems to run in families.

Nearly one-fifth of children with ODD have a parent who is alcoholic and who has had problems with the legal system.

WHAT IS THE TREATMENT FOR ODD?

It is important to thoroughly evaluate a child when ODD is suspected. Most children with ODD also have other psychiatric disorders such as ADHD or mood disorders (depression or anxiety). If another disorder is diagnosed along with ODD, it must be treated as well.

Most parents of children with ODD have a very difficult time dealing with their kids. Some hope their children will grow out of the condition as they grow older, but this is not usually the case. Most children continue to have ODD, and for some it develops into conduct disorder. Children with CD are at risk for developing even more serious

Phobias

WHAT IS A PHOBIA?

A phobia is an extreme fear of a specific situation (e.g., flying in a plane or standing on a high bridge) or thing (e.g., dogs, cats, mice, or birds). If the person is exposed to the situation or thing, he or she feels extreme anxiety and perhaps panic. While most older children and adolescents with phobias know that these fears are extreme and irrational, they are unable to control them. As a result, they dread and attempt to avoid the thing or situation that is the object of fear.

Sometimes a child's fear is so strong that it interferes with his or her daily life, school, social relationships, and so forth. The child's life may be affected in a variety of ways, such as missing school or being unable to go to certain

SEE THESE HANDOUTS ON RELATED TOPICS

Anxiety in Children

Helping Your Child or Teen Manage Stress

How to Build Your Child's Self-Esteem

How to Cope When Parenting Seems Overwhelming

Positive Reinforcement (for Parents)

When Kids Don't Want to Go to School

WHERE CAN I GO FOR MORE INFORMATION?

Anxiety Disorders Association of America (www.adaa.org).

Anxiety Panic Internet Resource (www.algy.com/anxiety).

Internet Mental Health (www.mental-health.com).

National Institute of Mental Health (www.nimh.nih.gov/anxiety).

Bassett, Lucinda. *From Panic to Power: Proven Techniques to Calm Your Anxieties, Conquer Your Fears, and Put You in Control of Your Life.* New York: Quill, 1997.

Bourne, Edmund J. *The Anxiety and Phobia Workbook.* Oakland, CA: New Harbinger, 2000.

Ross, Jerilyn. *Triumph Over Fear: A Book of Help and Hope for People with Anxiety Disorders.* New York: Bantam Books, 1995.

other places. The fear may also cause extreme distress. Such fears are considered phobias if they are not reasonable.

Phobias often begin in childhood and may be triggered by a traumatic event. A fear of birds, for example, may begin with a bird flying into the house and frightening a child. Many phobias that begin in childhood fade away by adulthood.

> Many phobias that begin in childhood fade away by adulthood.

WHAT IS THE TREATMENT FOR PHOBIAS?

> Phobias of specific things or situations often begin in childhood and may begin with a traumatic event. Many phobias that begin in childhood fade away by adulthood.

Most children and adolescents who suffer from phobias begin to feel better when they receive the proper treatment. It can be difficult to identify the correct treatment, however, because each person's phobia is caused by a unique set of factors. It can be frustrating when treatment is not immediately successful or takes longer than hoped for. Some patients feel better after a few weeks or months of treatment, while others may need a longer time to improve.

While a treatment plan must be specifically designed for each individual, there are a number of standard approaches. Mental health professionals who specialize in treating anxiety disorders (including phobias) most often use a combination of the following treatments (there is no single correct approach):

> Most children and adolescents who suffer from phobias begin to feel better when they receive the proper treatment. It can be difficult to identify the correct treatment, however, because each person's phobia is caused by a unique set of factors.

The patient is exposed to anxiety-producing stimuli one small step at a time, which gradually increases his or her tolerance to situations that have produced disabling anxiety.

Cognitive Therapy. The patient learns how to identify and change unproductive thought patterns by observing his or her feelings and learning to separate realistic thoughts from unrealistic ones.

Relaxation Training. Many children with anxiety disorders, including phobias, benefit from self-hypnosis, guided visualization, and biofeedback. Relaxation training is often part of treatment.

Medication. Antidepressant and antianxiety medications can help restore chemical imbalances that cause symptoms of anxiety. This is an effective treatment for many people, especially in combination with psychotherapy.

The treatment for a phobia depends on the severity and length of the disorder. The patient's willingness to actively participate in treatment is also an important factor. When a person with phobia is motivated to try new behaviors and practice new skills and techniques, he or she can learn to change the way the brain responds to familiar thoughts and feelings that previously caused anxiety.

> **Behavior Therapy.** This treatment helps the client alter and control unwanted behavior. **Systematic desensitization** is a type of behavior therapy often used to help people with phobias.

> **Systematic desensitization** is a type of behavior therapy often used to help people with phobias.

Posttraumatic Stress Disorder (PTSD)

WHAT IS PTSD?

Posttraumatic Stress Disorder (PTSD) develops in response to a traumatic or life-threatening event that is outside the normal range of human experience. It can arise when a person (child, adolescent, or adult) **experiences or witnesses** an event such as any of the following:

- Sexual abuse
- Rape
- Life-threatening injury or illness
- Murder
- Violence
- Being threatened with a weapon
- Terrorism
- War
- Natural disaster (e.g., tornado, hurricane, earthquake)
- Early and traumatic loss of a parent

Family therapy. The entire family is affected when a child experiences trauma. A skilled family therapist can help family members provide support for the victim and deal with their own feelings.

Support groups. A support group that includes other kids who have had similar experiences, and who are struggling with similar problems, can be very healing.

Eye movement desensitization reprocessing. EMDR is a fairly new therapeutic tool that has been shown to be effective in treating victims of trauma. A licensed, experienced therapist who has been trained in this technique may be able to relieve the symptoms of PTSD.

Relaxation training. Since many victims of trauma have a difficult time relaxing, special training may be helpful.

Physical exercise. An active exercise program is an excellent way to relax and relieve stress.

Medication. Antidepressant medications can help relieve the symptoms of depression and anxiety and encourage sleep.

Early treatment is best. Ideally, the victim of trauma should receive supportive treatment at the earliest possible time. Victims benefit from the support of their family members, friends, and mental health professionals. The most important element of any treatment plan is to create a sense of safety.

WHERE CAN I GO FOR MORE INFORMATION?

National Center for PTSD (www.NCPTSD.org).

For free information about posttraumatic stress disorder and related conditions, see www.PTSD.com.

Rothschild, Babette. *The Body Remembers: The Psychophysiology of Trauma and Trauma Treatment.* New York: W.W. Norton & Company, 2000.

Wilson, John, Friedman, Matthew, Lindy, Jacob, Editors. *Treating Psychological Trauma and PTSD.* New York: Guilford Press, 2001.

SEE THESE HANDOUTS ON RELATED TOPICS

Anxiety in Children

Children, Teens, and Suicide

Depression in Children and Teens

Helping Kids Manage Angry Feelings

How to Build Your Child's Self-Esteem

How to Cope When Parenting Seems Overwhelming

Positive Reinforcement (for Parents)

PTSD symptoms may impact the child's ability to carry on a normal life because he or she may be unable to do things like go to school or maintain friendships.

Children who develop PTSD may have both psychological and physical symptoms. The disorder often occurs along with other conditions like depression, substance abuse, memory and thinking problems, and other problems of physical and mental health. The symptoms may impact the child's ability to carry on a normal life because he or she may be unable to do things like go to school or maintain friendships.

WHAT ARE THE SYMPTOMS OF PTSD?

Some symptoms of PTSD may become apparent immediately, and some may be delayed until adulthood. The symptoms of PTSD may last from several months to many years and may include the following:

- Dissociation
- Withdrawal, detachment
- Flashbacks and memories of the event
- Avoidance of specific places and situations
- Acting out the event in play situations
- Nightmares and disturbing dreams
- Dreading that the event will happen again
- Fearing imminent death
- Being less interested in activities that once were enjoyable
- Headaches, stomachaches, or other physical symptoms
- Insomnia
- Inability to concentrate

HOW IS PTSD DIFFERENT FROM NORMAL REACTIONS TO STRESS?

Not every child who experiences or witnesses a life-threatening or traumatic act develops PTSD. After such an experience, most children experience the symptoms of acute stress. This begins with a sense of numbness or shock and perhaps confusion, sadness, and anxiety. They may have any of the symptoms on the preceding list. These signs of acute stress are normal, and if they disappear after about a month they are not PTSD. If they worsen and last longer than a month, PTSD could be the diagnosis.

Not every child who experiences or witnesses a life-threatening or traumatic act develops PTSD. After such an experience, most children experience the symptoms of acute stress.

WHY DO SOME CHILDREN DEVELOP PTSD WHILE OTHERS DON'T?

Several factors determine whether a person suffers from PTSD following a traumatic experience. The most important ones are:

The nature and the extent of the trauma. The more horrific the experience, the greater the impact it will have on anyone who experiences it.

Coping skills. Some people have developed a better ability to cope with stress and will have fewer and milder symptoms.

Previous experiences. Others who may have experienced other traumatic events in the past may be at greater risk.

Current stress level. When a child or adolescent is already experiencing great stress in his or her life, he or she is likely to be more vulnerable in the face of a traumatic event. For example, a child whose parents are divorcing and whose family is already in an upheaval and then experiences an earthquake is more likely to develop an extreme response like PTSD.

Support system. Those who have parents, teachers, and others who will listen and offer a shoulder to lean on will have a much easier time recovering from a traumatic experience.

Family and social environment. Victims who are made to feel ashamed or guilty are much more likely to experience PTSD. Those who are treated with empathy and understanding have a much better chance of complete recovery.

When a child or adolescent is already experiencing great stress in his or her life, he or she is likely to be more vulnerable in the face of a traumatic event.

WHAT ARE THE TREATMENTS FOR PTSD?

Individual psychotherapy. A therapist who specializes in working with children who are victims of trauma can help the patient talk about the event. The patient can also be encouraged to write about it. The therapist may use behavior modification techniques and cognitive therapy to alleviate the child's fears and worries.

A skilled family therapist can help them provide support for the victim and deal with their own feelings.

- Confusion
- Agitation, hyperarousal
- Fear and anxiety
- Feeling helpless
- Anger and irritability
- Sadness and depression
- Shock, apathy, or numbness

Psychosis

WHAT IS PSYCHOSIS?

Psychosis is a serious mental illness that affects mostly adults. Fortunately, this illness affects very few children or adolescents. The key characteristic is a loss of contact with reality. When a child is experiencing psychosis, it means that he or she:

- Does not understand what is real and what is not real
- Has hallucinations and delusions (see list of symptoms in next section)
- Is confused and unable to think clearly
- Is unable to communicate properly with others
- Behaves in an odd, strange, or inappropriate way

Several mental disorders may include psychotic features. These include the following:

- Depression
- Manic depression (bipolar disorder)
- Schizophrenia
- Drug and alcohol abuse

2. **Acute psychosis.** The symptoms become more pronounced and obvious. The person may experience confused thinking, hallucinations, and delusions.

3. **Recovery.** The person's symptoms disappear and he or she returns to normal.

WHAT CAUSES PSYCHOSIS?

There are many possible causes for psychosis. The psychotic symptoms may be a part of another disorder such as those listed on the first page of this handout (depression, bipolar disorder, schizophrenia, etc.). The psychotic symptoms may be caused by drugs or alcohol, may be a response to major stress, or may have an organic (physical) cause such as a head injury or tumor.

WHAT IS THE TREATMENT FOR PSYCHOSIS?

Psychosis is a treatable illness, and most people recover from it. The course of recovery varies from person to person and is based on each person's individual diagnosis. Many people who experience one episode of psychosis recover and never experience another.

It is critical to recognize the psychotic symptoms as early as possible and to obtain proper treatment immediately. After being assessed by a qualified medical professional, a person with psychotic symptoms may be treated with a combination of hospitalization, medication, counseling, and group support.

WHERE CAN I GO FOR MORE INFORMATION?

National Institute of Mental Health (www.nimh.gov).

National Mental Health Association (www.nmha.org).

Torrey, E. Fuller. *Surviving Schizophrenia: A Manual for Families, Consumers, and Providers.* New York: Quill, 2001.

Woolis, Rebecca, and Hatfield, Agnes. *When Someone You Love Has a Mental Illness: A Handbook for Family, Friends, and Caregivers.* New York: Jeremy Tarcher, 1992.

SEE THESE HANDOUTS ON RELATED TOPICS

How to Cope When Parenting Seems Overwhelming

Living with Your Child's Serious Medical Condition

Mania and Hypomania

Confused thoughts. The person's thoughts are muddled and don't fit together. He or she may have a hard time following a conversation and may become forgetful. He or she may say things that don't make sense.

Emotional changes. A person experiencing psychosis may feel alienated from others or cut off emotionally. He or she may feel like everything is moving slowly. Mood swings, from depressed to anxious to elated, are another example.

Behavioral changes. The child acts different from his or her normal way of behaving. He or she may respond to normal experiences in odd or bizarre ways, such as suddenly becoming upset or laughing inappropriately. The child's strange behavior also may be in response to delusions or hallucinations.

Delusions. A person who is in a psychotic episode may be completely certain that things that are not true are true. Examples include believing that he or she is being watched or being plotted against, or that he or she is has a terminal illness.

Hallucinations. A psychotic person may see, hear, feel, or taste something that is not really there. For example, he or she may see people or animals that are not present, or hear voices that tell him or her to carry out certain instructions.

Thought disorders. These can include thought insertion, thought broadcasting, or ideas of reference:

HALLUCINATIONS AND DELUSIONS

These are the hallmarks of psychosis that affect many more adults than children.

Hallucination: Seeing, hearing, feeling, or smelling something that is not really there. For example, a person with auditory hallucinations hears voices when no one is talking. A person with kinesthetic (feeling) hallucinations may be convinced that insects are crawling on his body.

Delusion: Firmly holding a false belief. Delusional beliefs are usually odd or unusual, not ordinarily held by members of the person's cultural group. Delusions may be paranoid (believing that people are out to get you in some way), grandiose (having exaggerated ideas of your importance), or somatic (believing that you have a serious illness even though you are perfectly healthy). Nihilistic delusions are beliefs that one's body is decomposing or rotting inside.

- **Thought insertion** is feeling that one's thoughts are not his or her own. These patients become convinced that someone else has inserted thoughts into their minds. These thoughts may be very demanding or controlling, and the patient may behave in unusual ways in response. These patients become very confused and have a hard time organizing or controlling their thoughts.

- **Thought broadcasting** is feeling that one's thoughts are being broadcast to others. It is confusing to hold a conversation with these patients because they believe that they only have to think their part of the conversation for it to be

---

heard. It is quite upsetting to the patient to think that others can hear all of his or her thoughts.

- **Ideas of reference** mean that the patient thinks that ordinary, harmless things (e.g., events or conversations having nothing to do with him or her) have some kind of special significance to him or her.

Most episodes of psychosis have three phases. The length of each phase varies with each person. They include:

> *Psychosis is a treatable illness, and most people recover from it. The course of recovery varies from person to person. Many people who experience one episode of psychosis recover and never experience another.*

1. **Prodrome.** In the early stage of psychosis, there are slight changes in the way the person behaves and thinks. He or she may become depressed, anxious, irritable, or suspicious, and may experience changes in appetite, have disturbed sleep, or be subject to mood swings. The person may become withdrawn, and work or studies may suffer. Things may just feel different, as if the world around him or her has changed in some way. As the person's behavior changes, the people around him or her often are the first to realize that something is wrong.

Runaway Kids

WHY DO CHILDREN RUN AWAY FROM HOME?

According to the U.S. Department of Justice, nearly half a million children run away from home each year. Some leave for a short time, such as overnight or for a few days, while others are gone much longer. Sadly, some never return home. In some cases, children escape to

This list could fill a hundred books, since the ways to raise responsible, happy children are limited only by our imagination. (See the handout "How to Build Your Child's Self-Esteem" for a list of ideas.)

WHERE CAN I GO FOR MORE INFORMATION?

National Center for Missing and Exploited Children (www.missingkids.com).

National Runaway Hot Line: 1-800-HIT-HOME (24 hours).

Runaway Help Line: 1-800-621-4000 (24 hours).

Branden, Nathaniel. *The Six Pillars of Self-Esteem*. New York: Bantam, 1994.

Briggs, Dorothy Corkville. *Celebrate Your Self: Making Life Work for You*. Garden City, NY: Doubleday, 1977.

SEE THESE HANDOUTS ON RELATED TOPICS

Helping Kids Manage Angry Feelings

Helping Your Child or Teen Manage Stress

How to Build Your Child's Self-Esteem

How to Cope When Parenting Seems Overwhelming

How to Help a Friend through a Crisis (for Teens)

How to Help Victims Of Child Abuse

Positive Reinforcement (for Parents)

What to Do about Teen Chemical Dependence

When Kids Underachieve

relatives or their noncustodial parents; others travel far away to distant locations and live on the streets.

There are many reasons that children and adolescents leave home without permission, causing their families tremendous angst. The most common reasons include the following:

- **Major family changes.** Separation, divorce, or remarriage generally cause upheaval in a family. These changes and the emotions surrounding them are very upsetting to the child and cause him or her to want to escape.

- **Parental alcohol or drug abuse.** When parents abuse alcohol or drugs, the home may become unsafe and the child decides that escape is the best option.

- **Alcohol or drug abuse by the child.** Kids who begin abusing substances begin to associate with other kids who have similar problems. Some-

times leaving home without permission becomes part of the experience.

- **Physical or sexual abuse.** When kids are being harmed at home, sometimes the only safe option they can see is to leave.

Divorce and remarriage, drug or alcohol abuse, and physical or sexual abuse are all very serious and must be addressed. In addition, the parents' parenting skills must be strengthened.

have caused the child to need to escape.

HOW CAN YOU PREVENT YOUR CHILD FROM RUNNING AWAY?

Unless the causes of the runaway behavior are addressed, it is unlikely that the problem will be solved. Since the problems underlying the runaway behavior are so severe, it is almost always recommended that the family seek professional assistance. An experienced family therapist can help in the following ways:

- Help the parents strengthen their parenting skills.
- Help the family communicate better and resolve the issues that have caused discord.
- Help the child or adolescent who has run away to develop alternative responses to stress and stronger self-esteem.

HOW CAN I BUILD TRUST AND SELF-ESTEEM?

The most important issue is to address the dysfunctional behaviors that are occurring within the family that may

> Parents who know how to effectively communicate with and discipline their children are more likely to prevent extreme behavior such as running away from home.

> The most important issue is to address the dysfunctional behaviors that are occurring within the family that may have caused the child to escape.

> Parents who know how to effectively communicate with and discipline their children are more likely to prevent extreme behavior such as running away from home. Practicing effective parenting skills helps build trust in the family and strengthen the self-esteem of the children.
>
> There are hundreds of ways that parents can convey the message "You are worthwhile" to their children.

> There are hundreds of ways that parents can convey the message "You are worthwhile" to their children.

Separation Anxiety

WHAT IS SEPARATION ANXIETY?

It is normal for a child to feel fearful or anxious when separated from his or her primary care-takers (usually the parents) and immediate family members. These people (called *attach-ment figures* by psychologists) are very impor-tant to the emotional growth and development of the child. Showing some anxiety when a parent or favorite adult leaves is a positive sign that the child has developed healthy attach-ments. This ability is an important step in the process of developing a healthy personality and is a building block in the ability to trust and love others.

SEE THESE HANDOUTS ON RELATED TOPICS

Anxiety in Children
Depression in Children and Teens
Helping Your Child or Teen Manage Stress
How to Build Your Child's Self-Esteem
How to Cope When Parenting Seems Over-whelming
Positive Reinforcement (for Parents)

- Avoid making the child feel bad about being anxious.

- Tell your child that you are confident that the anxious feelings will pass.

- Avoid rewarding the child for hiding his or her anxious feelings.

- Manage your feelings of guilt. Watch for signs that your child is learning to manipu-late you when you feel guilty.

- If your child continues to show separation anxiety after two weeks in a new situation, reconsider the arrangements. Perhaps the situation is unworkable, and it would be better to try something else.

If professional treatment is needed, the treatment plan will be based on what is discov-ered in the diagnosis. Treatment may include the following components:

- Psychological testing
- Medication for anxiety disorder
- Individual counseling
- Family counseling
- Parenting skills training

WHERE CAN I GO FOR MORE INFORMATION?

Bowlby, John. *Separation: Anxiety and Anger.* New York: Basic Books, 2000.

Crary, Elizabeth. *Mommy, Don't Go.* Seattle: Parenting Press, 1996.

While it is normal to feel some anxiety when being separated from one's family, separation anxiety is excessive and inappropriate for the child's level of development.

Feeling anxious and upset when being separated from one's mother, father, or other beloved adult is understandable. This is especially true when a situation is new or if a small child has had few such experiences. When a child is faced with an unfamiliar situation, it is to be expected that he or she will feel anxious because he or she has no way of predicting what will happen.

A child who has separation anxiety disorder feels extremely anxious when faced with being separated from the people to whom he or she is attached.

A child who has **separation anxiety disorder** feels extremely anxious when faced with being separated from the people to whom he or she is attached. This usually includes parents and family members. While it is normal to feel some anxiety when being separated from one's family, separation anxiety is **excessive** and **inappropriate** for the child's level of development.

To be diagnosed with separation anxiety disorder, a child under the age of 18 must demonstrate three or more of the following behaviors on an ongoing basis for four weeks or more:

- The child repeatedly feels distressed when separated from attachment figures.
- The child constantly worries that the attachment figures will be harmed or lost.
- The child constantly worries that he or she will be lost or kidnapped, resulting in separation from attachment figures.
- The child refuses to go to school or other places for fear of being separated from the attachment figures.
- The child doesn't want to be home alone or away from home without the attachment figures.
- The child won't go to sleep without the attachment figure nearby.
- The child has nightmares about being lost or separated from the attachment figures.
- When the child anticipates being separated from the attachment figures, he or she becomes physically ill.
- These worries cause a significant amount of distress in the child's ability to carry on a normal life.

WHAT CAUSES SEPARATION ANXIETY DISORDER?

Separation anxiety disorder may have any of the following causes:

- The child is not securely attached to his or her primary caretakers.
- The child is experiencing major life changes such as moving to a new home or starting at a new school.
- The child has experienced losses of important people through death or divorce.

WHAT IS THE TREATMENT FOR SEPARATION ANXIETY DISORDER?

The following suggestions may be helpful in assisting your child to recover from separation anxiety disorder:

- Anticipate when your child will need to face new experiences. Introduce your child to the new situations slowly and gradually. Avoid leaving your child alone in the new situation before this gradual introduction.

If your child continues to show separation anxiety after two weeks in a new situation, reconsider the arrangements. Perhaps the situation is unworkable, and it would be better to try something else.

Be empathic with your child when he or she is feeling anxious about being separated from someone important. Show that you understood and accept your child's feelings.

- Be empathic with your child when he or she is feeling anxious about being separated from someone important. Show that you understand and accept your child's feelings.

Sexual Acting Out

WHAT IS SEXUAL ACTING OUT?

Sexual acting out can include any of the following behaviors:

- Having sexual intercourse with more than one partner without an emotional connection.

- Having sexual intercourse without using birth control when one is not prepared to care for a baby.

- Having sexual intercourse without protecting oneself from sexually transmitted diseases or pregnancy.

- Engaging in sexual activity while under the influence of drugs and alcohol.

- Regularly dressing in a provocative way in public.

SEE THESE HANDOUTS ON RELATED TOPICS

Anxiety in Children

Attention-Seeking with Disruptive Behavior

Conduct Disorder

Depression in Children And Teens

Helping Kids Manage Angry Feelings

How to Build Your Child's Self-Esteem

How to Help Victims of Child Abuse

Life Skills (for Teens)

Managing Family Conflict

Oppositional Defiant Disorder (ODD)

Positive Reinforcement (for Parents)

What Teens Need to Know about HIV and AIDS

WHERE CAN I GO FOR MORE INFORMATION?

Focus Adolescent Services (www.focusas.com).

Beyond the Big Talk: Every Parent's Guide to Raising Sexually Healthy Teens—from Middle School to College. New York: Newmarket Press, 2001.

Haffner, Debra, Tartaglione, Alissa Haffner. *From Diapers to Dating: A Parent's Guide to Raising Sexually Healthy Children.* New York: Newmarket Press, 2000.

Schwartz, Pepper, and Cappello, Dominic. *Ten Talks Parents Must Have with Their Children about Sex and Character.* New York: Hyperion, 2000.

- Openly sharing information about one's sexual experiences and partners without concern for one's reputation or the reputation of one's partners.
- Showing a strong interest in pornography.

2 WHAT CAUSES KIDS TO ACT OUT SEXUALLY?

Adolescents act out sexually for many different reasons. The most common ones are:

- The child has been sexually abused and has not received proper treatment.
- The child has a brain dysfunction that causes impaired impulse control and an inability to understand social rules. Such dysfunction may be caused by fetal alcohol syndrome or another disorder.
- The teen is unable to deal with frustration and has learned to act it out sexually rather than confronting it in a healthy way. When the teen experiences painful feelings like anxiety, anger, and depression, he or she has a sexual encounter to ward off and contain the feelings and release the tension.

3 WHAT IS THE TREATMENT FOR SEXUAL ACTING OUT?

The specific treatment of sexual acting out behavior depends on the causes. If the behavior is caused by brain dysfunction, the following steps may be taken:

- Teach the adolescent about the brain disability. He or she needs to know that the brain dysfunction is the cause of the problem, not the fact that he or she is a bad person.

- Teach the teen the proper way to interact with people. Demonstrate how to keep clear boundaries and keep a respectful and safe distance from people.

> Teach the teen the proper way to interact with people. Demonstrate how to keep clear boundaries and keep a respectful and safe distance from people.

WHAT IS NORMAL TEEN SEXUAL BEHAVIOR?

Teens participate in any of the following behaviors. While some of these behaviors may be contrary to the beliefs and values of your family, they are all normal and should not be considered sexual acting out:

- Talking openly with friends about sex
- Making jokes with sexual references
- Using sexual terms in conversation with other teens
- Being flirtatious with other teens
- Showing interest in sexual publications
- Masturbating when alone
- Kissing
- Holding hands
- Hugging
- Engaging in consensual petting, fondling, and mutual masturbation
- Having intercourse with a single partner to the exclusion of other partners

- Practice alternative ways to manage situations that have presented problems in the past.
- Medication may be helpful in keeping problem behaviors in check.
- Explain the child's problem to his or her teachers and others who interact with him or her.
- Supervise the teen closely.
- Monitor the teen's environment for potential problem situations and help him or her avoid them.

If the behavior is caused by a history of sexual abuse, make certain that the abuse has been reported. As soon as the abuse is discovered, arrange for the child to receive professional treatment. It is important that all members of the victim's family be included in the treatment plan. Without treatment, child victims of sexual abuse are very likely to develop severe emotional problems that can last a lifetime. With the proper treatment and family support, most victims can recover their self-esteem and heal from the effects of the trauma.

> It is important that all members of the victim's family be included in the treatment plan.

Sleep Disturbances

WHAT ARE THE MOST COMMON SLEEP DISTURBANCES IN CHILDREN?

Sleeping well is important for a child's growth and emotional well-being, and also for the well-being of the parents. However, it is not unusual for children to experience some kind of sleep disturbance during childhood or adolescence. This could include any of the following:

- Having a hard time falling asleep
- Waking up often during the night
- Waking up early
- Talking while asleep
- Crying during the night

Spock, Benjamin, and Parker, Stephen. *Dr. Spock's Baby and Child Care.* New York: Pocket Books, 1998.

Weissbluth, Marc. *Healthy Sleep Habits, Happy Child.* New York: Fawcett Books, 1999.

SEE THESE HANDOUTS ON RELATED TOPICS

Anxiety in Children

Depression in Children and Teens

Do things in the child's room to alleviate the things he or she may be afraid of.

- Have a night-light or flashlight handy, play soft music, provide stuffed animals, and so forth to increase his or her comfort level.
- Do your best to avoid lying down with your child or allowing him or her to sleep with you. Once you begin doing this, it will be difficult to break the habit.
- If your child wakes up during the night, engage in as little conversation as possible. Give the child what he or she needs and go back to bed.

If you are concerned that your child's sleep problem is more than a passing phase, ask your doctor to evaluate the situation.

WHERE CAN I GO FOR MORE INFORMATION?

The National Sleep Foundation (www.sleepfoundation.org).

- Wetting the bed
- Having bad dreams

Every child has his or her own pattern of sleeping. What is fine for one child may be a problem for another. The most important thing is whether the child seems to be alert and happy during his or her waking hours. If the child seems to be healthy and thriving, unusual sleep behavior may not be cause for alarm.

NIGHTMARES

It is quite common for children to have bad dreams. If these dreams are frequent and very frightening, they can prevent the child from getting enough rest.

Parasomnias are a group of sleep disturbances that include sleepwalking, sleep talking, and terrors. These disorders seem to run in families but are fairly rare. A child with sleep terrors screams hysterically and seems to be awake but is unable to describe what is happening. Like those with sleep terrors, kids who sleepwalk seem to be awake as they move around, but they are really asleep. This can be dangerous because these children may hurt themselves.

If a child has a parasomnia that occurs frequently, the parents should consult the child's pediatrician.

WHAT ARE THE CAUSES OF SLEEP PROBLEMS?

There are many different causes of sleep problems in children. These are a few of the most common difficulties:

- Inconsistent sleeping habits
- Feeling fearful about going to bed alone
- Fear of being separated from the primary caregiver (usually the mother or father)
- Other common childhood fears (e.g., fear of the dark, monsters, storms)
- Physical illness
- Emotional disorders
- Alcohol and drug abuse (mostly in adolescents)
- Attention-deficit/hyperactivity disorder (ADHD)
- General feelings of anxiety

HOW CAN I HELP MY CHILD SLEEP WELL?

- Get professional help to rule out physical and emotional disorders as the cause of your child's sleep problems.
- Keep your child from drinking beverages containing caffeine during the six hours before bedtime.
- Make sure your child gets exercise on a regular basis, but not just before bedtime.
- Do things in the child's room to alleviate the things he or she may be afraid of.
- Have a routine where you put your child to bed and wake your child up at the same times every day, if possible.
- Help the child slow down at the end of the day. Encourage him or her to sit quietly while you read, or watch television together, or take a bath.

Get professional help to rule out physical and emotional disorders as the cause of your child's sleep problems.

Social Anxiety Disorder (Shyness)

 ## WHAT IS SOCIAL ANXIETY?

Social anxiety or social phobia (shyness) is the fear of being around other people. Children who suffer from this disorder are extremely apprehensive in social situations and may have tantrums and cling to their caregivers. Most of these children want to be able to interact with others but are unable to do so, freezing up and becoming withdrawn.

Older children and teens with social anxiety always feel uncomfortable and self-conscious around others. They may have the feeling that everyone is constantly staring at them and being critical in some way. Because the anxiety is so painful, they learn to stay away from social situations and avoid other people. Some eventually need to be alone at all times, in a room with the door closed. The feeling is pervasive and constant, and it even happens with people they know.

Small children with social anxiety become very upset when in unfamiliar social situations. They may experience a sense of intense fear, along with

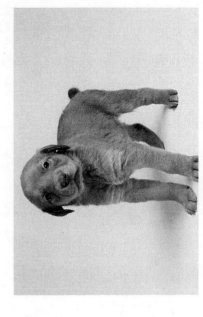

SEE THESE HANDOUTS ON RELATED TOPICS

Anxiety in Children
How to Build Your Child's Self-Esteem
Positive Reinforcement (for Parents)
When Kids Don't Want to Go to School

Cognitive therapy. The client learns how to identify and change unproductive thought patterns by observing his or her feelings and learning to separate realistic thoughts from unrealistic ones. Most experts agree that this type of therapy is the most effective one in treating social anxiety.

Group therapy. People with social anxiety benefit from being in an ongoing therapy group with other clients who also have the disorder. The best type of group is one in which the focus is learning new skills and overcoming the isolation that people with this disorder feel.

Relaxation training. Many people with social anxiety disorders benefit from self-hypnosis, guided visualization, and biofeedback. Relaxation training is often part of psychotherapy.

Medication. Antidepressant and antianxiety medications can help reverse chemical imbalances that cause symptoms of social anxiety. This is an effective treatment for many people, especially in combination with psychotherapy.

WHERE CAN I GO FOR MORE INFORMATION?

Social Phobia/Social Anxiety Association (www.socialphobia.org).

Burns, David. *Ten Days to Self-Esteem.* New York: William Morrow, 1993.

Zimbardo, P. *Shyness: What It Is and What to Do About It.* Reading, MA: Addison-Wesley, 1987.

Books for Kids:

Best, Cari. *Shrinking Violet.* New York: Farrar Straus & Giroux, 2001.

Lovell, Patty. *Stand Tall, Molly Lou Melon.* New York: Putnam, 2001

Raschka, Chris. *The Blushful Hippopotamus.* London, England: Orchard, 1996.

shaking, rapid heartbeat, blushing, dry mouth, difficulty in swallowing, and other symptoms of extreme nervousness. The prevailing feeling is intense, overwhelming anxiety. Most sufferers realize that their feelings are irrational, but this does not help relieve them.

> Help your child accept being shy. If you speak of shyness as a normal and acceptable way of being, your child will learn to accept it.

Social anxiety or shyness may be caused by any combination of the following factors:

- The child has a genetic predisposition to shyness. Many personality factors are inherited. On a continuum from introverted to extraverted, the child may be naturally shy.
- The attachment between the child and his or her parents is weak at best.
- The child has not learned adequate social skills.
- The child has been criticized and teased by family members and has learned that it is punishing to express him- or herself.

WHAT CAN PARENTS DO TO HELP THE SOCIALLY ANXIOUS CHILD?

Shyness can be extremely painful for a child, teen, or adult. Parents can help shy children be more comfortable around people by trying a few of the following ideas.

> Don't refer to your child as "shy." When you give a child a label, he or she may feel stuck with this identity and hopeless about learning different behaviors.

- Be empathic when your child is fearful around others. For example, if your child is afraid to go to a friend's house, you could say, "You seem to be feeling a little upset about this. It's okay to feel that way. I used to be a bit nervous about going to someone's house, too."
- Help your child accept being shy. If you speak of shyness as a normal and acceptable way of being, your child will learn to accept it. Tell your child about times when you felt shy and what you did to cope with it.
- Talk about learning some new behaviors, and help your child learn them. If you want your child to learn to be more outgoing, be outgoing yourself.
- Gradually introduce your child to new situations. Take small steps and talk about them before they happen. After each step, talk to your child about what happened.
- Set small and manageable goals—things like making eye contact and saying one word during a conversation. When your child learns the new behavior, give plenty of praise and acknowledge how challenging it was.
- Describe the value of learning to be more outgoing. Give your child some reasons to learn to overcome his or her shyness, such as having more friends and enjoying school more.
- Don't refer to your child as "shy." When you give a child a label, he or she may feel stuck with this identity and hopeless about learning different behaviors.
- When you and your child are together and encounter an outgoing person, talk about it afterward. Point out the outgoing behaviors without making a comparison to your child.
- Provide opportunities for your child to work on an activity with one other child.
- Read books to your young child about shy children who learn to be more outgoing. See the list at the end of this handout for a few recommendations.
- Protect your child from being teased by other kids.

- Talk to your child about feelings and show him or her how to express them. When your child is feeling afraid or self-conscious, help him or her to describe the feelings and put them into words. Talk about your own feelings. Such discussions help normalize these emotions and make the child feel less isolated.
- Ask other adults for their help. Explain what you are doing with your child and ask them to help in specific ways.
- Seek the assistance of a mental health professional. Sometimes parents need help with helping their children. If you try the ideas on this list and believe your child needs more than you can offer, ask your family doctor for a referral to a licensed mental health professional who specializes in working with kids.

WHAT KIND OF PROFESSIONAL TREATMENT HELPS SHY KIDS?

Most people who suffer from anxiety disorders begin to feel better when they receive the proper treatment. It can be difficult to identify the correct treatment, however, because each person's anxiety is caused by a unique set of factors. It can be frustrating for the client when treatment is not immediately successful or takes longer than hoped for. Many clients feel better after a few weeks or months of treatment. If a person has an anxiety disorder in combination with another disorder (such as depression), treatment is more complicated and takes longer.

> Most people who suffer from anxiety disorders begin to feel better when they receive the proper treatment.

Although a treatment plan must be specifically designed for each individual, a number of standard approaches exist. Mental health professionals who specialize in treating anxiety most often use a combination of the following treatments (there is no single correct approach):

What to Do About Teen Chemical Dependence

 INTRODUCTION

Addiction to alcohol and other drugs is a chronic disease. It is progressive, continuous, and long-term. *Alcohol or drug abuse* means that a person still has control over whether he or she drinks alcohol or uses drugs. *Chemical dependence* means that a teen has lost all control over his or her drinking or using behavior.

 WHAT IS ADDICTIVE BEHAVIOR?

Teens who suffer from addictive diseases engage in compulsive behavior and gradually lose control of their lives. They continue to drink or use drugs even when they know that doing so will lead to negative consequences. They tend to have low self-esteem and almost inevitably suffer from anxiety and depression.

If a teen in your life suffers from addictive

SEE THESE HANDOUTS ON RELATED TOPICS

Anxiety in Children

Depression in Children and Teens

Helping Kids Manage Angry Feelings

Helping Your Child or Teen Manage Stress

How to Build Your Child's Self-Esteem

How to Cope When Parenting Seems Overwhelming

How to Help a Friend through a Crisis (for Teens)

Life Skills (for Teens)

What Teens Need to Know about HIV and AIDS

---

lies of Chemically Dependent Persons. Washington, DC: The Johnson Institute, 1989.

West, James, and Ford, Betty. *The Betty Ford Center Book of Answers: Help for Those Struggling with Substance Abuse and for the People Who Love Them.* New York: Pocket Books, 1997.

 **WHAT CAN I DO WHEN SOMEONE WON'T STOP DRINKING ALCOHOL OR USING DRUGS?**

Sometimes the alcoholic or addict is in such a strong state of denial that the best alternative is to arrange an intervention. This process involves arranging for a professional interventionist to organize a meeting of the family, friends, and employer of the patient. The interventionist helps the group prepare a confrontation that will be followed by the patient entering a treatment center. The patient's family members and friends usually write brief statements describing how the drinking or drug use has affected them. The interventionist and the group then meet with the patient and read their statements to him or her with the guidance of the interventionist. These interventions, when managed by professionals from respected treatment organizations, often result in successful treatment of the addiction.

WHERE CAN I GO FOR MORE INFORMATION?

About (www.alcoholism.about.com).

Alcoholics Anonymous (www.alcoholics-anonymous.org).

National Center on Addiction and Substance Abuse at Columbia University (www.casacolumbia.org).

National Council on Alcoholism and Drug Dependence (www.ncadd.org).

National Institute on Alcohol Abuse and Alcoholism (www.niaaa.nih.gov).

Substance Abuse and Mental Health Services Administration (www.health.org).

Jay, Jeff, and Jay, Debra Erickson. *Love First: A New Approach to Intervention for Alcoholism and Drug Addiction.* Center City, MN: Hazelden, 2000.

Johnson, Vernon. *Intervention: How to Help Someone Who Doesn't Want Help: A Step-By-Step Guide for Fami-*

disease, you have experienced his or her extreme behavior, which can range from depression to exhilaration. You probably have also experienced the person's state of denial ("I can quit anytime" or "I don't have a problem"), dishonesty, frequent disappointments, and series of ruined relationships. These are the hallmark behaviors when a person suffers from addiction to alcohol or drugs.

WHO IS AFFECTED BY CHEMICAL DEPENDENCE?

Alcoholism and drug addiction affect people from all parts of society. They affect rock stars, writers, artists, and homeless people. Victims also include stay-at-home moms, teenagers, and corporate executives. There are addicts who are students at top universities and who are physicians in your local hospital. They may be teachers at your neighborhood school, or salespeople at the local hardware store.

Studies have shown that there is a genetic predisposition to alcoholism. About half of all alcoholics had an alcoholic parent. Men seem to be more vulnerable than women to the alcoholic traits of their parents. Women may be more affected by environmental factors (such as financial and life circumstances) than by inherited factors.

WHAT ARE THE PHYSICAL EFFECTS OF CHEMICAL DEPENDENCE?

Chronic alcohol abuse produces long-lasting damage in many areas of brain functioning. It damages the person's capacity for abstract thinking, problem solving, memory, and physical dexterity. It also impairs verbal, visual, and spatial ability. The extent of damage to the brain tissue depends on the extent of heavy alcohol abuse. When the drinking stops, a certain amount of healing is possible.

WHAT ABOUT PRESCRIPTION DRUGS?

Prescription and illegal drugs with psychoactive side effects target the brain and can change a person's mood. This causes these drugs to be potentially addicting. Some people think that if a doctor has prescribed a drug, it is not addictive. This is not true. It is important to tell your doctor if you:

- Are an alcoholic (using or in recovery)
- Have ever been addicted to any drug
- Have taken more than the prescribed dose of a prescribed drug
- Have taken a prescribed drug for a long time
- Take a prescribed drug with alcohol

WHAT IS THE TREATMENT FOR CHEMICAL DEPENDENCE?

Addictive diseases are often progressive and can be fatal. Fortunately, with the right treatment, recovery is possible. Treatment includes:

- **Detoxification.** The first phase of treatment of addictive disease focuses on controlling and reversing the physical effects of alcohol or drug use. This can include detoxification or treating life-threatening disorders such as liver failure.

SIGNS OF DRUG OR ALCOHOL ABUSE

Using alcohol or drugs every day

Regularly using alcohol or drugs until intoxicated

Hanging around with friends who abuse alcohol and drugs

Leaving drug paraphernalia in one's bedroom, locker, or backpack.

Noticeable behavioral changes that include withdrawing from family and friends, sleeping more and falling grades

Mood swings

Frequently absent from or late for school

Low self-esteem; describing oneself as a loser

Steals alcohol

Family history of drug or alcohol dependence

Sometimes the alcoholic or addict is in such a strong state of denial that the best alternative is to arrange an intervention. When they are managed by professionals from respected treatment organizations, interventions often result in successful treatment of the addiction.

- **Psychotherapy.** Since addictive disease is primarily a brain disease that results in behavioral symptoms, the main treatment is psychosocial therapy. Treatment usually focuses on identifying and eliminating the irrational feelings and distorted thinking that accompany chronic alcohol or drug abuse.

- **12-step program.** Alcoholism and drug addiction are chronic diseases that require a lifetime recovery plan. Most successful treatment plans include a focus on the 12 steps of Alcoholics Anonymous and involve ongoing, long-term participation in self-help groups. People who have been hospitalized for treatment often continue group and individual psychotherapy after they leave the hospital, in addition to attending 12-step meetings.

WHAT ABOUT THE FAMILY?

Addiction affects every member of the adolescent alcoholic or addict's family. As the disease progresses and the teen continues to drink or use drugs, it causes a range of emotional, spiritual, and financial problems for almost everyone involved, including family, friends, and coworkers. When the family is ready to begin the recovery process, Al-Anon and Alateen are excellent resources. A qualified family therapist who understands the process of addiction and recovery may also be consulted to work with the family.

When Kids Don't Want to Go to School

WHAT IS SCHOOL REFUSAL?

Nearly one-third of all children go through a phase when they don't want to go to school. This happens most often in kids who are between 5 and 7, and between 11 and 14. They may develop a fear of leaving the shelter

SEE THESE HANDOUTS ON RELATED TOPICS

Anxiety in Children

Depression in Children and Teens

Helping Kids Manage Angry Feelings

Helping Your Child or Teen Manage Stress

Helping Your Child Succeed in School

How to Build Your Child's Self-Esteem

How to Cope When Parenting Seems Overwhelming

Life Skills (for Teens)

Positive Reinforcement (for Parents)

When Kids Underachieve

- Parent training to deal effectively with negative behaviors and to reward positive behaviors.

- Family counseling to help the family manage conflict and communicate effectively

WHERE CAN I GO FOR MORE INFORMATION?

McEwan, Elaine. *When Kids Say No to School: Helping Children at Risk of Failure, Refusal, or Dropping Out.* Colorado Springs, CO: Harold Shaw Publishing, 1998.

Heyne, David, and Rollings, Stephanie. *School Refusal: Parent, Adolescent and Child Training Skills.* Malden, MA: Blackwell Publishers, 2002.

of their home and may insist that they feel sick. Their behavior may include any of the following:

- Anxiety
- Excessive crying
- Temper tantrums
- Refusing to stay alone in their rooms
- Following the parent through the house
- Wanting to be held
- Worrying about the parents' safety
- Worrying about their own safety
- Fears of animals and monsters
- Inability to fall asleep
- Bad dreams

If the children are allowed to stay home, they seem to calm down and feel better quickly.

Many parents have a hard time dealing with this behavior when it becomes a daily struggle. In many cases, this type of behavior starts right after the child has been at home with the parents for several days or weeks, such as on a vacation, or it may happen after a stressful event or change in the family, such as moving to a new home and school or the death of a family member or pet.

> *School refusal behavior includes any problem relating to attending school that lasts longer than two weeks. It can range from refusing to attend school at all to attending under strong protest.*

> *If school refusal behavior lasts more than two weeks, it is important to seek treatment to prevent the development of more serious emotional and academic problems.*

A child who refuses to go to school for several weeks or longer may develop both social and academic problems. If the child's feelings of fear and anxiety are not addressed, he or she is at risk for developing an anxiety disorder. Older children and adolescents who refuse to go to school generally need more serious treatment.

School refusal behavior includes any problem relating to attending school that lasts longer than two weeks. It can range from refusing to attend school at all to attending school under strong protest. Some kids protest and argue every morning, but do attend; others go to school but regularly leave during the day. They may continually look for ways to avoid school and plead with their parents to be allowed to stay home. To be considered school refusal, the behavior must be initiated by the child and not be the result of problems at home that prevent the child from attending school.

⚜ WHY DO KIDS REFUSE TO GO TO SCHOOL?

Children may refuse to go to school for many reasons. The most common ones include the following:

- Wishing to avoid situations at school that cause feelings of anxiety or depression
- Wanting to avoid certain people whom the child dislikes
- Wanting to avoid situations that cause discomfort, such as taking tests or having to speak in front of the class
- Wanting to get the attention of family members
- Wanting to spend school time doing more enjoyable things with one's parents or family members

⚜ WHAT IS THE TREATMENT FOR SCHOOL REFUSAL?

If school refusal behavior lasts more than two weeks, it is important to seek treatment for the child to prevent the development of more serious emotional and academic problems. The following steps should be considered:

- Meet with the child's teacher and discuss his or her view of the problem and its causes.
- Ask the school psychologist to assist with the assessment of the situation. He or she may interview the child and administer one or more assessment questionnaires to determine the causes and recommend a treatment plan.

Depending on the diagnosis, the treatment may include any of the following:

- Medication to treat an underlying anxiety disorder or depression
- Relaxation training
- Positive reinforcement for gradually returning to normal school attendance
- Individual counseling to explore feelings about negative situations at school
- Training to develop social and problem-solving skills

When Kids Underachieve

WHAT IS ACADEMIC UNDERACHIEVEMENT?

One of the more frustrating experiences of being a parent is when one's son or daughter does not achieve up to his or her ability in school. Regardless of the child's ability, doing less than he or she is capable of is confusing and frustrating. If the under-achievement is severe and lasts for more than a school year, or if it causes the student distress, it should be considered a problem. There are many possible causes for underachievement and just as many different solutions. If the problem is consid-ered objectively and the student is provided with adequate support, the chances are very good that the problem can be resolved. It is important to address issues of underachievement because they can quickly lead to a child losing self-esteem and coming to believe that he or she is not capable of doing well academically.

SEE THESE HANDOUTS ON RELATED TOPICS

Anxiety in Children

Attention-Seeking with Disruptive Behavior

Depression in Children and Teens

Helping Kids Manage Angry Feelings

Helping Your Child Succeed in School

How to Build Your Child's Self-Esteem

How to Cope When Parenting Seems Over-whelming

Positive Reinforcement (for Parents)

When Kids Don't Want to Go to School

---

1. Meet with your child's teacher(s) and discuss the problem. Keep the mindset that you and the teacher are allies to help your child suc-ceed.

2. Ask the teacher to communicate regularly with you about the problem and its progress.

3. Educate yourself by reading books, exploring the Internet, and talking with other parents and education professionals.

4. Encourage your child to identify and pursue his or her interests.

5. Talk to your child about his or her life. Ask questions, avoid being judgmental, and listen carefully.

6. When one thing doesn't work, try another. There is almost always a solution. It requires persistence and the belief that your child can be helped.

7. If your child is an adolescent, it's easy to get caught up in the power struggle and forget that the teen years comprise one of the most stressful times in a person's life. While your teen may come across as being angry or lazy, he or she may actually be depressed and con-fused by all of the changes in his or her life.

WHERE CAN I GO FOR MORE INFORMATION?

American Academy of Child and Adolescent Psy-chiatry (www.aacap.org)

Holt, John. *How Children Fail.* Cambridge, MA: Perseus Press, 1995.

McEwan, Elaine. *When Kids Say No to School: Helping Children at Risk of Failure, Refusal, or Dropping Out.* Wheaton, IL: Harold Shaw Publishing, 1998.

WHAT ARE COMMON SIGNS OF ACADEMIC UNDERACHIEVEMENT?

A combination of the following signs usually points to a problem:

- Grades have gradually gotten worse
- Does well on intelligence tests but does poorly in school
- Receives grades that are one full grade level below his or her ability level
- Is disorganized
- Shows little or no interest in school
- Makes excuses about his or her performance
- Doesn't finish assignments
- Loses papers and assignments
- Socializes too much or too little
- Avoids doing schoolwork by escaping into reading or playing games on the computer
- Doesn't put forth enough effort
- Gives up easily
- Has low self-esteem
- Seems depressed
- Has an inflated view of his or her abilities
- Underestimates the amount of work required to complete assignments properly
- Doesn't relate well with others of his or her own age group
- Is uncooperative
- Does not plan ahead
- Avoids working on things considered boring or too difficult
- Seeks individual attention from teachers; seems lost in a classroom full of other kids.

WHAT CAUSES ACADEMIC UNDERACHIEVEMENT?

Academic underachievement may be caused by disorders such as learning disabilities, neurological problems, or other conditions such as attention-deficit disorder (ADD) or attention-deficit/hyperactivity disorder (ADHD). If a child is tested and found to have any of these conditions, they should be addressed first and the problem may clear up.

Most students who achieve below their ability level could be considered normal students who come from families where academic achievement is valued. This makes the problem all the more frustrating. The causes may be a combination of factors, and it is important to carefully assess the situation and not rush into an explanation of the causes. The following kinds of factors may be contributing to the student's situation in some combination:

School Factors:

- The work is not challenging enough.
- The school is too competitive.
- The school is not competitive enough.
- The student dislikes the teacher.
- The student has just moved from another school.
- The child is feeling pressure from other students to slack off or socialize.
- The student is expected to conform to the teacher's guidelines; creativity is discouraged or stifled.
- The student's learning style doesn't fit with the classroom environment and teaching methods.
- The subjects don't match the student's abilities and interests.

Home Factors:

- There is an atmosphere of discord at home.
- The parents are too involved and controlling.
- The parents give the student too much freedom to determine how much time should be spent studying versus socializing.
- The student has too many responsibilities and stresses at home.
- The student is ill.

Student Factors:

- The student has ADD or ADHD that has not been diagnosed.
- The student lacks proper study skills.
- The student is depressed or anxious and unable to concentrate.
- The student has poor self-esteem and has given up on himself or herself.
- The student abuses drugs and/or alcohol.
- The student is involved in too many extracurricular activities.
- The student has to work many hours to earn money for the family.
- The student fears success because it would mean being expected to continue a pattern of success. To avoid this, the student sets himself or herself up to fail.
- The student is agonizing over identity issues and has no energy left for focusing on studies.
- The student fears the independence that might result if he or she achieves success. Failure allows the student to remain dependent on his or her parents and other adults.
- The student feels overly pressured and doubts his or her abilities.
- The parents expect the student to work too hard and too long.
- The parents discourage the student from spending much time on schoolwork.

HOW CAN AN UNDERACHIEVER BE HELPED?

The most important thing to do with a child or adolescent who is achieving below his or her ability level is to carefully assess the situation and determine the causes. This can be difficult to do, and you may want to seek the assistance of your child's teachers, school psychologist, or a mental health professional who specializes in working with children or adolescents.

The following are some of the steps to be taken:

Section II

Life Skills Handouts

Assertiveness Skills (for Teens)

INTRODUCTION

Assertive communication is a constructive way of expressing feelings and opinions. People are not born assertive; their behavior is a combination of learned skills. Assertive behavior enables you to:

- Act in your own best interests
- Stand up for yourself without becoming anxious
- Express your honest feelings
- Assert your personal rights without denying the rights of others

Assertive behavior is different from passive or aggressive behavior in that it is:

- Self-expressive
- Honest

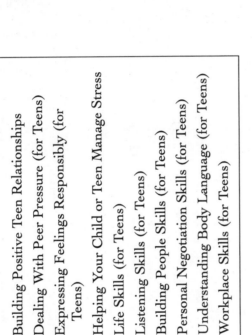

Let's look at some examples.

You-message: "You need to be here by 9:00 A.M. tomorrow."

Sample I-message: "I appreciate it when people come to work on time because we get all the stock work done before the store opens."

You-message: "You are too quiet when my mother is around."

Sample I-message: "When you don't express your opinion to my mother, I feel disappointed because you have such great ideas and she doesn't get to hear them."

You-message: "Here is what you ought to do."

Sample I-message: "If you would follow this plan, I would feel much more comfortable, because that is what Chris asked us to do."

You-message: "You should have chosen a better gift for Danny."

Sample I-message: "When you give a CD with a Parental Advisory label, it means he won't be able to show his parents or play it at home. I'm disappointed that he'll have to keep it a secret."

WHERE CAN I GO FOR MORE INFORMATION?

Alberti, Robert, and Emmons, Michael. *Your Perfect Right.* San Luis Obispo, CA: Impact Publishers, 2001.

Bower, Sharon, and Bower, Gordon. *Asserting Yourself: A Practical Guide for Positive Change.* New York: Perseus, 1991.

Elgin, Suzette Haden. *The Gentle Art of Verbal Self-Defense at Work.* Englewood Cliffs, NJ: Prentice Hall, 2000.

Gordon, Thomas. *Leader Effectiveness Training.* New York: Bantam Doubleday Dell, 1986.

SEE THESE HANDOUTS ON RELATED TOPICS

Building Positive Teen Relationships

Dealing With Peer Pressure (for Teens)

Expressing Feelings Responsibly (for Teens)

Helping Your Child or Teen Manage Stress

Life Skills (for Teens)

Listening Skills (for Teens)

Building People Skills (for Teens)

Personal Negotiation Skills (for Teens)

Understanding Body Language (for Teens)

Workplace Skills (for Teens)

- Direct
- Self-enhancing
- Constructive, not destructive

AGGRESSIVE, PASSIVE, OR ASSERTIVE?

Assertive behavior includes both **what** you say and **how** you say it. Let's look at some examples. Read each of the following short conversations and decide whether each illustrates aggressive, passive, or assertive behavior:

> Assertive behavior includes both **what** you say and **how** you say it.

Example 1

Lisa: "Listen, I've got a big problem with what you did. I've had it with these stupid mistakes you keep making. You either stop screwing up, or you're finished!"

Schuyler: "Give me a break, Lisa. You know it wasn't my fault."

Lisa: "Yeah, right! All I ever hear from you is excuses!"

Schuyler: "Those aren't excuses, Lisa. They're facts."

Lisa: "When are you going to do it the way I told you to do it?"

Lisa's behavior is **aggressive.**

Example 2

Lisa: "Schuyler, I wish you'd be more careful when you fill out these forms."

Schuyler: "I told you, Lisa, it wasn't my fault."

Lisa: "Oh, I'm sorry. You're right."

Lisa's behavior in this example is **passive.**

Example 3

Lisa: "Schuyler, these mistakes created a big problem for me. I turned in the sheet with your numbers on it and now I feel very embarrassed."

Schuyler: "I told you, Lisa, it wasn't my fault."

Lisa: "I know you've had some problems, Schuyler. But I have to ask you to double-check your work in the future, and make sure it's correct. Will you agree to do that?"

Schuyler: "Sure, I think I can agree to that."

Lisa: "Thanks, Schuyler. I hope this solves the problem."

In this example, Lisa's behavior is **assertive.**

WHAT ARE I-MESSAGES?

The I-message is a communication skill that can help you communicate assertively. Let's illustrate how they work with some examples. Think about how you would feel if your supervisor at work spoke to you like this:

"You need to check in with me more often."

"You were rude to that teacher."

"You sure made the wrong decision that time."

Most people would feel talked down to, disrespected, and blamed. These kinds of messages are called **you-messages,** since they begin with "you."

> I-messages are a more effective way of communicating than you-messages because they convey less blame and less negativity.

A more effective way to assertively speak to another person is with the **I-message.** Here are some examples:

"When I'm not kept informed about what's going on in your study group, I get worried and start imagining that you're having problems that are not getting solved."

"When you said, 'No, we're all out' without checking the back stock first, the customers thought you didn't care about helping them get what they're looking for."

"When I saw that you'd kept filling in the condiments during that rush of customers, I was upset that you didn't come up front right away."

I-messages are a more effective way of communicating than you-messages because they convey less blame and less negativity. Starting a statement with "I" indicates taking responsibility for the statement. Starting a statement with "you" conveys a feeling of finger-pointing and is likely to make the listener feel defensive.

I-messages have three components:

> **THREE COMPONENTS:**
>
> **Behavior**
>
> plus
>
> **Feelings**
>
> plus
>
> **Effect on you**

1. Identify the **behavior** that concerns you.
2. Describe your **feelings** about it.
3. Describe the **effect** the person's actions have on you.

Building People Skills (for Teens)

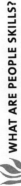

WHAT ARE PEOPLE SKILLS?

How would you like to get along even better with others in your family, in relationships with friends, and at school? Getting along well with people sounds kind of general and is difficult to do much about, so let's break it down into some manageable and specific skills. By building the following skills, you will get along well with others:

- Building others' self-esteem.
- Showing empathy for others.
- Encouraging people to cooperate with each other.
- Communicating assertively.
- Asking productive questions and demonstrating listening skills.
- Responding productively to emotional statements.

help you show that you are hearing and understanding another person and are interested in what he or she has to say.

Responding productively to emotional statements. A communication skill called *active listening* is especially useful in emotional situations because it enables you to demonstrate that you understand what the other person is saying and how he or she is feeling about it. Active listening means restating, in your own words, what the other person has said. It's a check on whether your understanding is correct. This demonstrates that you are listening and that you are interested and concerned. Active listening responses have two components:

- Naming the feeling that the other person is conveying
- Stating the reason for the feeling

Here are some examples of active listening statements:

- "Sounds like you're upset about what happened at school."
- "You're annoyed by my lateness, aren't you?"
- "You sound really confused about how to solve this problem."
- "It makes you angry when you find errors on my homework."
- "Sounds like you're really worried about Wendy."
- "I get the feeling you're awfully busy right now."

Active listening is not the same as agreement. It is a way of demonstrating that you intend to hear and understand another's point of view.

The ability to get along well with people is a set of learned skills. No one is born knowing how to build others' self-esteem, show empathy, encourage cooperation, communicate assertively,

ask productive questions, or respond productively to emotional statements. But with some practice these skills can be learned and developed. By taking the time to develop these skills, you will be able to build better relationships at home and at work.

WHERE CAN I GO FOR MORE INFORMATION?

Covey, Sean. *The 7 Habits of Highly Effective Teens: The Ultimate Teenage Success Guide.* New York: Simon and Schuster, 1998.

McGraw, Jay, and McGraw, Phillip. *Life Strategies for Teens.* New York: Fireside, 2000.

SEE THESE HANDOUTS ON RELATED TOPICS

Assertiveness Skills (for Teens)

Building Positive Teen Relationships

Dealing with Peer Pressure (for Teens)

Expressing Feelings Responsibly (for Teens)

Life Skills (for Teens)

Listening Skills (for Teens)

Personal Negotiation Skills (for Teens)

Understanding Body Language (for Teens)

Workplace Skills (for Teens)

People skills (which are also known as *emotional intelligence*) can be thought of as six specific skills. Let's take a brief look at each one.

Building others' self-esteem. When you are in a situation in which you are made to feel good about yourself, you feel good. You can do the same with others by doing the following kinds of things:

- Make eye contact with others.
- Call others by their names.
- Ask others their opinions.
- Compliment others' work.
- Tell people how much you appreciate them.
- Write notes of thanks when someone does something worthwhile.
- Make people feel welcome when they come to your home or workplace.

> *Empathy* means recognizing emotions in others. It is the capacity to put yourself in another person's shoes and understand how they view their reality and how they feel about things.

- Pay attention to what is going on in people's lives. Acknowledge milestones and express concern about difficult life situations such as illness, deaths, and accidents.
- Introduce your family members to acquaintances when you meet them out in public.
- Encourage people you care about to explore their talents and interests.
- Share your friends' excitement when they accomplish something.
- Honor people's needs and wants.

- Take responsibility for your choices and actions, and expect others to do the same.
- Take responsibility for the quality of your communications.

Showing empathy for others. *Empathy* means recognizing emotions in others. It is the capacity to put yourself in another person's shoes and understand how he or she feels about things.

Being aware of our emotions and how they affect our actions is a very important ability in today's world, both at school and at work. People who are cut off from their emotions are unable to connect with people. It's as if they were emotionally tone deaf. No one wants to be around such people, because they have no idea how they affect others. You have probably met a few people who fit this description.

Encouraging people to cooperate with each other. When you are working or engaging in activities with others in a group, there are some specific things you can do to help create an environment where you will all work together well:

- Don't play favorites. Treat everyone the same. Otherwise, some people will not trust you.

> People who are cut off from their emotions are unable to connect with people. It's like they are emotionally tone deaf.

- Don't talk about people behind their backs.
- Ask for others' ideas. Participation increases commitment.
- Follow up on suggestions, requests, and comments, even if you are unable to carry out a request.

- Check for understanding when you make a statement or announcement. Don't assume everyone is with you.
- Make sure people have clear instructions for tasks to be completed. Ask people to describe what they plan to do.
- Let people know you appreciate it when they are cooperative. Don't take it for granted.

Communicating assertively. Assertive communication is a constructive way of expressing feelings and opinions. People are not born assertive; their behavior is a combination of learned skills. Assertive behavior enables you to:

- Act in your own best interests
- Stand up for yourself without becoming anxious
- Express your honest feelings
- Assert your personal rights without denying the rights of others

Assertive behavior is different from passive or aggressive behavior in that it is:

- Self-expressive
- Honest
- Direct
- Self-enhancing
- Constructive, not destructive

Active listening responses have two components:

- Naming the feeling that the other person is conveying
- Stating the reason for the feeling

Assertive behavior includes both *what* you say and *how* you say it.

Asking productive questions and demonstrating listening skills. Listening skills

Building Positive Teen Relationships

INTRODUCTION

Sixteen-year-old Lisa spends most of her free time with her friends, Beth and Nancy. Today she is feeling upset because last weekend, her two friends went on line and bought tickets to a concert with their favorite band. They didn't tell Lisa they were planning to buy the tickets, but asked another girl to go with them. Lisa feels extremely hurt and thinks she should look for new friends.

Seventeen-year-old Doug is annoyed with his girlfriend, Whitney. Most of the time things between them are fine, but they got into a pretty big fight yesterday. He wanted to spend some time with his friends Chris, Stacy, and Rob. Chris and Stacy don't get along with Whitney, so Doug did not invite her. Whitney became very upset with Doug and told him that if he really cared about her, he would not hang out with people like Chris and Stacy. Doug is feeling very controlled by Whitney and is thinking about breaking up with her.

Fifteen-year-old Katie is furious with her friend Joel. She discovered that he gave her older brother Sam a pack of cigarettes, even though Joel knew that Sam is trying to quit. Her parents found the cigarettes and there was a huge argument at home about it. Katie is writing Joel an e-mail expressing how angry she is. She ends it with, "Thanks a lot for being a terrible friend."

These are three examples of common problems that teens experience in their relationships with their friends. Each example illustrates a dilemma

---

 Look for ways to build your self-esteem. If you love yourself, you will be more likely to seek out people who will respect you. You will also be less likely to tolerate negative behavior from others.

> Be willing to end relationships that are not working for you. You can do this with dignity and respect. You have the right to choose your friends, and you also have the right to end relationships that don't make you feel good.

- Get to know yourself well. Explore your beliefs and values and identify the things that you look for in a friend.

- Develop your ability to take responsibility for yourself and your actions.

- Set goals for yourself and make plans to reach them.

- Find people who can be positive role models for you.

- Learn to identify and express your feelings.

- Learn the skills of managing disagreements and conflicts.

- Develop your listening skills.

- Trust your feelings. If you are uncomfortable with a person, pay attention to your feelings and figure out why.

- Be willing to end relationships that are not working for you. You can do this with dignity and respect. You have the right to choose your friends, and you also have the right to end relationships that don't make you feel good.

WHERE CAN I GO FOR MORE INFORMATION?

Covey, Sean. *The Seven Habits of Highly Effective Teens: The Ultimate Teenage Success Guide.* New York: Simon and Schuster, 1998.

Kirberger, Kimberly. *Teen Love: On Relationships, A Book for Teenagers.* Deerfield Beach, FL: Health Communications, 1999.

McGraw, Jay, and McGraw, Phillip. *Life Strategies for Teens.* New York: Fireside, 2000.

SEE THESE HANDOUTS ON RELATED TOPICS

Assertiveness Skills (for Teens)

Building People Skills (for Teens)

Dealing with Peer Pressure (for Teens)

Expressing Feelings Responsibly (for Teens)

Goal Setting (for Teens)

Life Skills (for Teens)

Listening Skills (for Teens)

Personal Negotiation Skills (for Teens)

Workplace Skills (for Teens)

Understanding Body Language (for Teens)

that you may have faced yourself and raises questions about what you should be able to expect from a relationship. Let's explore some ideas about relationships and identify the factors that make them positive and healthy.

> You can tell if a relationship is positive by how you feel and behave when you are with the other person.

WHAT IS A POSITIVE RELATIONSHIP?

You can tell is a relationship is positive by how you feel and behave when you are with the other person. These are some signs to look for:

- You feel good when you are together.
- You both expect good things from each other.
- You give each other permission to be less than perfect.
- It is OK to disagree.
- You both feel free to do as you please without needing to ask for the other person's permission or being afraid that the other person will be upset.
- You always treat the other person with respect.

> If a relationship doesn't feel good to you, it might just need a little work to set things right.

- You consider the other person's needs and feelings when you do things that affect him or her.
- When the other person is upset, you listen with empathy.
- When either of you makes a mistake, you admit it.
- When you offend or hurt the other person, you apologize.
- Both of you pursue the things you are interested in. Sometimes this does not include the other person, and that is okay.

- You always tell your friend the truth.
- You never speak badly about your friend to others.
- You keep your friend's confidences.
- You encourage each other.
- You are excited and happy when your friend achieves something he or she considers important.
- You know you can count on your friend and do not attempt to control his or her activities or beliefs.
- You have things in common: beliefs, values, likes and dislikes, interests, goals.
- When you disagree on something, you talk about it and work out a compromise.
- When your friend wants you to do something that feels wrong, you speak up for yourself.
- Your friend does not pressure you to do things you don't want to do.
- Your relationship does not include abuse, intimidation, sarcasm, or put-downs.
- When one of you lends something to the other, it is promptly returned in the same condition as when it was lent.
- If your friend is your romantic partner, you have an agreement about whether you will date others and both of you honor that agreement.
- You trust your friend and do not check up on him or her.
- When you want to be alone, you spend time alone.
- When you must work and can't be with your friend, you feel free to work.
- It is okay for you to develop your own interests and talents apart from your friend.

Perhaps you would add a few things to this list. Check the items where your relationship could use some improvement. You can decide for yourself what you want to do about it.

WHAT ARE SIGNS OF A DESTRUCTIVE RELATIONSHIP?

If a relationship doesn't feel good to you, it might just need a little work to set things right. In some cases, however, there are enough bad things going on that

the relationship is downright destructive. These are some of the signs of such a relationship:

- One person feels bad (afraid, worthless, guilty, endangered) as a result of being in the relationship.
- One person insists on controlling the relationship.
- There is physical abuse (pushing, hitting, slapping, leaving bruises, throwing things, etc.)
- One person uses threats and intimidation to control the other. Any kind of threat is abusive.
- One person uses weapons against the other, or threatens to do so.
- One person forces him or herself upon the other in a sexual way.
- One person forces or intimidates the other into having unprotected sex.
- Yelling, screaming, swearing.
- Insulting or calling names.
- Keeping one's partner away from other people.
- Constantly checking up on the other person.
- Keeping control of money or possessions.
- Placing one's partner in physical danger by driving drunk or behaving unsafely.

> If you are experiencing even one of these warning signs, it is important to take action to improve or end the relationship.

If you are experiencing even one of these warning signs, it is important to take action to improve or end the relationship.

HOW CAN I BUILD HEALTHY RELATIONSHIPS?

There are some things you can do within yourself to become the kind of person who has healthy, positive relationships with others. These are some of the most important ways to do this:

Dealing with Peer Pressure (for Teens)

 **INTRODUCTION**

When 16-year-old Charlene came home from her friend Tamara's house, her mother said her clothes and hair smelled like smoke. "You've been smoking, haven't you," her mom said. It was true. For the first time, Charlene had given in to Tamara's pressure and smoked a cigarette.

Seventeen-year-old Richie was allowed to drive his parents' car under the condition that he carry no more than one passenger at a time. While it is legal in his state to have more people in the car, his parents established this rule until Richie had more driving experience. Today, however, when his friends Todd and Manuel begged him for a ride across town, he let them in, thinking his parents would never know. As he drove through the grocery store parking lot with his two friends in the car, who did he drive past but his mom? She took one look at him and motioned him over to her.

Scott, Sharon. *How to Say No and Keep Your Friends.* Amherst, MA: Human Resource Development Press, 1997.

SEE THESE HANDOUTS ON RELATED TOPICS

Assertiveness Skills (for Teens)

Building People Skills (for Teens)

Building Positive Teen Relationships

Expressing Feelings Responsibly (for Teens)

Goal Setting (for Teens)

How to Help a Friend through a Crisis (for Teens)

Life Skills (for Teens)

Listening Skills (for Teens)

Personal Negotiation Skills (for Teens)

Understanding Body Language (for Teens)

What Teens Need to Know about HIV and AIDS

Workplace Skills (for Teens)

"Thanks, but I've got homework to do."

"I don't want to hurt myself or anyone else."

"Nope, I don't want to get grounded."

"Sorry, I'm not willing to risk it."

"No way! I don't do that kind of stuff."

"I don't feel like it."

"Sorry, I have a bad feeling about this."

"I'm too tired. I'm going home."

"Are you nuts?"

"It's against my religion."

IT HELPS TO PLAN AHEAD

The best way to resist peer pressure is to have a plan. Think of the most challenging peer pressure situations that you've experienced so far and ask yourself these questions:

- Which situations did you resist successfully?

- Which situations did you give in to and what could you have done differently?

- What kinds of situations are most difficult for you to resist?

- Who handles peer pressure well? What can you learn by observing this person?

WHERE CAN I GO FOR MORE INFORMATION?

American Social Health Association (www.iwannaknow.org) has some good information on handling peer pressure, and other valuable information for teens.

Many articles for teens, including an excellent one on how to handle peer pressure, can be found at www.teenshealth.org/.

THIS IS WHAT PEER PRESSURE SOUNDS LIKE:

"Oh, come on. Don't worry about it so much. No one will ever find out."

"Please, just this once? Your mom will never know."

"Don't you want to relax and enjoy yourself?"

"You are really turning into a boring person, aren't you?"

"You used to be so much fun! What happened to you, anyway?"

"Do you want to lose all of your friends?"

"What are you, a baby? Can't you think for yourself?"

"When are you going to loosen up?"

You have probably done something like this yourself at one time or another. You know what the rules are and you have the best of intentions of following them, but for some reason you go against your better judgment and do the wrong thing. Why does this happen and what can you do to prevent it?

WHY IS PEER PRESSURE SO STRONG?

Peer pressure is such an issue for teens because adolescence is a time for experimentation—trying new things, having adventures, experiencing freedom. At the same time, the teen years are a time when it is important to belong to a group and to feel accepted. Put these two factors together, and you can see why peer pressure is such an issue for teens.

SO WHAT IF I GIVE IN TO PEER PRESSURE?

It is understandable that you may be tempted to just give in to the pressure and go along with your friends when they want you to do something that is against your rules. But it's impor-

tant to think ahead, into the future, and consider what the consequences of your actions might be. Of course, there is always a chance that no one will ever find out that you drank the alcohol, smoked the cigarettes, or let your friend drive your car. On the other hand, doing these things could lead to disaster. You have to ask yourself if the consequences would be worth the thrill. Would it still be worth it if you:

- Were arrested
- Had a police record and were unable to get certain jobs or join certain professions
- Were grounded
- Were kicked off your sports team
- Felt ashamed of yourself later, when you realize what you did
- Got into a really dangerous situation—one that is much more dangerous than you originally thought
- Were injured or killed

While it doesn't seem likely that any of these things would happen, the fact is that you just never know. So the first step in resisting peer pressure is to stop and consider the consequences. Some people call this a *worst-case scenario*—thinking of the worst that could happen, and thinking about what that would be like. If you think it can't happen to you, just read your

local newspaper for a few days and see that it has already happened to plenty of others, both teens and adults.

WHAT CAN I DO TO RESIST PEER PRESSURE?

There is no simple rule that will enable you to magically resist the pressure of your friends with no feelings of guilt or regret. It is not an easy thing to do. It takes a lot of courage and a strong sense of self, but you can learn to do it. Here are some things you can do:

1. Pay attention to how the people around you are behaving. If your friends are acting secretively or seem like they're trying to persuade you to do something, there may be something going on that you're going to want to avoid.

2. Trust your gut. If a situation sounds like trouble, it probably is. In her excellent book *How to Say No and Keep Your Friends*, author Sharon Scott advises that you avoid any situation that is against the law or that would result in a parent or other authority figure being angry.

3. Stop and think it through. Don't let yourself be swept along in the excitement of the moment. Take a minute to stop and think about whether you really want to participate in this. Consider the consequences of saying yes or saying no.

4. If you decide not to participate, take firm action. Tell your friend what you have decided to do, and do it. Having a list of ways to say no all ready in your head is tremendously helpful. Rather than waiting until you are in a pressure situation, think about ways you can say no to your friends. Rehearse them and have them ready. Here are some examples:

RESISTANCE STEPS

1. Pay attention to the behavior of those around you.
2. Trust your gut.
3. Stop and think it through.
4. If you decide not to participate, take firm action.

Expressing Feelings Responsibly (for Teens)

WHAT TRAPS DO TEENS FALL INTO WHEN THEY EXPRESS FEELINGS?

When it comes to expressing emotions, many teens—and adults—have a difficult time. Some go overboard, slipping into blame and anger. Others keep their feelings to themselves, and you never know where you stand. It is also not unusual for people to respond to emotions by denying them.

Let's consider an example. You come home from a long day at school, and you discover that your brother has had two friends over after he got home from his school. The house is a mess. There are dishes in the sink and crumbs sprinkled across the sofa. The smell of cigarette smoke hangs in the air. You feel very angry, because you were looking forward to a nice relaxing evening and can't stand the mess. You

You-Statement

"You made such a mess of this project!"

"You always leave me holding the bag when you commit to being part of a group project!"

"You said you'd call, but of course you didn't—you just can't be counted on!"

I-Statement

"I get frustrated after we put so much time into preparing for these projects and then they don't turn out as we'd planned."

"When I don't know where you are, I get upset because I don't know whether I should go about my business or not."

"When commitments are made and then I have to follow through, I get angry."

Expressing feelings responsibly with I-statements takes a bit of practice, but doing so helps to prevent conflicts and allows you to keep resentments from building.

WHERE CAN I GO FOR MORE INFORMATION?

Covey, Sean. *The 7 Habits of Highly Effective Teens: The Ultimate Teenage Success Guide.* New York: Simon and Schuster, 1998.

McGraw, Jay, and McGraw, Phillip. *Life Strategies for Teens.* New York: Fireside, 2000.

also hate smoking. There are several different ways to express your feelings of frustration:

- You yell, "How many times have I told you that you have to clean up after yourself? And what idiot has been smoking in this house?"

- You swallow your anger and say nothing. You clean up the mess yourself and refuse to speak to your brother until the next day.

- You say to your brother, "When I come home after a long day at school, I feel very angry to find the sink full of dirty dishes and the air smelling like cigarette smoke."

> Blaming and name-calling is easy to slip into because it allows you to release the emotions quickly and makes you feel powerful for a moment.

Most people probably choose the first option—blaming and name-calling. (This is true for teens and adults.) This behavior is the easiest one to slip into, because it allows you to release the emotions quickly and makes you feel powerful for a moment. However, it also makes the other person feel defensive and hurt and almost guarantees that the argument will escalate.

The problem with suppressing your feelings (as in the second option) is that you don't resolve them. They sit inside of you, and you find yourself feeling angrier at the other person and everyone around him or her. Until you express the feelings and get a satisfactory response from the other person, you have a difficult time being with him or her.

Besides blaming and denying, some other common ways of expressing feelings (especially negative ones) include:

- **Generalizing.** "You always do this to me!"
- **Name-calling.** "You are such an idiot!"
- **Accusing.** "You obviously don't care about this family!"
- **Commanding.** "You get in this room right now!"
- **Interrogating.** "Why do you always let your friends walk all over you? Don't you have any respect for yourself? Don't you have any respect for me?"
- **Disagreeing.** "That couldn't possibly be true!"
- **Put-downs.** "You wouldn't know about keeping this place clean! You can't even get yourself out of bed in the morning without Mom's help!"
- **Intimidating.** "You clean this dump up right now or I'll tell Dad that your friends were smoking here!"

All of these kinds of statements are destructive. They result in negative feelings and more anger, and are designed to exert power over the other person. Notice that most of them include the word *you*, which makes them seem more threatening and argumentative. A much more effective and productive way of expressing feelings is to use the *I-statement*.

> The most important feature of I-statements is that they are neutral. There is no effort to threaten, argue, or blame.

WHAT ARE I-STATEMENTS?

When you want to express a problem, use an I-statement instead of a you-statement. They

take some practice, but they can make a big difference in how successfully you communicate your feelings to others.

This is the formula: "I feel _____ when _____."

Here are some examples.

- "I feel angry when I come home and there are dirty dishes in the sink."
- "I feel upset when I know that you have been smoking in the house."
- "I get so excited when I see how much you enjoy working on your project."

You can also change the wording around like this:

- "When I have to stand out on the curb for an extra hour, I feel really frustrated."
- "When there are so many mistakes on your part of this project, I feel embarrassed and worried about what kind of grade we'll get."
- "Having so many friends over when Mom's not home makes me worry that things are going to get out of control."

The most important feature of I-statements is that they are neutral. There is no effort to threaten, argue, or blame in any of these statements. The speaker is simply making a statement and takes full responsibility for his or her feelings. They are an excellent way to express feelings in a nonintimidating, noncontrolling way.

HOW CAN I CHANGE YOU-STATEMENTS TO I-STATEMENTS?

Here are some examples of how you-statements can be changed to more productive and neutral I-statements. Notice how the revised statements are less blameful and hostile than the original statements:

Goal Setting (for Teens)

WHY IS IT IMPORTANT FOR TEENS TO HAVE GOALS?

It has been demonstrated that when people have goals to guide them, they are happier and achieve more than they would have without goals. This is true for teens and adults alike. There are several reasons for this:

Goals provide focus. Having no goals is like going on a trip without a map. When there is no destination, vision, or plan, most teens (and adults, for that matter) tend to drift.

Goals enable you to measure progress. It is impossible to measure how well you've performed if no goals have been set to measure progress against.

Goals are motivating. When there is a target, most teens feel driven to meet it.

Life Area: _____

Goal: _____

Life Area: _____

Goal: _____

Life Area: _____

Goal: _____
_____
_____

WHERE CAN I GO FOR MORE INFORMATION?

Blair, Gary Ryan. *Goal Setting 101: How to Set and Achieve a Goal.* Palm Harbor, FL: The Goals Guy, 2000.

Blair, Gary Ryan. *Goal Setting Forms: Tools to Help You Get Ready, Get Set, & Go for Your Goals.* Palm Harbor, FL: The Goals Guy, 2000.

Smith, Douglas. *Make Success Measurable: A Mindbook-Workbook for Setting Goals and Taking Action.* New York: John Wiley & Sons, 1999.

Goals enhance productivity. Having goals makes teens more productive than they would be without them.

Goals enhance self-esteem. Setting a goal and achieving it makes teens feel good about themselves.

Goals increase commitment. When teens have a vision of where they want to go, they tend to feel a greater sense of commitment than they would without the vision.

Goals motivate groups. Having group goals increases the sense of team. This is good for any group because teams tend to be more creative and productive than individuals.

FOR WHAT LIFE AREAS SHOULD I SET GOALS?

You can have goals that cover several different areas of your life. Here are some examples. To begin, choose five or six areas and use the guidelines in this handout to write some goals for yourself.

Knowledge	Service	Home
Adventure	Contribution	Clothes
Fantasy	Family	Spiritual
Emotional	Career	Church
Hobbies	Travel	Politics
Interest	Financial	Community
Study	Income	Clubs
Reading	College	Relationships
Exploring	Health	Future profession
Communication	Job	Life after school

HOW DO I WRITE GOALS THAT WILL MOTIVATE ME?

The best goals are fully defined visions of how you want things to be. The more specific, measurable, and challenging goals are, the more motivated you will be to attain them.

Good goals have these five elements:

1. They are expressed using **action verbs.**
2. They are written with **specific language.**
3. They specify **measurable outcomes.**
4. They **challenge** you without being unreachable.
5. They specify **completion dates.**

Let's look at each of these elements.

Necessary Ingredient: **For Example:**

Use action verbs
- *Paint* bedroom
- *Save* money
- *Enroll in* college classes

Use specific language
- Paint *my bedroom*
- Save *$500*
- Enroll in *English 201*

Specify measurable outcomes
- Paint *one wall each day beginning February 23, to be completed by February 28*
- Save *$500 by March 15*
- Enroll in *English 201 in the spring term at Community College*

Specify completion dates
- Paint *one wall each day beginning February 23, to be completed by February 28*
- Save *$500 by March 15*
- Enroll in *English 201 in the spring term at Community College by January 1*

Pick goals that challenge you without being unreachable
- *Paint one wall each day beginning February 23, to be completed by February 28,* **not** *Paint the entire room, closet and ceiling this weekend*
- *Enroll in English 201 in the spring term at Community College,* **not** *Enroll in five classes and audit two classes in the spring term at Community College*
- *Save $500 by March 15,* **not** *Save $2000 by March 15*

Try some for yourself. Remember to include all five elements:

1. Use action verbs
2. Use specific language
3. Specify measurable outcomes
4. Challenge without being unreachable
5. Specify completion dates

Helping Your Child or Teen Manage Stress

 INTRODUCTION

People feel stress when their resources (their ability to cope with things) do not match the demands of a specific situation. This is true for kids as teens as well as adults. Typical situations where people feel stressed include the following:

- Having to cope with too many distractions
- Being expected to meet unclear, confusing, or unrealistic goals
- Having too much or too little to do
- Having to do work that is overly complicated
- Having to do tasks that are boring, repetitive, or unpleasant

SEE THESE HANDOUTS ON RELATED TOPICS

Anxiety In Children

Assertiveness Skills (for Teens)

Building People Skills (for Teens)

Building Positive Teen Relationships

Dealing With Peer Pressure (for Teens)

Depression In Children And Teens

Expressing Feelings Responsibly (for Teens)

Goal Setting (for Teens)

Helping Kids Manage Angry Feelings

Helping Your Child Succeed In School

Helping Your Kids to Be Self-Confident

Helping Your Kids Manage the Relocation Blues

How to Build Your Child's Self-Esteem

How to Cope When Parenting Seems Overwhelming

How to Help a Friend through a Crisis (for Teens)

Life Skills (for Teens)

Listening Skills (for Teens)

Personal Negotiation Skills (for Teens)

Positive Reinforcement (for Parents)

Separation Anxiety

Social Anxiety Disorder (Shyness)

When Kids Don't Want to Go to School

When Kids Underachieve

Workplace Skills (for Teens)

---

and is not always ready to meet the demands of unfamiliar social situations. When he or she starts to feel stressed, it probably means that pent-up feelings need to be let out. Besides being available yourself, encourage your teen to look for help from people like these:

- Other relatives
- Your minister or rabbi
- The family doctor
- A mental health professional with experience working with adolescents
- Teachers
- The school psychologist
- Guidance counselors
- Friends
- Friends' parents
- Neighbors

WHERE CAN I GO FOR MORE INFORMATION?

Cunningham, J. Barton. *The Stress Management Sourcebook.* Los Angeles: Lowell House, 1997.

Hanson, Peter G. *Stress for Success.* New York: Doubleday, 1989.

Hanson, Peter G. *The Joy of Stress.* Kansas City, MO: Andrews & McMeel, 1985.

Kelly, Kate. *The Complete Idiot's Guide to Parenting a Teenager.* New York: Alpha Books, 1996.

Law, Felicia, and Parker, Josephine (eds.). *Growing Up: A Young Person's Guide to Adolescence.* Chippenham, Wiltshire, UK: Merlion Publishing, Ltd., 1993.

McCoy, Kathy, and Wibbelsman, Charles. *The New Teenage Body Book.* New York: Putnam, 1992.

- Having to deal with too many changes (e.g., in the rules, in one's situation, in how the work needs to be done)
- Being expected to do tasks without the required skills, training, or background
- Having to spend time with abusive, negative, or unreliable people (other kids or authority figures)
- Fearing for one's safety
- Living, working, or going to school in a crowded space
- Being ill or just not feeling well
- Not getting enough exercise
- Not eating properly
- Not getting enough sleep
- Not having enough time to relax
- Abusing drugs or alcohol

HOW CAN I HELP MY CHILD MANAGE STRESS?

The following tips may assist you in helping your child or teen identify the sources of stress in his or her life and to manage them better.

1. Work with your child to figure out what is causing him or her to feel stressed out. Use the preceding list to help identify the stressors.

   - Suggest that younger children draw pictures that illustrate their bad feelings.

> *Suggest that younger children draw pictures that illustrate their bad feelings.*

   - Older children and adolescents can write about their feelings in a private journal. Teens might make a list of people who cause them stress, and explore what the issues are.

2. Help your child decide what to do about each of the sources of stress. Look for areas where you can help him or her. For example:

   - If the child is stressed because another child is bullying him in class, suggest that you talk to the teacher together.

   - If your teen is anxious because she is falling behind in Spanish class, discuss the options for helping her. Let her choose the best one.

3. If relating to others is one of the problems, help your child or teen build stronger people skills. These may include the areas of communication, assertiveness, problem solving, and/or managing conflict. People skills are learned; no one is born knowing how to get along well with others.

> *People skills are learned; no one is born knowing how to get along well with others. Help your child identify the skills he or she needs to develop, and help make a plan for learning them.*

4. Teach your child to steer clear of toxic people and situations. Explain that there will always be individuals who seem to have a negative effect on others. Discuss with your child how to limit the amount of time spent with these people. He or she might consider declining their invitations to play or ask the teacher to be moved to a different part of the classroom. Explain to your children that they don't have to feel guilty about avoiding anyone who makes them feel bad about themselves.

5. Help your child look for ways to seek out positive people and situations. This is the reverse of the idea above. Talk to your child about spending more time in situations that make him or her feel good.

6. Check your child's diet. Some foods actually amplify the stress response:

   - Caffeine stimulates the release of stress hormones. This increases blood pressure, heart rate, and the flow of oxygen to the heart. Ongoing exposure to caffeine can also harm the heart tissues.

   - Refined sugar and processed flour are stripped of important vitamins. In times of stress, some of these vitamins are needed to help the body maintain the nervous and endocrine systems.

   - Complex carbohydrates (fruits, vegetables, whole breads, cereals and beans) are better for the body and help it resist the effects of stress.

7. Encourage your child to exercise. This is one of the simplest and most effective ways to respond positively to stress. Physical activity provides a natural release for the body during its fight-or-flight state of arousal. When the body returns to its normal state of equilibrium after exercising, one feels relaxed and refreshed.

> *Physical activity provides a natural release for the body during its fight-or-flight state of arousal.*

8. Help your child look for ways to let go of tension and anxiety. Meditation and progressive relaxation are two valuable ways to regenerate and refresh oneself. Even children can benefit. You can purchase meditation and relaxation audiotapes (there are some titles created especially for kids) or record your own. This is especially important because health and long life depend on minimizing stress and achieving a sense of balance and well-being.

9. Make sure that your teen has someone to talk to. Adolescence can be a highly emotional time. Your teen is encountering new things every day

Helping Your Child Succeed in School

 ## INTRODUCTION

Every parent wants his or her child to succeed in school. There are some specific things every parent can do to stack the deck in favor of the child's success. They are:

1. Build your child's self-esteem.
2. Know your child.
3. Set goals.
4. Turn disappointments into learning opportunities.
5. Make reading important in your family.
6. Pay attention to your child's work and ask to see it.
7. Provide positive reinforcement.

Let's take a look at each one of these strategies.

 ## BUILD YOUR CHILD'S SELF-ESTEEM

Kids with high self-esteem generally do better in school (and in just about everything else they want to accomplish in life). There are hundreds of ways to convey the message "You are worthwhile" to your children. You are limited only by your imagination. Here are some places to begin.

1. Spend time with your child. If you are absent most of the time, he or she notices, and probably thinks it's because he or she isn't important enough.

Dreikurs, Rudolph. *Children: The Challenge.* New York: Plume, 1991.

Dinkmeyer, Don, and McKay, Gary. *Parenting Young Children: Systematic Training for Effective Parenting (STEP) of Children Under Six.* Circle Pines, MN: American Guidance Service, 1997.

SEE THESE HANDOUTS ON RELATED TOPICS

Assertiveness Skills (for Teens)

Building People Skills (for Teens)

Building Positive Teen Relationships

Dealing with Peer Pressure (for Teens)

Expressing Feelings Responsibly (for Teens)

Goal Setting (for Teens)

Helping Your Child or Teen Manage Stress

Helping Your Kids Manage the Relocation Blues

Helping Your Kids to Be Self-Confident

How to Build Your Child's Self-Esteem

Kids Who Sexually Abuse Other Kids

Life Skills (for Teens)

Listening Skills (for Teens)

Personal Negotiation Skills (for Teens)

Positive Reinforcement (for Parents)

Teaching Your Child to Respect Others

Understanding Body Language (for Teens)

When Kids Underachieve

PROVIDE POSITIVE REINFORCEMENT

Don't forget to give your child a pat on the back when he or she does something well or completes a tough assignment. By pointing out what was done and taking the time to give a compliment, you will motivate your child to continue to do good work. Keep in mind the following guidelines for positively reinforcing your child:

1. Be specific in your praise. Say what you are recognizing and why it is significant. Instead of saying to your daughter: "You always do such good work," say this instead: "You got your book report done one day early, and it follows the assignment guidelines exactly. Good job." Your daughter will know exactly what you are praising her for and she will be more likely to do the same thing next time.

2. Praise right away. Don't wait a day or a week to compliment a job well done. The closer the behavior is to its positive consequence, the more meaning it will have for the person being reinforced.

3. Praise publicly. When your daughter gets an A in Algebra after a semester of struggling, you can post a note on the refrigerator (for all to see) saying, "Susan, great job in Algebra."

4. Be on the lookout for things to compliment. You don't want to overdo it so that your praise becomes meaningless, but there is no reason to hold it back when it is deserved.

> Be on the lookout for things to compliment.

5. Do something special. Bake a cake or cookies and bring it in for your kids' teachers when they do something out of the ordinary for your child, such as patiently helping her learn a difficult concept or arranging for special help when it's needed. When your team at work accomplishes something special, you can do this for them, too.

WHERE CAN I GO TO LEARN MORE?

Branden, Nathaniel. *The Six Pillars of Self-Esteem.* New York: Bantam, 1994.

Briggs, Dorothy Corkville. *Celebrate Your Self: Making Life Work for You.* Garden City, NY: Doubleday, 1977.

Burns, David D. *Ten Days To Self-Esteem.* New York: William Morrow, 1993.

2. Look at your child when you speak to him or her. This conveys, "This is important and you are important."

3. Look at your child when he or she speaks to you. This conveys, "What you are saying is important. You are important."

4. Explain *why.* It takes more time, but it conveys that your child is important enough for you to spend the time helping him or her to understand. When you explain why, you are also saying, "I understand that you need to know why. I am going to help you get your needs met."

> Explain *why.* It takes more time, but it conveys that your child is important enough for you to spend the time helping him or her to understand.

5. When your child tells you about something that happened at school, ask how he or she feels about it. Take the time to listen to the answer.

6. When you ask your child a question, encourage him or her to elaborate. Say, "Tell me more about that."

7. When you ask a question, don't interrupt when your child is answering.

8. Take your child seriously.

9. Give your child a private space where he or she can express himself or herself.

10. When you are giving feedback, describe specific behavior. For example, "I like how you asked the question so politely" or "You still need to pick up the towels off the floor."

11. When there is a problem, focus on the issue, not the child. For example, "You didn't do the last 10 problems on this assignment" is more constructive than "You never finish anything."

12. Give your child a hug at least every few days.

> When there is a problem, focus on the issue, not the child.

13. Say nice things about your child and let him or her overhear you.

14. Go in and say goodnight before your child goes to sleep. (This is easy to forget once your children become teenagers.)

15. Look up and smile when your child walks into the room.

16. Ask your child to tell you about the book he or she is reading or the video his or her class saw today in school.

KNOW YOUR CHILD

Each kid has a unique personality, style of learning, talents, interests, and abilities. Some children have no trouble succeeding in school, while others have a tougher time. Find out what aspects of the school experience are most difficult for your child and work with the teacher to set your child up to do well.

> Find out what aspects of the school experience are most difficult for your child and work with the teacher to set your child up to do well.

SET GOALS

It is never too early to help your child learn to set and achieve goals. You can set daily, weekly, and monthly goals. These can focus on not just grades, but on projects, skills to be learned, assignments to complete, and other school-related challenges. Be sure to check on how your child is progressing toward meeting each goal and reinforce every step toward success.

---

your child and the teacher. Use this as an opportunity to teach your child that no one is always perfect and that it's okay to stumble and make mistakes. Find out your child's view on what went wrong and where the problems started. Ask questions and listen to make sure you understand. Talk about what can be done to solve the problem or to prevent it from happening again.

MAKE READING IMPORTANT IN YOUR FAMILY

Reading is such an important component of school success that you should do all you can to encourage your child to develop excellent reading skills. Spend time yourself reading and take your child to the library. Let your child read in bed on occasion. Give books as gifts. Read to your children before bed or while they eat breakfast. Ask your child to read to you. If you can afford it, make occasional trips together to the bookstore and buy books to build your family's library.

> Reading is such an important component of school success that you should do all you can to encourage your child to develop excellent reading skills.

PAY ATTENTION TO YOUR CHILD'S WORK AND ASK TO SEE IT

Ask to see your child's homework. Show interest and encourage your children to talk about what they are learning in school. Ask often about how they are progressing and what kinds of grades they expect to bring home. When you see that problems might be developing, talk about what is most challenging and ask how you can help.

> Ask to see your child's homework. Show interest and encourage your children to talk about what they are learning in school.

TURN DISAPPOINTMENTS INTO LEARNING OPPORTUNITIES

When your child is not doing especially well in a subject, find out exactly where the problems are. Talk to both

Helping Your Kids Manage the Relocation Blues

INTRODUCTION

Moving to a new town or city is "way up there" on the stress scale. After the strain of moving out of one house, traveling, and moving into a new place, most people vacillate between euphoria and despair. You know you should be excited and positive about this new life you're beginning, and there are days when you feel good about it. But you also have plenty of times when you find yourself wondering if this move was such a great idea.

It's normal to have mixed feelings. Leaving a familiar life behind produces a sense of loss, even if you wanted to move to the new town or city. Think of the changes you are facing, all at

---

Viorst, Judith. *Alexander, Who's Not (Do You Hear Me? I Mean It!) Going to Move.* New York: Aladdin Paperbacks, 1998.

Williamson, Greg, and Abele, Greg (Illustrator). *What's the Recipe for Friends?* New Orleans, LA: Peerless Publishing, 1999.

SEE THESE HANDOUTS ON RELATED TOPICS

Anxiety in Children

Depression in Children and Teens

Helping Children in Divorcing Families

Helping Kids Manage Angry Feelings

Helping Kids Recover from Loss

How to Build Your Child's Self-Esteem

Separation Anxiety

When Kids Don't Want to Go to School

Building Positive Teen Relationships

Positive Reinforcement (for Parents)

Helping Your Child or Teen Manage Stress

Helping Your Child Succeed in School

How to Cope When Parenting Seems Over-whelming

> It is important to encourage the child to talk about his or her feelings. Reassure the child that you accept his or her feelings and will help deal with them.

15. Talk with your children about their first day at the new school. Help them plan what to wear and make a plan for getting where they need to go.

16. Have special family meetings every week in the beginning. Devote most of the time to talking about how the move has gone and encourage everyone to bring up concerns. Reinforce each family member for making the adjustment. Talk about how difficult it is to move to a new place and acknowledge them for doing their best.

WHERE CAN I GO TO LEARN MORE?

Berenstain, Stan, and Berenstain, Jan. *The Berenstain Bears' Moving Day* (First Time Books). New York: Random House, 1981.

Carlisle, Ellen. *Smooth Moves.* Charlotte, NC: Teacup Press, 1999.

Carlstrom, Nancy White. *Boxes, Boxes, Boxes Everywhere.* New York: Aladdin Paperbacks, 1999.

Goodwin, Cathy. *Making the Big Move: How to Transform Relocation into a Creative Life Transition.* Oakland, CA: New Harbinger Publications, 1999.

McGeorge, Constance, and Whyte, Mary (Illustrator). *Boomer's Big Day.* San Francisco: Chronicle Books, 1994.

once—you may be sleeping in a different bed, going to a different grocery store, taking your clothing to a different cleaner, finding a new doctor and dentist, maybe getting used to different weather, different accents, finding new friends (not to mention doing a different job)—all of these changes are very stressful. And since you and your family members are human, you're bound to react to it. Don't be surprised if you or someone in your family comes down with a case of the Relocation Blues. Look for symptoms like these:

- Feeling sad
- Eating too much or too little
- Feeling irritable
- Drinking too much alcohol
- Feeling tired
- Sleeping too much or too little

Adjusting to life in a new place affects everyone differently. Some families notice more frequent arguments. Others say the experience eventually results in more closeness. It is important to remember that the Relocation Blues is a process, not a single event—it goes on for a year or two until everyone is comfortably settled in the new life. The symptoms may hit each family member at a different time, so just when you think you're going to be okay, another person in the family seems to have a meltdown. What can you do about it? Let's look at some ways to get through the tough times.

> Some families notice more frequent arguments. Others say the experience eventually results in more closeness.

SPECIAL TIPS FOR HELPING KIDS THROUGH A MOVING EXPERIENCE

You can expect your children's responses to the experience of moving to be different than the response of an adult. Being moved from one place to another can be a traumatic experience for a child, made worse if the parents do not handle it well. Here are some ideas for helping your kids make the transition without major problems:

> Being moved from one place to another can be a traumatic experience for a child, made worse if the parents do not handle it well.

1. Explain to the kids why your family is moving. It is unfair to wait until the last minute and then dive into the process. Give them as much notice as you can and take the time to explain why the move is necessary.

2. Make it safe for everyone in the family to express feelings and ask questions about the move. Talk about both the good things and bad.

3. As a family, make a list of things you want to find out about your new town or city.

4. Decide how you want to say good-bye to your friends and acquaintances. You may want to have a party, individual visits with people, or some combination of these.

5. Make a calendar of all of the steps of the moving process. Review it each week. Talk with your family about what happened during the week just ended and anticipate the events of the week ahead.

6. Look for books to read to the children about moving and transitions.

7. If you go to the new city without the kids to look for houses, take photos to bring back.

8. Talk about the stages of the packing process and encourage every family member to participate in it.

9. Encourage every family member to be present when the moving van comes to the house you are leaving.

10. Put special items in specially marked cartons so you will be able to identify them easily when they come off the van at the new house.

11. Set aside a few special things to take along on the plane or in the car.

12. Think of a way to make your first day at your new house special.

13. Schedule a few trips around your new neighborhood and town with the whole family. Talk about how to get from one place to the next. This will help everyone build confidence that they know where to go and won't become lost.

14. Expect the kids to experience some anxiety during the entire process. Sometimes symptoms emerge long after the move has been completed. It is important to encourage the child to talk about his or her feelings. Reassure the child that you accept his or her feelings and will help deal with them.

> Put special items in specially marked cartons so you will be able to identify them easily when they come off the van at the new house.

Helping Your Kids To Be Self-Confident

❋ INTRODUCTION

Self-confidence is not something people are born with. It results from a combination of factors:

- *Learned skill:* Self-confidence is a combination of skills, not just a single quality. People are not born with it or without it. It can be learned.

- *Practice:* Self-confidence comes from practice. It may appear to be spontaneous, but it isn't.

- *Internal locus of control:* Self-confidence results from what psychologists call an internal locus of control. (Locus means central point.) This means that people who are self-directing, who accept responsibility for their own results, have greater self-confidence.

❋ HOW TO HELP YOUR CHILD BUILD CONFIDENCE

1. Encourage your child to follow his or her strengths. Show your child that self-confidence comes from being the best "you" possible, not from trying to be someone else. It is the result of following paths like these:

❋

SEE THESE HANDOUTS ON RELATED TOPICS

Assertiveness Skills (for Teens)

Building People Skills (for Teens)

Building Positive Teen Relationships

Dealing with Peer Pressure (for Teens)

Expressing Feelings Responsibly (for Teens)

Goal Setting (for Teens)

Helping Your Child or Teen Manage Stress

Helping Your Child Succeed in School

Helping Your Kids Manage the Relocation Blues

How to Build Your Child's Self-Esteem

Life Skills (for Teens)

Listening Skills (for Teens)

Personal Negotiation Skills (for Teens)

Positive Reinforcement (for Parents)

Social Anxiety Disorder (Shyness)

Understanding Body Language (for Teens)

When Kids Don't Want to Go to School

When Kids Underachieve

Workplace Skills (for Teens)

assignment" is more constructive than "You never finish anything."

20. Ask your child to go with you on routine errands just because you want to spend some time with him or her.

21. Touch your child when you talk to him or her.

22. Give your child a hug at least every few days.

23. Go in and say goodnight before your child goes to sleep. (This is easy to forget once your children become teenagers.)

24. Look up and smile when your child walks into the room.

> Look up and smile when your child walks into the room.

25. Introduce yourself when your child is with a new friend.

26. Ask your child to tell you about the book he or she is reading or the movie he or she just saw.

27. Review child development literature regularly to stay updated on what is normal at each age and stage. It is important to recheck your standards and expectations to be sure they are realistic for the child's age and individual abilities.

28. Look for ways to maintain your own self-esteem. If you are unhappy, discontented, or disappointed in how your life is turning out, it will be difficult for you to build the self-esteem of your children.

29. If you show that you accept yourself and your actions, you give permission to your child to do the same.

❋ WHERE CAN I GO TO LEARN MORE?

Branden, Nathaniel. *The Six Pillars of Self-Esteem.* New York: Bantam, 1994.

Briggs, Dorothy Corkville. *Celebrate Your Self: Making Life Work For You.* Garden City, NY: Doubleday, 1977.

Burns, David D. *Ten Days To Self-Esteem.* New York: William Morrow, 1993.

De Angelis, Barbara. *Confidence: Finding It and Living It.* Carson, CA: Hay House, 1995.

> **Encourage your child to follow his or her strengths. Show your child that self-confidence comes from being the best "you" possible, not from trying to be someone else.**

- Doing what comes naturally
- Developing his or her talents
- Following his or her convictions
- Expressing his or her own style

2. Show your child how to plan ahead for challenging situations. When a person is prepared for a challenging situation, he or she is much more likely to feel confident and perform better. The most basic example is taking a test in school. Those who are better prepared almost always do better, which in turn builds self-confidence.

3. Encourage your child to take action. Being proactive almost always results in feeling more confident. Show her how to break a challenging situation into small steps and then to take that first step, no matter how small it seems.

4. Help your child to rehearse for success. One of the best ways to build self-confidence is to practice an important conversation before it's time for the real thing. For example, if your son wants to ask his teacher for a chance to retake a test he did poorly on, offer to play the role of the teacher in a practice run.

5. Encourage your child to be persistent. Explain to him or her that self-confidence is the result of a lot of hard work. In fact, it has been said that success is 99 percent persistence and 1 percent talent.

HOW IS SELF-CONFIDENCE RELATED TO SELF-ESTEEM?

Without self-esteem, it is difficult to really be confident. Self-esteem is the sense that a person carries inside that he or she is worthwhile. This feeling comes from a lifetime of experiences that convey that one is worthy. It starts with the relationship that a person has with his or her parents—so you, the parent, are the key factor.

One of the most important things you can do for your children is to convey the message "You are worthwhile." The ways to raise responsible, happy children are limited only by your imagination. You are probably already doing some of the things on the following list, but there may also be a few new ideas here that will help you build your child's self-esteem:

1. Tell your child on a regular basis that you love him or her. Actually say the words. If you think, "I don't have to tell her. She knows," you are wrong. It doesn't count if you think it but don't say it out loud.

2. Give your child an example to follow. Take the time to teach him or her the steps. Kids need models. It's unfair to expect that your child will know what to do in daily life if you haven't shown him or her how to do it.

> **Kids need models. It's unfair to expect that your child will know what to do in daily life if you haven't shown him or her how to do it.**

3. Spend time with your child. If you are absent most of the time, he or she notices, and probably thinks it's because he or she isn't important enough.

4. Look at your child when you speak to him or her. This conveys, "This is important and you are important."

5. Look at your child when he or she speaks to you. This conveys, "What you are saying is important. You are important."

6. Explain *why*. It takes more time, but it conveys that your child is important enough for you to spend your time helping him or her to understand. When you explain why, you are also saying, "I understand that you need to know why. I am going to help you get your needs met."

7. When your child tells you about something that happened, ask how he or she feels about it. And take the time to listen to the answer. This conveys that what he or she says is important.

8. When you ask a question, encourage your child to elaborate. Say, "Tell me more about that" or ask, "What was that like?" This is another way to convey that what he or she says is important.

9. When you ask your child a question, don't interrupt when he or she is answering.

10. When you ask a question, watch your responses. Don't disagree or criticize his or her answer. Doing so teaches that it isn't safe to be candid and will make your child edit what he or she tells you.

> **When you ask a question, watch your responses. Don't disagree or criticize his or her answer. Doing so teaches that it isn't safe to be candid and will make your child edit what he or she tells you.**

11. Set a positive example with your own behavior. You can only expect your child to behave with dignity and self-respect if he or she sees you behaving that way too.

12. When you lose your temper or make a mistake, apologize. Say that you are sorry; be specific about what you are sorry for, and give your child a chance to respond.

13. When you know that you have disappointed your child, acknowledge it. Ask him or her how he or she feels about it.

14. Give your child a private space where he or she can express himself or herself.

15. If your child did a good job on something, say so.

16. If your child didn't do such a good job on something, point out what he or she did well.

17. After a disappointment or failure, ask, "What did you learn from the experience?"

> **After a disappointment or failure, ask, "What did you learn from the experience?"**

18. When you are giving feedback, describe specific behavior. For example, "I like how you asked the question so politely" or "You still need to pick up the towels off the floor."

19. When there is a problem, focus on the issue, not the child. For example, "You didn't do the last 10 problems on this

How to Cope When Parenting Feels Overwhelming

INTRODUCTION

Most people who have been parents for a few years say that parenting is much more difficult and stressful than they had ever imagined it would be. Although they love their children and would never trade the experience for anything, there are times when every parent feels overwhelmed and unsure where to turn next.

Appreciate what you are doing well and forgive yourself for the mistakes you make along the way. Just keep learning and trying to do better. As with your job, you aren't going to enjoy every part of being a parent.

11. *Recognize when you are at the end of your rope and ask for help.* Sometimes parental stress becomes so overwhelming that it interferes with a person's quality of life or ability to function. If you are feeling like you are close to stepping over the edge, get help. Make an appointment with a mental health professional who specializes in parenting issues, or speak to a member of the clergy or join a parenting support group. Don't attempt to go it alone when you are at the high end of the stress scale.

12. *Remind yourself that these feelings will not last forever.* Each stage of parenting is temporary. The children grow and develop, and their behavior changes. Parents learn new skills or become more experienced and the stressors have less of an impact. This too shall pass.

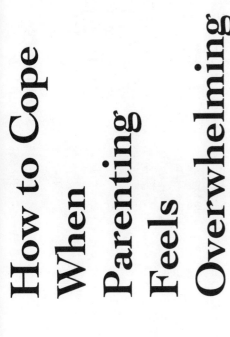 WHERE CAN I GO TO LEARN MORE?

Bolton, Michele Kremen. *The Third Shift: Managing Hard Choices in Our Careers, Homes, and Lives as Women.* New York: Jossey-Bass, 2000.

Brawner, Jim, Brawner, Suzette, and Smalley, Gary. *Taming the Family Zoo: Maximizing Harmony and Minimizing Family Stress.* Colorado Springs, CO: Navpress, 1998.

Gordon, Thomas, *Parent Effectiveness Training: The Proven Program for Raising Responsible Children.* New York, NY: Three Rivers Press, 2000.

Peters, Joan, *When Mothers Work: Loving Our Children Without Sacrificing Ourselves.* Cambridge, MA: Perseus Books, 1998.

SEE THESE HANDOUTS ON RELATED TOPICS

Helping Your Child or Teen Manage Stress

Helping Your Child Succeed In School

Helping Your Kids to Be Self-Confident

Helping Your Kids Manage the Relocation Blues

Managing Family Conflict

Managing the Stepfamily

Positive Reinforcement (for Parents)

Teaching Your Child to Respect Others

This handout addresses some of the key parental stress issues and offers several ideas to help parents regain a sense of control and equilibrium:

1. *Identify what you are actually feeling.* The most important step to take when you are feeling parental stress is to stop and consider what you are actually feeling. Here are some examples of negative feelings that might be behind your stress:

   - Anger
   - Anxiety, fear
   - Dejection, despair, hopelessness
   - Sadness, sorrow, grief
   - Guilt, shame

2. *Pay attention to your body sensations.* They will also provide clues about why you are feeling so stressed. An emotion is an experience that involves feelings and sensations. Pay attention to your emotions and keep from becoming overwhelmed.

> Pay attention to your emotions and keep from becoming overwhelmed.

3. *Learn to calm yourself down.* When you are calm, you are less likely to say and do things you'll later regret—things that could be destructive to your relationship with your children and your partner. You will be also less likely to become defensive and shut others out. Examples of ways to

calm yourself and keep from getting carried away with emotion include the following:

   - Pay attention to your physical responses. Is your heart racing? Are you breathing faster? If you are, take a time out.
   - Leave the room. Go for a drive. Do something relaxing. Listen to music or do relaxation exercises.
   - Make a conscious effort to calm yourself down. Say things to yourself like, "I'm very upset right now, but it'll be okay. I still love her." "Even though we disagree, we still have a good relationship." "We can work this out. We're partners." The feelings underlying your stressed-out state are important to identify. This step will help you decide the best course for you to take to return to a sense of calm and control.

4. *Focus on things you can do something about.* Make a list of the things stressing you out and cross off the items you have no control over. Choose the smallest and easiest thing to do and do it.

5. *Take a break.* Think of a way to get away periodically. If you have small children and if you can afford a sitter, hire one. If you can't, ask another parent to exchange babysitting with you. Do what you need to do to provide some breathing room to enable you to regain your perspective.

> Do what you need to do to provide some breathing room to enable you to regain your perspective.

6. *Take care of your body.* Parenting takes an enormous amount of energy. You need to feed your body properly and give it adequate rest. If you don't, you won't be up to the job.

7. *Vent your feelings to someone you can trust.* It is important not to keep feelings of frustration bottled up inside. Call all the person who loves you the most and is never judgmental with you. Ask if he or she will listen while you vent for 10 minutes.

8. *Look for ways to head off trouble at the pass.* Sometimes if you think ahead, you can anticipate places where things will go wrong. If you make plans now to avoid those places, you will save yourself some stressful moments later. For example, if you argue with your daughter each morning over what she is going to wear to school, consider asking her to make her choices the night before.

9. *Stay away from people and situations that make you feel bad.* You have probably heard the expression "toxic people." We all have people in our lives who make us feel bad when we are around them. When you are feeling stressed, it is important to avoid them if you can.

10. *Review your expectations of yourself.* Many parents stress themselves because they expect themselves to perform as if they were at work or at school. That isn't possible. Other parents become frustrated because they don't think they are as good a parent as the person next door or their sister-in-law or someone else. Expecting to be perfect is setting yourself up for disappointment.

How to Help a Friend through a Crisis (for Teens)

❧ INTRODUCTION

The teen years are a time of major changes and challenges. While it is normal to face plenty of ups and downs during this time, some teens get into major crises and really need help from their friends and families. If you have a friend who seems to be in crisis, and you are worried about him or her, there are some things you can do to help.

> Even if your friend withdraws from you or seems reluctant to talk, don't give up. Call and check on him or her and repeat your invitation to do things together.

12. If you friend mentions suicide, take it seriously. Tell your friend that you are very worried about him or her and that he or she needs to get help immediately.

13. If your friend asks you not to tell anyone that he or she is having suicidal thoughts, don't keep the secret. Keeping it secret will not help him or her, and if your friend commits suicide you will have to carry the knowledge that you had been warned.

14. If your friend refuses to get help, ask a trusted adult.

15. Call a hotline and ask for help.

16. If you are extremely concerned, tell another adult that your friend is in danger. Call your friend's parent(s), the police, 911, your doctor, or a hospital.

❧ WHERE CAN I GO TO LEARN MORE?

American Academy of Child and Adolescent Psychiatry (www.aacap.org)

Burns, David. *Feeling Good: The New Mood Therapy.* New York: Avon Books, 1980.

Covey, Sean. *The Seven Habits of Highly Effective Teens: The Ultimate Teenage Success Guide.* New York: Simon and Schuster, 1998.

Marcus, Eric. *Why Suicide? Answers to 200 of the Most Frequently Asked Questions About Suicide, Attempted Suicide, and Assisted Suicide.* San Fransisco: Harper San Fransisco, 1996.

WHAT SHOULD I DO IF MY FRIEND IS DEPRESSED?

Depression is a serious illness that affects as many as 5 percent of children in this country. It is always troubling, and for some teens it can be disabling. Depression is more than just sadness or "the blues." It can have an impact on nearly every aspect of a person's life. A teen who suffers from depression may experience feelings of despair and worthlessness, and this can have an enormous impact on his or her relationships as well as on the person's physical body, behavior, thought processes, and mood.

WHEN SHOULD I ASK AN ADULT FOR HELP?

If your friend is depressed and shows any of the following signs, it is extremely important that he or she obtain the assistance of a medical or mental health professional. If your friend is reluctant to seek help on his or her own and if you think that his or her life is in danger, you should not hesitate to get help on your friend's behalf.

> *If your friend is reluctant to seek help on his or her own and if you think that his or her life is in danger, you should not hesitate to get help on your friend's behalf.*

- *Thoughts about death or suicide.* This is always dangerous. Your friend should see a professional therapist immediately.

CLINICAL DEPRESSION SYMPTOMS

Children and adolescents who are diagnosed with clinical depression have a combination of symptoms from the following list.

- Feeling sad, crying
- Low self-esteem, feelings of worthlessness or hopelessness
- Anger, irritability, hostility
- Isolating oneself from others
- Having a hard time getting along with others
- Fatigue, low energy
- Restlessness, boredom
- Much less interest or pleasure in most regular activities
- Excessive or inappropriate guilt
- Difficulty concentrating and making decisions
- Feeling sick much of the time; headaches and stomachaches
- Change in appetite or sleeping patterns
- Excessive school absences
- Running away from home
- Recurrent thoughts of death
- Suicidal thoughts, a specific plan for committing suicide, or a suicide attempt

- *Symptoms of depression have continued for a long time.* Acute responses to events are normal, but they should not last beyond a reasonable time.
- *The person's ability to function has become impaired.* Seek help before your friend's life situation deteriorates to a serious level.
- *The person has become so isolated that he or she has no one with whom to reality test.* Advise

your friend to seek someone out to share thoughts and feelings with. This could be a mental health professional, clergy member, teacher, or friend.

- *The depressive symptoms have become severe.*

WHAT CAN I DO TO HELP?

The following list will give you some ideas for helping your friend who is in crisis:

1. Tell your friend that you are available to listen and help.

2. Listen carefully and do not judge him or her.

3. Take your friend seriously, even if you think the problem is not so bad.

4. Don't try to cheer him or her up. Doing so would tell your friend that you don't really understand how serious the problem is.

5. Suggest that your friend talk to a trusted adult who can help. This could be a parent, teacher, school counselor, or therapist.

6. Offer to go along with your friend to talk to the adult helper.

7. Share books and articles that you think may be helpful.

8. Suggest that your friend keep a journal for recording private thoughts and for writing about what is bothering him or her.

9. Talk with your friend about constructive ways to deal with stress and anger. (See related handouts on these subjects.)

10. Suggest that you and your friend share in an activity that he or she particularly enjoys.

11. Even if your friend withdraws from you or seems reluctant to talk, don't give up. Call and check on him or her and repeat your invitation to do things together.

I'm Planning to Come Out to My Family. What Should I Expect?

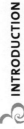 **INTRODUCTION**

Although you may have known for most of your life that you are gay or lesbian, it may come as a surprise to the people in your family. Almost every gay and lesbian person at some point in his or her life faces the challenge of coming out to friends and family members. For some, this experience is relatively painless, and for others, it is extremely difficult. The degree of challenge depends on many factors. When the news is a complete surprise, it usually takes some time for the person receiving it to process it, and the experience is often very much like a loss. The person is losing the image or view he or she once had of the person coming out and

---

SEE THESE HANDOUTS ON RELATED TOPICS

Assertiveness Skills (for Teens)

Building People Skills (for Teens)

Building Positive Teen Relationships

Dealing with Peer Pressure (for Teens)

Expressing Feelings Responsibly (for Teens)

Goal Setting (for Teens)

How to Help a Friend through a Crisis (for Teens)

Life Skills (for Teens)

Listening Skills (for Teens)

Personal Negotiation Skills (for Teens)

Positive Reinforcement (for Parents)

Understanding Body Language (for Teens)

What Teens Need to Know about HIV and AIDS (for Teens)

---

11. Look for ways to build cohesiveness in the family. The family has changed as a result of your news. Some rebuilding may be needed.

> The family has changed as a result of your news. Some rebuilding may be needed.

12. If the family has trouble recovering from your announcement, you may need the help of a family therapist to resolve things.

13. Invite family members to participate in a support group for family members of gays and lesbians.

14. Discuss ways to gradually involve same-gender partners and gay friends into family activities.

WHERE CAN I GO FOR MORE INFORMATION?

Gay and Lesbian Alliance Against Defamation (GLAAD) (www.GLAAD.org)

American Civil Liberties Union (ACLU) (www.ACLU.org)

The Advocate (www.Advocate.com)

Borhek, Mary. *Coming Out to Parents: A Two-Way Survival Guide for Lesbians and Gay Men and Their Parents.* Cleveland, OH: Pilgrim Press, 1993.

Kübler Ross, Elisabeth. *On Death and Dying.* New York: Scribner, 1997.

Signorile, Michelangelo. *Outing Yourself: How to Come Out as Lesbian or Gay to Your Family, Friends, and Coworkers.* New York: Fireside, 1996.

must replace it with a different image or view. For some people, this is an extremely emotional experience.

As with any significant loss, many people experience reactions like these:

- *Shock.* The first reaction may be numbness or denial. The person may ask, "Are you sure?" or say, "It can't be true!" He or she may feel nothing for several days, claiming to have no reaction at all.

- *Anger.* After the shock wears off, people usually become angry. They may say or think, "Why me? Why does this have to happen to me?" or "What did I do to deserve this?" or "After all I've done for her!"

- *Bargaining.* The person may start to think that he or she can do something to change the fact of your gayness. He or she may say, "Why don't you take a nice vacation with the family? I'm sure you'll feel differently about this after a good rest," or pray to God, "Please just make this go away and I'll never say a bad word to him again."

- *Depression.* Sadness and lethargy may follow next. The person may feel guilty and sad for a long time, wishing that things could be different.

- *Acceptance.* After a time, most people come to accept the news. They may cycle through the stages a few times, but eventually the facts sink in and the person is ready to accept them and move on.

These five reactions form a process that was first described by Elisabeth Kübler Ross in her work on death and dying. She and others discovered that people experience the same five stages in response to any kind of loss, including hearing the news that a son or daughter is gay or lesbian.

> After a time, most people come to accept the news. They may cycle through the stages a few times, but eventually the facts sink in and the person is ready to accept them and move on.

HOW CAN I HELP MY FAMILY LEARN TO ACCEPT MY SEXUAL ORIENTATION?

For some families, it is difficult to accept the fact that a son or daughter is gay or lesbian. Some family members process the news quickly and seem to accept it with little problem. Others have a very difficult time and may even never completely understand or like what they have learned. You can do several things to make the process less difficult for yourself and your family members:

1. Have and use a support system. Don't expect to be able to have this experience on your own. Discuss it with others who care about you and who have gone through the experience themselves. Meet with a counselor or therapist and talk through your feelings.

2. Decide how candid and open you can safely be. You don't have to tell or explain everything.

> Decide how candid and open you can safely be. You don't have to tell or explain everything.

3. State that you are asking for the support and understanding of everyone in the family.

4. Don't take your family members' reactions personally. Their reactions are not about you; they are about them.

5. Ask them a lot of questions to learn what they are thinking and feeling, and why. If you can give them a chance to express their thoughts and feelings, they will more easily be able to let them go.

6. Be prepared to do a lot of listening. Listening is a way to maintain your sense of dignity and power. When you are listening, you are in control.

> Be prepared to do a lot of listening. Listening is a way to maintain your sense of dignity and power.

7. Accept their reactions. You don't have to agree with those reactions or like them, but you can accept them.

8. Help your friends and family learn about what it means to be gay or lesbian. Gather some things for them to read.

9. Tell the members of your family that it's not their fault. It's not anyone's fault, it just is.

10. Expect family members to say hurtful things they will take back later. You can choose whether you want to continue to expose yourself to such anger if it becomes especially hurtful. Sometimes it makes sense to take a vacation from each other until the others regain control of their emotions.

Life Skills (for Teens)

INTRODUCTION

Whether you have supportive parents or not, the teen years can be tough. Some kids are lucky enough to have parents and other adults in their lives who show them the way, coaching them toward a successful and productive adulthood. Other kids aren't so lucky—they are pretty much left to learn life's lessons on their own.

STEPS TO LEARNING LIFE SKILLS

Regardless of what kind of parental environment you live in, the following strategies can help you survive your teen years:

1. *Understand what emotional changes to expect.* It always helps to know what you're getting into. When you know what to expect, the changes of adolescence don't come as such a surprise. It's like seeing the trailer before you see the movie, or reading the table of contents before you start a book. It gives you a sense of what's to come, so you feel prepared.

2. *Get to know yourself better.* The teen years can be very confusing. You may often feel like you're not the same person you were when you got up this morning. How do you keep track of your changing self? One way is to keep a journal—a private notebook where you write about your feelings.

It's very important to have someone you can talk to during this time.

- Your parents
- Your siblings
- Your relatives
- Your minister or rabbi
- Your doctor
- Psychotherapists
- Police officers
- Your teachers
- The school psychologist
- Your guidance counselor
- Your friends
- Your friends' parents
- Your neighbors

13. *Learn teamwork skills.* Being a part of a team is an important skill, and it will become even more important when you are an adult. Teamwork skills include things like these:

- Cooperating
- Making decisions
- Being loyal
- Encouraging others
- Planning
- Problem solving
- Supporting
- Trusting

WHERE CAN I GO TO LEARN MORE?

Kelly, Kate. *The Complete Idiot's Guide to Parenting a Teenager.* New York: Alpha Books, 1996.

Law, Felicia, and Parker, Josephine (eds.). *Growing Up: A Young Person's Guide to Adolescence.* Chippenham, Wiltshire, UK: Merlion Publishing, Ltd., 1993.

McCoy, Kathy, and Wibbelsman, Charles. *The New Teenage Body Book.* New York: Putnam, 1992.

SEE THESE HANDOUTS ON RELATED TOPICS

Assertiveness Skills (for Teens)

Building People Skills (for Teens)

Building Positive Teen Relationships

Dealing with Peer Pressure (for Teens)

Expressing Feelings Responsibly (for Teens)

Goal Setting (for Teens)

How to Help a Friend through a Crisis (for Teens)

Listening Skills (for Teens)

Personal Negotiation Skills (for Teens)

Understanding Body Language (for Teens)

What Teens Need to Know about HIV and AIDS (for Teens)

Workplace Skills (for Teens)

How do you keep track of your changing self? One way is to keep a journal—a private notebook where you write about your feelings.

3. *Look for positive influence.* The teen years can be less stressful if you have a role model. This is someone you would value as a mentor, or someone worthwhile you could pattern yourself after. Role models are important because they set an example for you to follow. If you admire someone and model yourself after him or her, this process can give you some direction and goals. Think about the people who are positive influences in your life. They might be family members, teachers, leaders, or famous people you will never meet but whom you admire just the same.

4. *Practice thinking for yourself.* Thinking for yourself is a sign of strong self-esteem. It means that you know you matter, and that you value your ability to think. It means that you ask questions about things rather than just accepting what people tell you.

5. *Learn to be assertive.* Assertive behavior is another sign of self-esteem. It usually means that a person values him or herself. Assertiveness is standing up for yourself and protecting your own interests.

Assertiveness is standing up for yourself and protecting your own interests.

6. *Learn to present yourself with confidence.* Here is one way to develop confidence. First, make a list of at least five things you do well. Then make a list of at least five things you *don't* do very well. Choose something to do from the first list every day. This will make you feel good about yourself. Then, when you're feeling good, do something from the second list. You will see that the way you feel about yourself at the moment can greatly affect how you perform.

7. *Learn to express your opinions.* Here are some tips:
   - Know what you want to say. Organize your facts and arguments.
   - Choose the best moment. Having good timing can make a huge difference in the impact your statement makes.
   - Look friendly. People will be more receptive to you if you smile.
   - Develop your listening skills.
   - Watch your voice. Speak clearly and not too loudly.
   - When you disagree, do so in a pleasant and polite way. Being rude or unfriendly turns people off and lessens your impact.
   - Know the difference between facts and opinions. Facts will help you win your argument.
   - Acknowledge the other point of view. People may not agree with you. You have more power when you acknowledge that others have a right to a different point of view.

8. *Find out what you believe in.* One of the tasks of adolescence is to discover what you believe in—what you value in life. This process involves questioning the ideas of people around you, especially your parents. It is understandable that you will reject some of the values and beliefs of your parents, but there are constructive ways of disagreeing.

One of the tasks of adolescence is to discover what you believe in—what you value in life.

9. *Learn to disagree productively.* There are plenty of nonproductive ways to disagree with parents and other authority figures, such as temper tantrums, violent or rebellious behavior, or disobeying laws. You will have more success if you learn the more productive ways to disagree, such as developing your negotiation skills or by forming or joining an action group.

10. *Create your own private place.* As you grow older, you have a greater need for a private place that is all you own. You need it as a place to escape to, and also as a place where you can create your own life. At the end of adolescence you will be an adult,

At the end of adolescence you will be an adult, ready to go out into the world.

ready to go out into the world. You will need to be ready to stand on your own as an independent and responsible person. It helps if you have some things you can call your own, such as:
   - A private space
   - A place to play music
   - A place to study and read
   - A place to write down your thoughts and feelings, such as a private journal
   - Places to meet friends
   - Your own money
   - Your own possessions

11. *Make a few good friends.* Making new friends takes some effort. Some people seem to make friends quite easily, while others find it difficult. It's mostly a matter of learning a few skills. See if you can develop behaviors like these:
   - Smile; appear friendly
   - Say "Hi"
   - Ask questions
   - Give compliments
   - Join groups
   - Ask for information ("Where did you get your jacket?")
   - Be interested

12. *Find someone you can talk to.* Just in case you hadn't noticed, adolescence can be a highly emotional time. You are learning new things every day and you are not always ready to meet the demands of social situations. It's very important to have someone you can talk to during this time. Different people can help you with different kinds of problems. The important thing is that when you start to feel stressed, it means you probably need to let it out. Look for help from people like these:

Listening Skills (for Teens)

WHAT ARE THE BENEFITS OF DEVELOPING GOOD LISTENING SKILLS?

Listening skills help you show that you are hearing and understanding another person and are interested in what he or she has to say. Developing strong listening skills is good for relationships because:

- When you make an effort to understand what someone is thinking and feeling, it creates good feelings in the other person and makes you feel good about yourself.

- Listening carefully and checking for understanding enhances communication and results in fewer misunderstandings.

- In an emotional situation, using good listening skills has a calming effect and helps deescalate anger.

SEE THESE HANDOUTS ON RELATED TOPICS

Assertiveness Skills (for Teens)

Building People Skills (for Teens)

Building Positive Teen Relationships

Dealing with Peer Pressure (for Teens)

Expressing Feelings Responsibly (for Teens)

Life Skills (for Teens)

Personal Negotiation Skills (for Teens)

Understanding Body Language (for Teens)

Workplace Skills (for Teens)

- Reflective statements are *not* the same as agreement. They are a way of demonstrating that you intend to hear and understand another's point of view.

Examples:

"Sounds like you're upset about what happened at work."

"You sound really confused about how to solve this problem."

"It makes you angry when you find errors on my homework."

"Sounds like you're really worried about Wendy."

"I get the feeling you're awfully busy right now."

WHERE CAN I GO FOR MORE INFORMATION?

Covey, Sean. *The 7 Habits of Highly Effective Teens: The Ultimate Teenage Success Guide.* New York: Simon and Schuster, 1998.

McGraw, Jay, and McGraw, Phillip, *Life Strategies for Teens.* New York: Fireside, 2000.

WHAT ARE THE KEY LISTENING SKILLS?

1. Ask open-ended questions
2. Use summary statements
3. Use neutral questions and phrases
4. Use reflective statements

Listening Skill 1: Ask Open-Ended Questions

What they are: Open-ended questions begin with *what, why, how do,* or *tell me*. These questions cannot be answered with a simple *yes* or *no*. Their purpose is to encourage the other person to open up and elaborate on the topic.

What they do:

- Asking open-ended questions gets the other person involved in your conversation by giving him or her a chance to tell what he or she thinks or knows.

- Open-ended questions are useful when the other person is silent or reluctant to go into detail.

- These questions help you deal with negative emotions, such as anger or fear. This is because they encourage the other person to vent feelings and get them out on the table.

Examples:

"How do you feel about what she said?"

"Tell me how you put away those books so quickly."

"What do you think about the new plants in the garden?"

Listening Skill 2: Use Summary Statements

What they are: A statement that summarizes the facts you gathered.

What they do:

- Summary statements help you focus on facts, not emotions.

- They help the other person clarify his or her own thinking by hearing your summary.

- They help eliminate confusion by focusing on the relevant facts.

- They help you separate the important issues from the trivial.

- They enhance the other person's self-esteem by showing that you are listening carefully.

Examples:

"So, you're saying you want to finish the book report before you go to dinner. Then you plan to start your chemistry assignment."

"You're saying that you tried your best, but it was beyond your control."

"Give me some more reasons why we should put this off until tomorrow."

"Tell me more about why you want to buy the new car now rather than waiting until spring."

- They help the other person understand what you are interested in hearing more about.

- They benefit communication because they help you gain more information.

Listening Skill 3: Use Neutral Questions and Phrases

What they are: Neutral questions and phrases get the other person to open up and elaborate on the topic you are discussing.

What they do:

- These questions are more focused than open-ended questions.

Examples:

Listening Skill 4: Use Reflective Statements

What they are: Reflective statements involve restating, in your own words, what the other person has said. The most effective reflective statements have two components:

1. Name the feeling that the other person is conveying.
2. State the reason for the feeling.

What they do:

- Reflective statements help you check whether your understanding of a message is correct.

- Reflective statements enable you to demonstrate that you are listening and that you are interested and concerned.

Personal Negotiation Skills (for Teens)

INTRODUCTION

Negotiating skills can help teens manage lots of different kinds of life situations, both in school and in personal relationships. Here are a few examples of where these skills can help you build an even better life for yourself:

- Many family situations require negotiating with others. Deciding which movie to see, planning how to spend money, choosing a vacation spot,

WHERE CAN I GO FOR MORE INFORMATION?

Fisher, Roger, and Ury, William. *Getting to Yes: Negotiating Agreement Without Giving In.* New York: Penguin, 1991.

SEE THESE HANDOUTS ON RELATED TOPICS

Assertiveness Skills (for Teens)

Building People Skills (for Teens)

Building Positive Teen Relationships

Dealing with Peer Pressure (for Teens)

Expressing Feelings Responsibly (for Teens)

Goal Setting (for Teens)

Life Skills (for Teens)

Listening Skills (for Teens)

Understanding Body Language (for Teens)

Workplace Skills (for Teens)

> With practice, you can learn to use these simple skills to get more of what you want in life—without coming across like a bully.

A attacks B.
B defends herself and attacks A.
A defends herself and attacks B.
B defends herself and attacks A.

We've all experienced being caught in one of these spirals and know how nonproductive they are. Rather than perpetuating such a process, the successful negotiator puts a stop to it by choosing to avoid saying anything that would be perceived as aggressive or defensive.

Example A:
Jim: "I can't believe you are being so rigid."
Anne: "Rigid! You should talk! You are completely bullheaded."
Jim: "Right! You should try listening to yourself. You are impossible."

Example B:
Jim: "I can't believe you are being so rigid."
Anne: "You're not happy with what I've asked for."
Jim: "You're damn right! You have to consider what I want."
Anne: "Tell me more about it, then. I'll be happy to listen."

In Example A, Jim and Anne dig themselves in deeper with each statement. In Example B, Anne blocks the defend/attack spiral and makes it possible for communication to resume.

With practice, you can learn to use these simple skills to get more of what you want in life—without coming across like a bully. In fact, these skills help you reach agreements that are more likely to satisfy both parties while maintaining a positive relationship. Try them in your work life or at home—they work equally well in either setting.

and many other decisions work best when you have these skills.

- Being a good negotiator enables you to get what you want more often without resorting to becoming aggressive or pushy. Negotiating with others is more effective than simply demanding what you want or just caving in.

- You will be more successful at school and at your job if you know how to negotiate. These skills enable you to stand up for yourself and get what you want more often without harming relationships with bosses and coworkers.

> Being a good negotiator enables you to get what you want more often without resorting to becoming aggressive or pushy.

- Negotiation skills increase your personal effectiveness in any group situation (e.g., school groups, volunteer groups, church or synagogue groups).

- Knowing how to negotiate lessens the chances that others will take advantage of you.

- Negotiating a fair solution makes you feel good about yourself and increases others' respect for you.

WHAT DO SUCCESSFUL NEGOTIATORS DO?

What exactly is negotiation? It is a set of skills that any teen can learn. When researchers have observed the behavior of negotiators, they learned that the most successful negotiators do the following things:

1. Skillful negotiators plan ahead. Successful negotiations are rarely spontaneous. Taking the time to analyze the situation and think through your strategy is perhaps the most important element of negotiating success. This is true if you are negotiating a better grade in a class or negotiating your vacation plans with your family.
   Example: Anthony is a junior in high school and he wants to get the best possible grades this year because he plans to apply to some top colleges. He has been working part-time at a nearby restaurant but wants to work fewer hours so he can study more. He anticipates that his parents will resist this idea because they expect him to earn his own spending money. For a while, he avoids the subject, fearing that it will turn into an argument. Then he starts to feel angry and resentful. He decides to negotiate with his parents and begins by making a list of his needs and wants, as well as their needs and wants.

> The most successful negotiators are open-minded. They avoid being locked in to one outcome. They are willing to consider many possibilities and combinations of options.

2. Skillful negotiators are willing to consider a wide range of outcomes and options rather than rigidly insisting on a specific result. Negotiators who are most successful are open-minded and avoid being locked in to one outcome. They are willing to consider many possibilities and combinations of options.
   Example: Lisa is feeling very stressed by the demands of participating on the yearbook staff. She was thinking of giving it up until she decided to make a list of other options. She came up with several alternatives to present to her journalism teacher, including being able to come in on some Saturdays instead of staying after school, taking on a smaller role on the yearbook rather than the editor position she is now in, and being able to recruit a few more classmates to help with the yearbook.

3. Skillful negotiators look for common ground rather than areas of conflict. Pointing out areas where you and the other person are already in agreement conveys an attitude of cooperation and lessens any feeling of opposition.
   Example: Sandy wants her first car to be a sporty one. Her parents want her to drive their old Volvo because of their reputation for safety. She says, "Let's talk about what we agree on. First, we agree that the car has to have a strong safety record. Second, we want it to be a used car because they are more affordable. And third, we've set our price range as $10,000 or less."

4. Skillful negotiators discuss the key issues in order of priority. Have a clear idea of what the two or three key issues are and which is the most important issues and proceed to those that matter less. If you can reach agreement on the most important things, the lesser issues will most likely be easier to resolve.
   Example: Carol wants to go to a special teen program this summer, her last before she finishes high school. Her parents want her to stay home and work to save money. She sees the key issues as follows: (1) She will never have a chance to attend a program like this one again, since it is only for high school students; (2) she needs money to pay her car insurance; (3) her grandfather has agreed to pay for half of the program.

> Skillful negotiators avoid behavior that the other person is likely to consider annoying.

5. Skillful negotiators avoid behavior that the other person is likely to consider annoying. This includes any of the following kinds of behavior: having an aggressive or intimidating manner, using sarcasm, using negative body language, talking loudly. Not only do skillful negotiators avoid such behavior, they work hard at conveying an attitude of cooperation, reasonableness, openness, and friendliness.
   Example: Caesar wants to finish high school one semester early so that he can work to earn money for college the following fall. He has enough credits and the school will allow him to do it. His mother is resisting the idea. Caesar says, "I thought you would be more understanding about my wanting to finish school and earn some money. Any reasonable parent would agree to this." This sarcastic remark is likely to create some doubts in his mom's mind rather than convince her to let Caesar do what he wants.

6. Skillful negotiators avoid participating in a defend/attack spiral. You know what this sounds like:

Positive Reinforcement (for Parents)

WHAT IS POSITIVE REINFORCEMENT?

The best way to define positive reinforcement is to provide some examples. Positive reinforcement is all of these:

- When your son finishes a meal and clears his dishes and puts them in the dishwasher, you say, "Thank you for cleaning up after yourself. I really appreciate it."

- You look your daughter in the eyes and say, "You did such a good job on this report. I saw that you worked very hard on it and made the deadline with plenty of time to spare."

no reason to hold it back when it is deserved.

Have a list of behaviors you want your children to demonstrate. These could include cleaning up after themselves, doing homework promptly, answering the phone politely. Tell your children that you expect them to demonstrate these behaviors, and reinforce them when they do. The reinforcement could be saying "Good job" after the job is completed, and giving the thumbs-up sign.

Do something special. Bake a cake or cookies and bring the treat to school for your kids' teachers when they do something out of the ordinary for your child, such as patiently helping her learn a difficult concept or arranging for special help when it's needed. When your team at work accomplishes something special, you can do this for them, too.

WHERE CAN I GO FOR MORE INFORMATION?

Dinkmeyer, Don, and McKay, Gary. *Parenting Young Children: Systematic Training for Effective Parenting (STEP) of Children Under Six.* Circle Pines, MN: American Guidance Service, 1997.

Dreikurs, Rudolph. *Children: The Challenge.* New York: Plume, 1991.

SEE THESE HANDOUTS ON RELATED TOPICS

Helping Kids Manage Angry Feelings

How to Build Your Child's Self-Esteem

Managing Family Conflict

- You write a thank-you note to your daughter-in-law after she has cooked a delicious dinner for you and your family.

- When your son brings home grades that were higher than his goal, you write him a note that says, "Congratulations. I am very proud of your hard work."

Positive reinforcement is saying or doing something that will **encourage** a person to repeat a desirable behavior. It is the opposite of punishment, which is providing a consequence that **discourages** a person from repeating an unwanted behavior.

People want and need to be appreciated for their efforts. There are few things more motivating than a pat on the back or a few words of appreciation from those in charge. Conversely, when basic appreciation and recognition are missing from a work or personal relationship, it is demotivating and demoralizing. Since something so powerful takes so little effort and costs nothing, it is hard to understand why more people don't take advantage of it both at home and in the workplace.

HOW CAN I USE POSITIVE REINFORCEMENT?

You can positively reinforce people in countless ways. Here are some examples to stimulate your imagination:

Person	Situation	Ideas for positive reinforcement
Your child	Gets a part in the school play.	• Tell him or her how proud you are. • Take pictures of the event and send them to relatives and friends.
	Cleans up his or her room without being asked.	• Tell him or her how pleased you are. • Offer to take him or her for a special treat.
Your spouse	Having a difficult time at work.	• Hug him or her and say, "I'm so happy you made it through this week. I know how hard it has been for you. You have been working very hard."
	Buys you a nice birthday present.	• Say, "Thank you so much for remembering me with such a perfect gift. It makes me feel very special."
	Cooks a nice dinner for you.	• Say, "This was a delicious dinner. Thank you so much for taking the time to make it special. Now I'll clean up while you relax."

> Don't wait a day or a week to thank someone for a job well-done. The closer the behavior is to its positive consequence, the more meaning it will have for the person being reinforced.

WHAT ARE THE GUIDELINES FOR USING POSITIVE REINFORCEMENT?

Whether it's at home or at work, there are a few simple guidelines for using positive reinforcement that will help you maximize its effectiveness:

Be specific in your praise. Say what you are recognizing and why it is significant. Instead of saying to your daughter, "You always do such good work," say this instead: "You got your book report done one day early and it follows the assignment guidelines exactly. Good job." Your daughter will know exactly what you are praising her for and she will be more likely to do the same thing next time.

Praise right away. Don't wait a day or a week to thank someone for a job well-done. The closer the behavior is to its positive consequence, the more meaning it will have for the person being reinforced.

Praise publicly. When your daughter Susan gets an A in Statistics after a semester of struggling, you can post a note on the refrigerator (for all to see) saying, "Susan, great job in Statistics."

Be on the lookout for things to compliment. You don't want to overdo it so that your praise becomes meaningless, but there is

Teaching Your Child to Respect Others

INTRODUCTION

Respect is an attitude that is conveyed by one's actions. Respect is shown in different cultures in different ways. In the American culture, people show respect through behaviors like these:

- Using good manners.
- Saying *"please"* and *"thank you."*
- Waiting your turn.
- Being on time. Calling if you are going to be late.
- Listening when a person is speaking.
- Responding when someone asks you a question.
- Treating a person's possessions with care.
- Treating animals with care.
- Valuing others the same as you value yourself.

SEE THESE HANDOUTS ON RELATED TOPICS

Assertiveness Skills (for Teens)

Attention-Seeking with Disruptive Behavior

Building People Skills (for Teens)

Building Positive Teen Relationships

Conduct Disorder

Dealing with Peer Pressure (for Teens)

Expressing Feelings Responsibly (for Teens)

Helping Your Child Succeed in School

Helping Your Kids to Be Self-Confident

How to Build Your Child's Self-Esteem

Life Skills (for Teens)

Listening Skills (for Teens)

Managing Family Conflict

Personal Negotiation Skills (for Teens)

Understanding Body Language (for Teens)

Workplace Skills (for Teens)

---

important. You must also *show* your child how to behave respectfully.

Most important, you must show respect toward others. If you don't, you will have a hard time raising a child who is respectful. When you see other people behaving either respectfully or disrespectfully—on television, in public, at the child's school—look for examples of respectful behavior and talk with your child about them.

4. *Act immediately when your child is disrespectful.* When you see your child behaving disrespectfully, it is important to take immediate action. Be sure to demonstrate respect for the child as you deal with the situation. If you can, do the following:

- Take the child away from the situation.
- Explain what behavior was unacceptable.
- Explain why.
- State what the child should do instead.
- Give the child a chance to respond.
- If appropriate, ask the child to apologize to the other person.

It is important to speak firmly, convey that you are serious, and be clear that you will not tolerate disrespectful behavior. Of course, you must tailor your actions to the child's age and to the situation itself.

WHERE CAN I GO TO LEARN MORE?

Borba, Michele. *Parents Do Make a Difference: How to Raise Kids with Solid Character, Strong Minds, and Caring Hearts.* New York: Jossey-Bass, 1999.

McKay, Gary, et al. *Raising Respectful Kids in a Rude World: Teaching Your Children the Power of Mutual Respect and Consideration.* Rocklin, CA: Prima Publishing, 2001.

HOW CAN I TEACH MY CHILD TO BE RESPECTFUL?

You are your child's most important teacher. Here are a few very important things you can do to encourage him or her to develop into a respectful person:

1. *Set a positive example.* Children learn to respect others mainly by the examples that are set in their family. They observe their parents' behavior and family interactions, and learn from these how to interact with other people. If parents treat their children respectfully and expect the children to treat others the same way, the children will learn respect.

> If parents treat their children respectfully and expect the children to treat others the same way, the children will learn respect.

Children will learn to respect others if they see their parents and other authority figures behave according to the examples listed at the beginning of this handout. They will be less likely to grow into respectful adults, however, if they see their parents engage in behaviors like these:

- Behaving rudely
- Making fun of others
- Demanding to be first
- Teasing
- Refusing to wait
- Not taking care of others' possessions
- Insulting others
- Pushing to the front of a line
- Cheating
- Trying to get away with things
- Lying
- Being late for appointments
- Gossiping
- Yelling at a person in front of others
- Not following through on promises
- Trying to get something for nothing
- Being impatient
- Taking things that don't belong to them

Even if the parents say that respectful behaviors (like those on the first page of this handout) are important, it is the parents' *actions* that have the strongest influence on their children.

2. *Set clear expectations.* Be specific about what kinds of behavior you expect from your child. Specify what kinds are not acceptable, too. For example:

> Be specific about what kinds of behavior you expect from your child. Specify what kinds are not acceptable, too.

- When your child has a friend over, say, "I expect you to let Maria play with your trucks."
- When you visit your mother, say, "Remember to be very careful when you're playing with Grandma's tea set."
- When you go to a restaurant, say, "When you tell the waitress what you'd like to eat, say 'Please.' And when she brings you your food, say 'Thank you.'"

3. *Show children what you mean by respect.* Telling your child to be respectful is

---

- Avoiding behavior that demeans another person.
- Explaining what you mean.
- Looking at a person when you speak to him or her.
- Being quiet when another person is speaking.
- Using a friendly tone of voice.
- Asking a person's opinion.
- When you use another person's idea, giving him or her credit.
- Thanking people for contributing their ideas and opinions.
- Spending time with people you care about, even if you don't feel like it.
- Being alert to a person's body language.
- When you are talking to someone, interrupting your conversation when a third person enters the room or needs your attention.
- Excusing yourself if you must inconvenience another person.
- Apologizing for bad behavior or misunderstandings.

Respectful behavior stems from a person's values. If you believe that other people are just as worthy as you are, you will treat them with respect. You will also treat yourself with respect and not tolerate poor treatment from others.

> Respectful behavior stems from a person's values. If you believe that other people are just as worthy as you are, you will treat them with respect.

Understanding Body Language (for Teens)

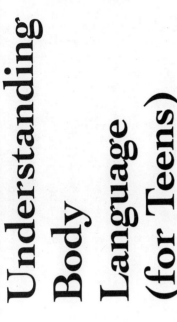

WHAT IS BODY LANGUAGE AND WHY IS IT IMPORTANT?

Body language is the nonverbal part of communication. It is the way a person moves his or her body when communicating with another person. It involves any kind of movement—the way a person sits, stands, looks, or listens. If you think about it for a minute, you will understand why body language is such an important part of communication. Think of a time when you were talking with someone and he or she did any of the following:

your clothes, your jewelry, or the coins in your pocket. This is distracting to the other person, and he or she will be less able to focus on your message.

7. Keep your facial expressions friendly or neutral. Make sure that your face is sending the same message as your words.

8. Show that you are interested when you are listening to another person by looking at him or her as he or she is speaking.

Looking elsewhere creates the impression that you are not interested. You don't have to stare (which can also make the other person uncomfortable), but it is important to maintain eye contact.

9. If you like to crack your knuckles, save it for a time when you are by yourself.

These suggestions are just a beginning. You will think of more by paying attention to others and noticing what effect their body language has on you. You can also ask a teacher, parent, sibling, or friend to coach you. Ask him or her to give you feedback on the strengths and weaknesses of your body language. You may be doing things that you are not aware of, for better or worse.

WHERE CAN I GO FOR MORE INFORMATION?

Glass, Lillian. *I Know What You're Thinking: Using the Four Codes of Reading People to Improve Your Life.* New York: John Wiley and Sons, 2002.

Wainwright, Gordon. *Teach Yourself Body Language.* New York: McGraw Hill, 2000.

- Rolled her eyes while you were talking
- Avoided making eye contact with you
- Tapped his foot while you talked
- Leaned forward while making a point
- Stood up while you were talking to him, although you were still seated
- Stood too close to you while you talked

> Show that you are interested when you are listening to another person by looking at him or her as he or she is speaking. Looking elsewhere creates the impression that you are not interested.

- Sat at a desk with his back to you as you walked into his office, and didn't get up after you entered
- Kept her arms crossed tightly across her chest while you asked her questions
- Kept his hand over his mouth while he spoke
- Looked out the window while you talked

These are just a few examples of how a person's body language might be sending a message that is very different from the verbal message. How a person uses his or her body can make you feel uncomfortable, confused, and angry, or it can place you at ease.

WHAT DOES IT MEAN?

While it's dangerous to make assumptions about any situation, it is important to realize that your body language has an effect on anyone you interact with, and that others may draw certain conclusions about you based on it. Let's return to the examples on the first page of this handout. Think about what effect each of the behaviors could have on another person.

When the other person:	It could mean that he or she:
Rolls his or her eyes as you speak	Is annoyed, disagrees, is making fun of your point, is disrespecting you
Avoids eye contact	Is shy, guilty, nervous, fearful
Taps his or her foot	Is impatient, nervous, preoccupied
Leans forward while making a point	Is enthusiastic, bossy, pushy, emphatic
Stands up before the conversation is finished	Is in a rush, is ready to end the conversation, wants you to leave
Stands too close to you	Is from another culture, is trying to intimidate you
Sits with his or her back to you after you enter the room	Does not respect you, is too busy to talk to you, doesn't want you to stay long, is engrossed in something else
Keeps his or her arms crossed tightly across the chest	Is feeling self-protective, is nervous, angry, afraid . . . may also be cold
Speaks with a hand over his or her mouth	Doesn't want you to listen too closely, lacks confidence in what he or she is saying, is concerned about his or her breath
Looks continually out the window during the conversation	Is preoccupied, is not listening to you, feels more powerful than you, wants you to feel uncomfortable, wants to be somewhere else

It is important to remember that no single gesture or movement always means the same thing. It is important to consider the overall feeling of a conversation, including the words being spoken, the tone of voice and the situation or context.

TIPS FOR USING BODY LANGUAGE TO STRENGTHEN YOUR COMMUNICATIONS

The following suggestions will help you communicate effectively with others:

1. Make eye contact with the other person. When you look a person in the eyes, you come across as more powerful, positive, and sincere. The other person will be more likely to take you seriously and will be less likely to disregard your message.

2. Turn your body toward the other person. This is a sign that you want him or her to hear you and take your message seriously.

3. Stand up straight. You will come across as more confident than if you slouch.

4. Allow a respectful distance between yourself and the other person. If you sense that the other person is uncomfortable, back up a little.

5. Keep your body open. Keep your arms relaxed.

6. Avoid nervous movements like fiddling with a pencil, your hair, the buttons on

What Teens Need to Know about HIV and AIDS

The Nemours Foundation's Center for Children's Health Media (www.kidshealth.org/teen)

SEE THESE HANDOUTS ON RELATED TOPICS

Assertiveness Skills (for Teens)

Building Positive Teen Relationships

Dealing with Peer Pressure (for Teens)

How to Help a Friend through a Crisis (for Teens)

Kids Who Sexually Abuse Other Kids

Life Skills (for Teens)

Living with Your Child's Serious Medical Condition

Sexual Acting Out

What to Do about Teen Chemical Dependence

---

becomes your sexual partner has been tested. A person infected with HIV may have no obvious symptoms for a long time. When the symptoms do become apparent, they may include the following:

• Diarrhea for more than a week

• Feeling tired all the time

• Losing weight quickly

• Lymph glands swell

• Pneumonia

• Sweating at night

• White spots appear inside the throat or mouth

Since all of these symptoms can also be caused by other illnesses, don't alarm yourself if you or someone else has any of them. They do not necessarily mean that a person has HIV. To be certain, a person must be tested.

If you think you may have had contact with someone with HIV and may have been infected, arrange to be tested. The sooner a person receives a diagnosis, the sooner he or she can begin treatment. Early treatment is very important. There is no benefit in waiting and hoping that the virus will go away.

 **WHERE CAN I GO TO LEARN MORE?**

Starr, Robert. *AIDS: Why Should I Care?: Teens Across America Speak Out.* PTAAA Press (People Taking Action Against AIDS), 1999.

National Clearinghouse for Alcohol and Drug Information (www.health.org)

INTRODUCTION

HIV (Human Immunodeficiency Virus) causes AIDS (Acquired Immunodeficiency Syndrome). HIV is a virus and AIDS is the disease that can result from being infected by HIV. HIV weakens the immune system and makes a person more susceptible to infections and illnesses.

HOW DOES A PERSON GET HIV?

People get HIV when they make contact with the bodily fluids of a person who has the virus. The most common ways this happens are:

- Having sex without using a condom
- Sharing needles (usually when injecting drugs)
- Getting a blood transfusion
- Having contact with an open wound
- Being born to a mother who has the virus

HIV can be transmitted from an infected person to another through small cuts or sores on the genitals (penis, rectum, and vagina). It may also be transmitted through cuts or sores on and in the mouth. Some people may have tiny cuts, sores, or ulcers on or in their genitals without being aware of their existence. If they engage in sex, these people are at risk of being infected.

Some people may have tiny cuts, sores, or ulcers on or in their genitals without being aware of their existence. If they engage in sex, these people are at risk of being infected.

A person *cannot* get HIV from the following situations:

- Being bitten by a mosquito or other insect (bugs don't carry it)
- By casual contact such as holding hands or hugging
- By deep kissing (transmission by saliva)
- By touching a person's sweat
- From someone sneezing or coughing
- Sitting next to a person who has it

HIV affects people of all races, sexual orientations, and socioeconomic groups. Babies born from mothers with HIV and AIDS may be born with the virus.

HIV affects people of all races, sexual orientations, and socioeconomic groups.

HOW CAN I BE SAFE FROM HIV AND AIDS?

1. Don't abuse alcohol. When a person is intoxicated, he or she loses self-control and good judgment. It is much more likely that a person will engage in unsafe behaviors if he or she is drunk or high. This includes engaging in unprotected sex.

2. Don't do illegal drugs. Drugs that are not injected impair judgment and those that are injected carry the risk of spreading HIV and AIDS.

3. If you choose to be sexually active, use a latex condom. Use it properly and only use it once. It is safest to avoid sexual acts that are vaginal, anal, or oral. Be aware that using a condom does not provide 100 percent protection against contracting HIV; it is simply a barrier.

4. If you smoke, be aware that smokers with HIV develop AIDS much more quickly than nonsmokers.

5. Don't have sex or share a needle with anyone who hasn't been tested.

Don't have sex or share a needle with anyone who hasn't been tested.

HOW CAN I TELL IF SOMEONE HAS HIV?

You may not be able to tell. That's why it's so important to be sure that anyone who

Workplace Skills (for Teens)

Every teen wants to do well on his or her first job. You know it's important to make a good impression and do a good job performing the tasks that are assigned to you. This handout will give you some tips on how to make sure you do a good job and enjoy yourself, too.

BE POSITIVE WITH OTHERS

1. Introduce yourself to coworkers and customers or patients if they don't know you.
2. Make eye contact with people.
3. Smile.
4. If someone has a question and you don't know the answer, say, "I don't know the answer to that, but I'd be glad to find out." Then, find the answer.
5. Look for ways to be of service to others.
6. Thank people when they do something to help you.

BE COURTEOUS

1. When a coworker approaches you, look up immediately and give him or her your attention.
2. When the telephone rings while you are assisting a customer, say "Excuse me while I answer the phone" before you answer it.
3. Speak with sincerity. Beware of sounding like you've said "Thank you" or "Have a nice day" one hundred times today (even if you have).

WHERE CAN I GO FOR MORE INFORMATION?

Leland, Karen, and Bailey, Keith. *Customer Service for Dummies.* Foster City, CA: IDG Books Worldwide, 1995.

Nelson, Bob. *1001 Ways to Energize Employees.* New York: Workman Publishing, 1997.

Torres, Crescencio, and Fairbanks, Deborah. *The ASTD Trainer's Sourcebook/Teambuilding.* New York: McGraw-Hill, 1996.

SEE THESE HANDOUTS ON RELATED TOPICS

Assertiveness Skills (for Teens)

Building People Skills (for Teens)

Building Positive Teen Relationships

Dealing with Peer Pressure (for Teens)

Expressing Feelings Responsibly (for Teens)

Goal Setting (for Teens)

Life Skills (for Teens)

Listening Skills (for Teens)

Personal Negotiation Skills (for Teens)

Understanding Body Language (for Teens)

---

3. Make a list of five things you'd like to accomplish on the job and talk to your supervisor about how to make it happen.
4. Take your breaks and vacation. We all need to get away during the day and during the year.
5. Think of things to celebrate.
6. Look for ways to make team members feel needed and useful.
7. Ask for feedback about how you are doing. Know what's expected of you; make sure you're delivering; and relax.

> Make a list of five things you'd like to accomplish on the job and talk to your supervisor about how to make it happen.

MANAGE THE STRESS AT WORK

1. Take yourself out of the situation for a moment.
   - Take your break outside of the workplace.
   - Shift your focus and separate yourself from the situation for a moment.
2. Say to yourself, "This is only temporary. It will end soon."
3. Take a deep breath and stretch.
4. Look for the humor in the situation. Try not to take it too seriously.
5. Acknowledge what is happening. Denying it won't help.
6. If your workplace has customers who are waiting impatiently, say, "I apologize for the inconvenience, but I hope you can see that I'm doing the best I can to help you." Be sure to smile and speak with a friendly tone.
7. Don't sweat the small stuff.
8. Ask for help.
9. Don't blame yourself when things are stressful.

4. When you are in a hurry, avoid rushing through the office or brushing past people—unless it's an emergency.

5. If you work in a store or restaurant:

- Speak quietly when you discuss business with coworkers.

- Avoid personal conversations with coworkers or on the telephone while customers are present.

- If you must cross someone's path in the office or store, say "Excuse me."

DEVELOP YOUR TELEPHONE SKILLS

1. Answer the phone promptly.

2. If you are working with another person and the telephone rings, excuse yourself first before answering the phone.

3. Always answer the phone in the way you have been instructed. Many workplaces expect you to answer with your name and department.

4. If you must put a person on hold, ask, "May I put you on hold?" and wait for a response.

5. If you must put a person on hold, say how long he or she will have to wait. If it is going to take more than a minute, offer to call back.

6. If you have people waiting for you to finish your call, politely explain to the person on the telephone that you are working with someone and offer to call them back. Take their name

and phone number; call them back as soon as possible.

7. Smile when you speak to people on the phone. Your friendly manner will come through on the other end.

8. When you return to a person who was waiting for you, thank them for waiting.

9. If you need to transfer a call, explain what you are doing and ask the person if they mind being transferred. Explain why you are transferring them and to whom.

DEAL CONSTRUCTIVELY AND TACTFULLY WITH PEOPLE AT WORK WHO ARE UPSET

1. Let the person vent his or her feelings.

2. Ask questions.

3. Summarize what you hear.

4. Use active listening.

5. Maintain open body language.

6. Nod your head.

7. Say, "I can see that you're upset."

8. Take a deep breath.

9. Say, "I want to help you find a solution."

BE A TEAM PLAYER

1. Get to know your coworkers.

2. Be open to others' opinions and feelings, even if they are different from yours.

3. Show interest in what others say.

4. Look for ways to lessen the stress level on your work team.

5. Develop negotiation skills.

6. Admit your mistakes.

7. Respect and appreciate differences.

8. Celebrate everyone's successes.

LEARN HOW TO DO YOUR JOB

1. Ask what's expected of you.

2. Ask for training.

3. Ask for feedback on how you are doing.

4. If you don't know, ask.

5. Learn from your mistakes.

DEVELOP POSITIVE WORK HABITS

1. Start and end your work shift on time.

2. Complete assignments.

3. If you work with customers, always put them first.

4. Don't bring your problems to work.

5. Always be professional.

6. Stay off the phone.

7. Ask your friends not to come to your workplace.

8. Be positive.

9. When you can't finish a task or are having a problem, talk to your supervisor.

10. Keep busy. If you run out of things to do, try these ideas:

- Ask your supervisor how you can be helpful.

- Learn more about your job. If you work in a store, learn about the merchandise you sell. If you work in a restaurant, learn about the food. There is always something to learn.

- Look for ways to make the store, restaurant or office sparkle.

LEARN TO ENJOY YOURSELF AT WORK

1. If there are things that are bothering you, speak up. It is unlikely that much will change unless you express your feelings and opinions.

2. Look for ways to connect with coworkers.

> If you work with customers, always give them your attention first.

Helpful Books and Web Sites

ATTENTION DEFICIT HYPERACTIVITY DISORDER (ADHD)

Hartmann, T. *Attention Deficit Disorder: A Different Perception.* Grass Valley, CA: Underwood, 1997.

Hallowell, E., and Ratey, J. *Answers to Distraction.* New York: Bantam Books, 1996.

Hallowell, E., and Ratey, J. *Driven to Distraction.* New York: Pantheon Books, 1994.

Kelly, K., and Ramundo, P. *You Mean I'm Not Lazy, Stupid, or Crazy?* Cincinnati, OH: Scribner, 1995.

Children and Adults with Attention Deficit/Hyperactivity Disorder (chadd.org).

The National Attention Deficit Disorder Association (add.org).

ANXIETY IN CHILDREN

Beck, Aaron, Emery, Gary, and Greenberg, Ruth. *Anxiety Disorders and Phobias: A Cognitive Perspective.* New York: Basic Books, 1990.

Freeman, Arthur, and DeWolf, Rose. *Woulda, Coulda, Shoulda: Overcoming Regrets, Mistakes, and Missed Opportunities.* New York: Harperperennial Library, 1992.

Anxiety Disorders Association of America (www.adaa.org).

Free self-help for people with anxiety disorders (www.Anxieties.com).

The Anxiety Network (www.anxietynetwork.com).

The Anxiety Panic Internet Resource (TAPIR) (www.algy.com).

ASSERTIVENESS SKILLS (FOR TEENS)

Alberti, Robert, and Emmons, Michael. *Your Perfect Right.* San Luis Obispo, CA: Impact Publishers, 2001.

Bower, Sharon, and Bower, Gordon. *Asserting Yourself: A Practical Guide for Positive Change.* New York: Perseus, 1991.

Elgin, Suzette Haden. *The Gentle Art of Verbal Self-Defense at Work.* Englewood Cliffs, NJ: Prentice Hall, 2000.

Gordon, Thomas. *Leader Effectiveness Training.* New York: Bantam Doubleday Dell, 1986.

ATTACHMENT DISORDER

Gil, Eliana. *Outgrowing the Pain.* Rockville, MD: Laurel Press, 1983.

Jaratt, Claudia Jewett. *Helping Children Cope with Separation and Loss.* Harvard, MA: Harvard Common Press, 1982.

Turecki, Stanley. *The Difficult Child.* New York: Bantam Books, 1985.

ATTENTION SEEKING AND DISRUPTIVE BEHAVIOR

Dreikurs, Rudolf, and Soltz, Vicki. *Children: The Challenge.* New York: Plume, 1991.

Dreikurs, Rudolf, Cassel, Pearl, and Kehoe, David. *Discipline Without Tears.* New York: Plume, 1992.

AUTISM

Attwood, Tony, and Wing, Lorna. *Asperger's Syndrome: A Guide for Parents and Professionals.* London, England: Jessica Kingsley Publishers, 1997.

Wing, Lorna, Klin, Ami, and Volkmar, Fred. *The Autistic Spectrum: A Parents' Guide to Understanding and Helping Your Child.* Berkeley, CA: Ulysses Press, 2001.

Autism Society of America (www.autism-society.org).

BUILDING POSITIVE TEEN RELATIONSHIPS

Covey, Sean. *The Seven Habits of Highly Effective Teens: The Ultimate Teenage Success Guide.* New York: Simon and Schuster, 1998.

Kirberger, Kimberly. *Teen Love: On Relationships, A Book for Teenagers.* Deerfield Beach, FL: Health Communications, 1999.

McGraw, Jay, and McGraw, Phillip. *Life Strategies for Teens.* New York: Fireside, 2000.

CHILDHOOD SPEECH AND LANGUAGE DISORDERS

Apel, Kenn, and Masterson, Julie. *Beyond Baby Talk.* New York: Prima Publishing, 2001.

Martin, Katherine. *Does My Child Have a Speech Problem?* Chicago: Chicago Review Press, 1997.

Sowell, Thomas. *Late-Talking Children.* New York: Basic Books, 1998.

American Speech-Language-Hearing Association (www.ASHA.org).

Learning Disabilities Association of America (www.LDAnatl.org).

CHILDREN, TEENS AND SUICIDE

Marcus, Eric. *Why Suicide? Answers to 200 of the Most Frequently Asked Questions About Suicide, Attempted Suicide, and Assisted Suicide.* San Francisco: Harper San Francisco, 1996.

CONDUCT DISORDER

Katherine, Anne. *Boundaries: Where You End and I Begin.* New York: Simon and Schuster, 1991.

Rosellini, Gayle, Worden, Mark, and Rosell, Garth. *Of Course You're Angry: A Guide to Dealing With the Emotions of Substance Abuse.* San Francisco: Harper Hazelden, 1986.

Williams, Redford, and Williams, Virginia. *Anger Kills: Seventeen Strategies for Controlling the Hostility That Can Harm Your Health.* New York: Time Books, 1993.

DEALING WITH COMMON ADOPTION ISSUES

Brodzinsky, David, Schechter, Marshall, and Henig, Robin Marantz. *Being Adopted: The Lifelong Search for Self.* New York: Doubleday, 1992.

Lifton, Betty Jean. *Lost and Found: The Adoption Experience.* New York: Harper and Row, 1979.

Melina, Lois Ruskai. *Making Sense of Adoption.* New York: Harper and Row, 1989.

Melina, Lois Ruskai. *Raising Adopted Children* (rev. ed.). New York: HarperCollins, 1998.

Melina, Lois Ruskai, and Roszia, Sharon Kaplan. *The Open Adoption Experience: A Complete Guide for Adoptive and Birth Families—from Making the Decision Through the Child's Growing Years.* New York: HarperCollins, 1993.

Silber, Kathleen, and Dorner, Patricia Martinez. *Children of Open Adoption.* San Antonio, TX: Corona Publishing, 1990.

Silber, Kathleen, and Speedlin, Phyllis. *Dear Birthmother (Thank You for Our Baby).* San Antonio, TX: Corona Publishing, 1982.

www.raisingadoptedchildren.com

www.adopting.org

DEALING WITH PEER PRESSURE (FOR TEENS)

Scott, Sharon. *How to Say No and Keep Your Friends.* Amherst, MA: Human Resource Development Press, 1997.

Many articles for teens, including an excellent one on how to handle peer pressure, appear on the following web site: (www.teenshealth.org/).

American Social Health Association has some good information on handling peer pressure, and other valuable information for teens (www.iwannaknow.org).

DEPRESSION IN CHILDREN AND TEENS

Burns, David D. *Feeling Good: The New Mood Therapy.* New York: Avon Books, 1980.

Solomon, Andrew. *The Noonday Demon: An Atlas of Depression.* New York: Scribner, 2001.

Yapko, Michael. *Breaking the Patterns of Depression.* New York: Doubleday, 1997.

American Academy of Child and Adolescent Psychiatry
(www.aacap.org).

EATING DISORDERS

Costin, Carolyn. *The Eating Disorder Sourcebook: A Comprehensive Guide to the Causes, Treatments, and Prevention of Eating Disorders.* New York: McGraw Hill, 1999.

Siegel, Michelle, Brisman, Judith, and Weinshel, Margot. *Surviving an Eating Disorder: Strategies for Family and Friends.* New York: Harper-Collins, 1997.

Natenshon, Abigail. *When Your Child Has an Eating Disorder: A Step-by-Step Workbook for Parents and Other Caregivers.* New York: Jossey-Bass, 1999.

National Association for Anorexia Nervosa and Associated Disorders (ANAD) (www.ANAD.org)

Eating Disorders Awareness and Prevention (www.EDAP.org)

National Eating Disorders Screening Program
(www.NMISP.org/eat.htm)

Eating Disorders Association
(www.UQ.ENET.AU/EDA/documents/start.html)

ENCOPRESIS

Spock, Benjamin, and Parker, Stephen. *Dr. Spock's Baby and Child Care.* New York: NY: Pocket Books, 1998.

ENURESIS (BED WETTING)

Spock, Benjamin, and Parker, Stephen. *Dr. Spock's Baby and Child Care.* New York: Pocket Books, 1998.

EXPRESS YOUR FEELINGS RESPONSIBLY (JUST FOR TEENS)

Covey, Sean. *The Seven Habits of Highly Effective Teens: The Ultimate Teenage Success Guide.* New York: Simon and Schuster, 1998.

McGraw, Jay, and McGraw, Phillip. Life Strategies for Teens. New York: Fireside, 2000.

FIRE SETTING

Sakheim, George, and Osborn, Elizabeth. *Firesetting Children: Risk Assessment and Treatment.* Washington, DC: Child Welfare League of America, 1994.

GENDER IDENTITY DISORDER

Di Ceglie, Domenico, Freeman, David, and Money, John. *A Stranger in My Own Body: Atypical Gender Identity Development and Mental Health.* London, England: Karnac Books, 1998.

Zucker, Kenneth, and Bradley, Susan. *Gender Identity Disorder and Psychosexual Problems in Children and Adolescents.* New York: Guilford Press, 1995.

GOAL SETTING (FOR TEENS)

Blair, Gary Ryan. *Goal Setting 101: How to Set and Achieve a Goal.* Palm Harbor, FL: The Goals Guy, 2000.

Blair, Gary Ryan. *Goal Setting Forms: Tools to Help You Get Ready, Get Set, & Go for Your Goals.* Palm Harbor, FL: The Goals Guy, 2000.

Smith, Douglas. *Make Success Measurable: A Mindbook-Workbook for Setting Goals and Taking Action.* New York: John Wiley & Sons, 1999.

HELPING A CHILD RECOVER FROM SEXUAL ABUSE

Bass, E., and Davis, L. *The Courage to Heal: A Guide for Women Survivors of Child Sexual Abuse.* San Francisco: HarperCollins, 1988.

Bradshaw, John. *Healing the Shame That Binds You.* Deerfield Beach, FL: Health Communications, Inc., 1988.

Kleven, Sandy. *The Right Touch: A Read-Aloud Story to Help Prevent Child Sexual Abuse.* Bellevue, WA: Illumination Arts, 1998.

American Academy of Child and Adolescent Psychiatry Facts for Families (www.AACAP.org)

HELPING CHILDREN IN DIVORCING FAMILIES

Wallerstein, Judith, and Blakeslee, *Second Chances: Men, Women, and Children a Decade after Divorce.* Boston: Mariner Books, 1996.

Wallerstein, Judith, and Kelly, Joan Berlin. *Surviving the Breakup: How Children and Parents Cope with Divorce.* New York: Basic Books, 1996.

American Academy of Child and Adolescent Psychiatry (www.aacap.org).

HELPING KIDS MANAGE ANGRY FEELINGS

McKay, Matthew, Rogers, Peter, and McKay, Judith. *When Anger Hurts: Quieting the Storm Within.* Oakland, CA: New Harbinger Publications, 1989.

Rosellini, Gayle, and Worden, Mark. *Of Course You're Angry* (2nd. ed.). Center City, MN: Hazelden Foundation, 1997.

Tavris, Carol. *Anger: The Misunderstood Emotion.* New York: Touchstone, 1989.

HELPING YOUR CHILD OR TEEN MANAGE STRESS

Cunningham, J. Barton. *The Stress Management Sourcebook.* Los Angeles, CA: Lowell House, 1997.

Hanson, Peter G. *The Joy of Stress.* Kansas City, MO: Andrews & McMeel, 1985.

Hanson, Peter G. *Stress for Success.* New York: Doubleday, 1989.

Kelly, Kate. *The Complete Idiot's Guide to Parenting a Teenager.* New York: Alpha Books, 1996.

Law, Felicia, and Parker, Josephine, eds. *Growing Up: A Young Person's Guide to Adolescence.* Chippenham, Wiltshire, UK: Merlion Publishing, Ltd., 1993.

McCoy, Kathy, and Wibbelsman, Charles. *The New Teenage Body Book.* New York: Putnam, 1992.

HELPING YOUR CHILD SUCCEED IN SCHOOL

Branden, Nathaniel. *The Six Pillars of Self-Esteem.* New York: Bantam, 1994.

Briggs, Dorothy Corkville. *Celebrate Your Self: Making Life Work for You.* Garden City, NY: Doubleday, 1977.

Burns, David D. *Ten Days to Self-Esteem.* New York: William Morrow, 1993.

Dreikurs, Rudolph. *Children: The Challenge.* New York: Plume, 1991.

Dinkmeyer, Don, and McKay, Gary. *Parenting Young Children: Systematic Training for Effective Parenting (STEP) of Children under Six.* Circle Pines, MN: American Guidance Service, 1997.

HELPING YOUR KIDS MANAGE THE RELOCATION BLUES

Berenstain, Stan, and Berenstain, Jan. *The Berenstain Bears' Moving Day (First Time Books).* New York: Random House, 1981.

Carlisle, Ellen. *Smooth Moves.* Charlotte, NC: Teacup Press, 1999.

Carlstrom, Nancy White. *Boxes, Boxes Everywhere.* New York: Aladdin Paperbacks, 1999.

Goodwin, Cathy. *Making the Big Move: How to Transform Relocation into a Creative Life Transition.* Oakland, CA: New Harbinger Publications, 1999.

McGeorge, Constance, and Whyte, Mary (illustrator). *Boomer's Big Day.* San Francisco, CA: Chronicle Books, 1994.

Viorst, Judith. *Alexander, Who's Not (Do You Hear Me? I Mean It!) Going to Move.* New York: Aladdin Paperbacks, 1998.

Williamson, Greg, and Abele, Greg (illustrator). *What's the Recipe for Friends?* New Orleans, LA: Peerless Publishing, 1999.

HELPING YOUR KIDS TO BE SELF-CONFIDENT

Branden, Nathaniel. *The Six Pillars of Self-Esteem.* New York: Bantam, 1994.

Briggs, Dorothy Corkville. *Celebrate Your Self: Making Life Work for You.* Garden City, NY: Doubleday, 1977.

Burns, David D. *Ten Days to Self-Esteem.* New York: William Morrow, 1993.

De Angelis, Barbara. *Confidence: Finding It and Living It.* Carson, CA: Hay House, 1995.

HELPING KIDS RECOVER FROM LOSS

Deits, Bob. *Life After Loss.* Tucson, AZ: Fisher Books, 1992.

Kübler-Ross, Elisabeth. *On Death and Dying.* New York: MacMillan: 1969.

HOW TO BUILD YOUR CHILD'S SELF-ESTEEM

Branden, Nathaniel. *The Six Pillars of Self-Esteem.* New York: Bantam, 1994.

Briggs, Dorothy Corkville. *Celebrate Your Self: Making Life Work For You.* Garden City, NY: Doubleday, 1977.

Burns, David D. *Ten Days to Self-Esteem.* New York: William Morrow, 1993.

Sher, Barbara, with Gottlieb, Annie. *Wishcraft.* New York: Ballantine Books, 1979.

HOW TO COPE WHEN PARENTING FEELS OVERWHELMING

Bolton, Michele Kremen. *The Third Shift: Managing Hard Choices in Our Careers, Homes, and Lives as Women.* New York: Jossey-Bass, 2000.

Brawner, Jim, Brawner, Suzette, and Smalley, Gary. *Taming the Family Zoo: Maximizing Harmony and Minimizing Family Stress.* Colorado Springs, CO: Navpress, 1998.

Gordon, Thomas. *Parent Effectiveness Training: The Proven Program for Raising Responsible Children.* New York: Three Rivers Press, 2000.

Peters, Joan. *When Mothers Work: Loving Our Children Without Sacrificing Ourselves.* Cambridge, MA: Perseus Books, 1998.

HOW TO HELP A FRIEND THROUGH A CRISIS

American Academy of Child and Adolescent Psychiatry (www.aacap.org).

Burns, David. *Feeling Good: The New Mood Therapy.* New York: Avon Books, 1980.

Covey, Sean. *The Seven Habits of Highly Effective Teens: The Ultimate Teenage Success Guide.* New York: Simon & Schuster, 1998.

Marcus, Eric. *Why Suicide? Answers to 200 of the Most Frequently Asked Questions about Suicide, Attempted Suicide, and Assisted Suicide.* San Francisco, CA: HarperSan Francisco, 1996.

HOW TO HELP VICTIMS OF CHILD ABUSE

Jantz, Gregory. *Healing the Scars of Emotional Abuse.* Grand Rapids, MI: Fleming H. Revell Co., 1995.

Miller, Alice. *The Drama of the Gifted Child.* New York: Basic Books, 1996.

Monahon, Cynthia. *Children and Trauma: A Parent's Guide to Helping Children Heal.* New York: Lexington Press, 1983.

Child Help USA (www.childhelpusa.org).

I'M PLANNING TO COME OUT TO MY FAMILY. WHAT SHOULD I EXPECT?
Gay and Lesbian Alliance Against Defamation (GLAAD) (www.GLAAD.org).

American Civil Liberties Union (ACLU) (www.ACLU.org).

The Advocate (www.Advocate.com).

Borhek, Mary. *Coming Out to Parents: A Two-Way Survival Guide for Lesbians and Gay Men and Their Parents.* Cleveland, OH: Pilgrim Press, 1993.

Kübler-Ross, Elisabeth. *On Death and Dying.* New York: Scribner, 1997.

Signorile, Michelangelo. *Outing Yourself: How to Come Out as Lesbian or Gay to Your Family, Friends, and Coworkers.* New York: Fireside, 1996.

LIFE SKILLS (FOR TEENS)
Kelly, Kate. *The Complete Idiot's Guide to Parenting a Teenager.* New York: Alpha Books, 1996.

Law, Felicia, and Parker, Josephine, eds. *Growing Up: A Young Person's Guide to Adolescence.* Chippenham, Wiltshire, UK: Merlion Publishing, Ltd., 1993.

McCoy, Kathy, and Wibbelsman, Charles. *The New Teenage Body Book.* New York: Putnam, 1992.

LISTENING SKILLS (JUST FOR TEENS)
Covey, Sean. *The Seven Habits of Highly Effective Teens: The Ultimate Teenage Success Guide.* New York: Simon and Schuster, 1998.

McGraw, Jay, and McGraw, Phillip. *Life Strategies for Teens.* New York: Fireside, 2000.

LIVING WITH YOUR CHILD'S SERIOUS MEDICAL CONDITION
Capossela, Cappy, and Warnock, Sheila. *Share the Care: How to Organize a Group to Care for Someone Who Is Seriously Ill.* New York: Fireside Books, 1995.

Kubler-Ross, Elisabeth. *On Death and Dying.* New York: MacMillan, 1969.

Register, Cheri. *The Chronic Illness Experience.* Minneapolis, MN: Hazelden Information and Educational Services, 1999.

Well, Susan Milstrey. *A Delicate Balance: Living Successfully with Chronic Illness.* New York: Perseus Books, 1998.

MANAGING FAMILY CONFLICT
Gordon, Thomas. *Parent Effectiveness Training: The Proven Program for Raising Responsible Children.* New York: Three Rivers Press, 2000.

Ury, William. *Getting Past No: Negotiating Your Way from Confrontation to Cooperation.* New York: Bantam Doubleday Dell, 1993.

MANAGING THE STEPFAMILY
Kalter, Neil. *Growing Up with Divorce.* New York: Fawcett Books, 1991.

Norwood, Perdita Kirkness, and Wingender, Teri. *The Enlightened Stepmother; Revolutionizing the Role.* New York: Avon Books, 1999.

Visher, Emily, and Visher, John. *Stepfamilies: Myths and Realities.* Secaucus, NJ: Citadel Press, 1993.

MANIA AND HYPOMANIA
Fawcett, Jan, Golden, Bernard, Rosenfeld, Nancy, and Goodwin, Frederick. *New Hope for People with Bipolar Disorder.* Rocklin, CA: Prima Publishing, 2000.

Mondimore, Francis. *Bipolar Disorder: A Guide for Patients and Families.* Baltimore: Johns Hopkins University Press, 1999.

National Depressive and Manic-Depressive Association (www.ndmda.org).

MENTAL RETARDATION
Burack, Jacob, Hodapp, Robert, and Zigler, Edward (eds.). *Handbook of Mental Retardation and Development.* New York: Cambridge University Press, 1998.

Drew, Clifford, and Hardman, Michael. *Mental Retardation: A Life Cycle Approach.* Upper Saddle River, NJ: Prentice Hall, 1999.

Smith, Romayne, and Shriver, Eunice Kennedy. *Children with Mental Retardation: A Parents' Guide* (The Special Needs Collection). Bethesda, MD: Woodbine House, 1993.

The Arc of the United States (www.thearc.org).

OPPOSITIONAL DEFIANT DISORDER (ODD)

Barkley, Russell. *Defiant Children (2nd ed.)*. New York: Guilford Press, 1997.

Greene, Ross. *The Explosive Child*. New York: HarperCollins, 1998.

Koplewicz, Harold. *It's Nobody's Fault: New Hope and Help for Difficult Children and Their Parents*. New York: Random House, 1997.

PERSONAL NEGOTIATION SKILLS (JUST FOR TEENS)

Fisher, Roger, and Ury, William. *Getting to Yes: Negotiating Agreement Without Giving In*. New York: Penguin, 1991.

PHOBIAS

Bassett, Lucinda. *From Panic to Power: Proven Techniques to Calm Your Anxieties, Conquer Your Fears, and Put You in Control of Your Life*. New York: Quill, 1997.

Bourne, Edmund J. *The Anxiety and Phobia Workbook*. Oakland, CA: New Harbinger, 2000.

Ross, Jerilyn. *Triumph Over Fear: A Book of Help and Hope for People with Anxiety Disorders*. New York: Bantam Books, 1995.

Anxiety Disorders Association of America (www.adaa.org).

Anxiety Panic Internet Resource (www.algy.com/anxiety).

Internet Mental Health (www.mentalhealth.com).

National Institute of Mental Health (www.nimh.nih.gov/anxiety).

PRINCIPLES OF POSITIVE REINFORCEMENT (FOR PARENTS)

Dreikurs, Rudolph. *Children: The Challenge*. New York: Plume, 1991.

Dinkmeyer, Don, and McKay, Gary. *Parenting Young Children: Systematic Training for Effective Parenting (STEP) of Children Under Six*. Circle Pines, MN: American Guidance Service, 1997.

PSYCHOSIS

Torrey, E. Fuller. *Surviving Schizophrenia: A Manual for Families, Consumers, and Providers.* New York: Quill, 2001.

Woolis, Rebecca, and Hatfield, Agnes. *When Someone You Love Has a Mental Illness: A Handbook for Family, Friends, and Caregivers.* New York: Jeremy Tarcher, 1992.

National Institute of Mental Health (www.nimh.gov).

National Mental Health Association (www.nmha.org).

POST-TRAUMATIC STRESS DISORDER (PTSD)

Rothschild, Babette. *The Body Remembers: The Psychophysiology of Trauma and Trauma Treatment.* New York: W.W. Norton & Company, 2000.

Wilson, John, Friedman, Matthew, and Lindy, Jacob (eds.). *Treating Psychological Trauma and PTSD.* New York: Guilford Press, 2001.

National Center for PTSD (www.NCPTSD.org).

Free information about posttraumatic stress disorder and related disorders appears at the following web site: (www.PTSD.com).

RUNAWAY KIDS

Branden, Nathaniel. *The Six Pillars of Self-Esteem.* New York: Bantam, 1994.

Briggs, Dorothy Corkville. *Celebrate Your Self: Making Life Work For You.* Garden City, NY: Doubleday, 1977.

National Center for Missing and Exploited Children (www.missingkids .com).

National Runaway Hot Line: 1-800-HIT-HOME (24 hrs).

Runaway Help Line: 1-800-621-4000 (24 hrs).

SEPARATION ANXIETY

Bowlby, John. *Separation: Anxiety and Anger.* New York: Basic Books, 2000.

Crary, Elizabeth. *Mommy, Don't Go.* Seattle: Parenting Press, 1996.

SEXUAL ACTING OUT

Beyond the Big Talk: Every Parent's Guide to Raising Sexually Healthy Teens —from Middle School to College. New York: Newmarket Press, 2001.

Haffner, Debra, and Tartaglione, Alissa Haffner. *From Diapers to Dating: A Parent's Guide to Raising Sexually Healthy Children.* New York: Newmarket Press, 2000.

Schwartz, Pepper, and Cappello, Dominic. *Ten Talks Parents Must Have with Their Children about Sex and Character.* New York: Hyperion, 2000.

Focus Adolescent Services (www.focusas.com).

SLEEP DISTURBANCES

Spock, Benjamin, and Parker, Stephen. *Dr. Spock's Baby and Child Care.* New York: Pocket Books, 1998.

Weissbluth, Marc. *Healthy Sleep Habits, Happy Child.* New York: Fawcett Books, 1999.

The National Sleep Foundation (www.sleepfoundation.org)

SOCIAL ANXIETY DISORDER (SHYNESS)

Best, Cari. *Shrinking Violet.* New York: Farrar Straus & Giroux, 2001.

Burns, David. *Ten Days to Self Esteem.* New York: William Morrow, 1993.

Lovell, Patty. *Stand Tall, Molly Lou Melon.* New York: Putnam, 2001.

Raschka, Chris. *The Blushful Hippopotamus.* London, England: Orchard, 1996.

Zimbardo, P. *Shyness: What It Is and what to Do About It.* Reading, MA: Addison-Wesley, 1987.

Social Phobia/Social Anxiety Association (www.socialphobia.org).

TEACHING YOUR CHILD TO RESPECT OTHERS

Borba, Michele. *Parents Do Make a Difference: How to Raise Kids with Solid Character, Strong Minds, and Caring Hearts.* New York: Jossey-Bass, 1999.

McKay, Gary, McKay, Joyce, Maybell, Steven, and Eckstein, Daniel. *Raising Respectful Kids in a Rude World: Teaching Your Children the Power of Mutual Respect and Consideration.* Prima Publishing, 2001.

UNDERSTANDING BODY LANGUAGE (FOR TEENS)

Glass, Lillian. *I Know what You're Thinking: Using the Four Codes of Reading People to Improve Your Life.* New York: John Wiley and Sons, 2002.

Wainwright, Gordon. *Teach Yourself Body Language.* New York: McGraw Hill, 2000.

WHAT TEENS NEED TO KNOW ABOUT HIV AND AIDS

National Clearinghouse for Alcohol and Drug Information (www.health.org).

The Nemours Foundation's Center for Children's Health Media (www.kidshealth.org/teen).

Starr, Robert. *AIDS: Why Should I Care: Teens across America Speak Out.* PTAAA Press (People Taking Action Against AIDS), 1999.

WHAT TO DO ABOUT TEEN CHEMICAL DEPENDENCE

Jay, Jeff, and Jay, Debra Erickson. *Love First: A New Approach to Intervention for Alcoholism and Drug Addiction.* Center City, MN: Hazelden, 2000.

Johnson, Vernon. *Intervention: How to Help Someone Who Doesn't Want Help: A Step-by-Step Guide for Families of Chemically Dependent Persons.* Washington, DC: The Johnson Institute, 1989.

West, James, and Ford, Betty. *The Betty Ford Center Book of Answers: Help for Those Struggling with Substance Abuse and for the People Who Love Them.* New York: Pocket Books, 1997.

About (www.alcoholism.about.com).

Alcoholics Anonymous (www.alcoholics-anonymous.org).

National Center on Addiction and Substance Abuse at Columbia University (www.casacolumbia.org).

National Council on Alcoholism and Drug Dependence (www.ncadd.org).

National Institute on Alcohol Abuse and Alcoholism (www.niaaa.nih.gov).

Substance Abuse and Mental Health Services Administration (www.health.org).

WHEN KIDS DON'T WANT TO GO TO SCHOOL

McEwan, Elaine. *When Kids Say No to School: Helping Children at Risk of Failure, Refusal, or Dropping Out.* Colorado Springs, CO: Harold Shaw Publishing, 1998.

Heyne, David, and Rollings, Stephanie. *School Refusal: Parent, Adolescent and Child Training Skills.* Malden, MA: Blackwell Publishers, 2002.

WHEN KIDS SEXUALLY ABUSE OTHER KIDS

Morrison, Tony, Erooga, Marcus, and Beckett, Richard. *Sexual Offending Against Children: Assessment and Treatment of Male Abusers.* New York: Routledge, 1994.

WHEN KIDS UNDERACHIEVE

Holt, John. *How Children Fail.* Cambridge, MA: Perseus Press, 1995.

McEwan, Elaine. *When Kids Say No to School: Helping Children at Risk of Failure, Refusal, or Dropping Out.* Wheaton, IL: Harold Shaw Publishing, 1998.

American Academy of Child and Adolescent Psychiatry (www.aacap.org).

WORKPLACE SKILLS FOR TEENS

Leland, Karen, and Bailey, Keith. *Customer Service for Dummies.* Foster City, CA: IDG Books Worldwide, 1995.

Nelson, Bob. *1001 Ways to Energize Employees.* New York: Workman Publishing, 1997.

Torres, Crescencio, and Fairbanks, Deborah. *The ASTD Trainer's Sourcebook/Teambuilding.* New York: McGraw-Hill, 1996.

About the CD-ROM

INTRODUCTION

The files on the enclosed CD-ROM are saved in Adobe Acrobat (.PDF) format and require the Acrobat Reader in order for you to open and view the files.

SYSTEM REQUIREMENTS

- IBM PC or compatible computer
- CD-ROM drive
- Windows 95 or later
- Adobe Acrobat Reader*
- *For users who do not have Acrobat Reader installed on their computer you can download the Acrobat Reader for free from Adobe's website. The URL for the reader is:
  http://www.adobe.com/products/acrobat/readstep.html

USING THE FILES

Loading Files

To view the PDF's, launch Adobe Acrobat. Select **File, Open** from the pull-down menu. Select the appropriate drive and directory. Double click on the file you want to open. Edit the file according to your needs.

Printing Files

If you want to print the files, select **File, Print** from the pull-down menu.

Saving Files

When you have finished editing a file, you should save it under a new file name by selecting **File, Save As** from the pull-down menu.

USER ASSISTANCE

If you need assistance with installation or if you have a damaged CD-ROM, please contact Wiley Technical Support at:

Phone: (201) 748-6753

Fax: (201) 748-6450 (Attention: Wiley Technical Support)

URL: www.wiley.com/techsupport

To place additional orders or to request information about other Wiley products, please call (800) 225-5945.

For information about the CD-ROM see the **About the CD-ROM** section on page 145.

Publishers Since 1807